Praise for The 21ˢᵗ Cen[tury]
Leading Schools in Today's World

"Dr. Fowler has strategically pieced together a book that clearly embodies what it means to lead schools effectively in the 21ˢᵗ Century."
> ~ Deb Delisle (Executive Director and CEO of ASCD, former Assistant Secretary for Elementary and Secondary Education at the United States Department of Education)

"This is a significant contribution to the extant literature on school leadership that will help leaders ensure all children get what they need, including those on "the margins.""
> ~ Dr. Melody Musgrove (Former Director of the Office of Special Education at the United States Department of Education)

"The 21ˢᵗ Century School Leader serves as an accurate depiction of what it means to effectively lead schools in today's world."
> ~ Dr. James E. Berry (Executive Director of the International Council of Professors of Educational Leadership)

"A must-read for all aspiring and practicing school leaders."
> ~ Dr. Todd Whitaker (Leading author and speaker on Educational Leadership)

"It is my hope that any individual aspiring to the superintendency in the 21ˢᵗ Century will take the time to read this text."
> ~ Dr. Thomas Tucker (Two-time National Superintendent of the Year and current Superintendent)

"This book should be titled School Leadership 101. It clearly encompasses all aspects of school leadership from the building level to district office. Brilliant!"
> ~ Tom Burton (Former Principal of the Year and Teacher of the Year, and current Superintendent)

"Written from both a practitioner and scholarly perspective, Dr. Fowler has bridged the gap between theory and practice as it applies to school leadership in the 21ˢᵗ Century."
> ~ Dr. Jerry Johnson (Current President of the Florida Association of Professors of Educational Leadership and Professor of Educational Leadership, University of Central Florida)

"A perfect blend of practical strategies and advice grounded in sound theory and mindset; Dr. Fowler addresses the challenges of 21st Century schools by helping to equip both seasoned and aspiring school leaders with the tools for success. Dr. Fowler's work will no doubt find its way into the hands of countless school leaders around the globe and, in turn, positively impact the lives of countless students."
~ *Dr. Justin Tarte (Executive Director of Human Resources, Union R-XI School District)*

"With The 21st Century School Leader, Dr. Fowler articulates a clear path forward for all educational leaders seeking to make a difference in the lives of children. Fowler's work is a must read for aspiring and practicing school leaders."
~ *Dr. Chris Colwell (Chair of the Department of Education, Stetson University)*

"As a successful school principal and professor, I am extremely impressed with the accuracy, profoundness, and utility of The 21st Century School Leader. This book captures the essence of effective school leadership in the current age of accountability."
~ *Dr. Arvin Johnson (Former Principal and Current Assistant Professor of Educational Leadership at Kennesaw State University)*

"Dr. Fowler's work shines an important light on the necessary transition of modern educational leaders. This book provides a glowing marker on the educational landscape, utilizing practical advice and personal experience to guide current leadership practices for the success of today's students in tomorrow's world."
~ *Kenneth J. Hopkins Jr. (Former Assistant Principal of the Year and Current Principal, Rhode Island)*

"Dr. Fowler has assembled a genuine and relevant collection of knowledge that provides real-world advice for today's educational leaders. As the landscape of public education continues to change at such a rapid pace, it is my hope that all current and aspiring leaders take the time to read The 21st Century School Leader for valuable advice on how to meet the needs of ALL students."
~ *Dr. Robert F. Hill (Current Superintendent, Springfield, Ohio)*

"Dr. Fowler has purposefully presented the various components and mechanisms for what it takes to be an effective leader and advocate for students in today's schools."

~ *Dr. Sarah Graham (Assistant Professor of Educational Leadership & Policy Studies, California State University, Sacramento)*

"Dr. Fowler's work raises critical questions and prompts deep thinking for every school leader who understands the ever-changing role of technology in 21st Century schools.

~ *Jason Johnson (Current High School Principal, Columbus, Ohio)*

"At the heart of this book is the understanding that instructional leaders lead for the improvement of the quality of teaching and for the improvement of student learning."

~ *Dr. Valerie Storey (Associate Professor of Educational Leadership, University of Central Florida)*

"There is no more important time in education than today for our leaders to be prepared for the rigors and rewards that come with school leadership in the 21st Century. Dr. Fowler has pulled together the best research and practices in this new book. All aspiring school leaders, at any level, will be more effective for taking the time to read it."

~ *Dr. Trent Grundmeyer (Former High School Principal and current Assistant Professor of Educational Leadership, Drake University)*

"The 21st Century School Leader is a text that must be adopted in every school leader preparation program. The topics are spot on, from social media to work-life balance to leading for inclusiveness to school culture and everything in between. Dr. Fowler is at the forefront of ushering in a new era of school leadership!"

~ *Dr. David DeJong (Assistant Professor of Educational Leadership, The University of South Dakota)*

"Dr Fowler's work will undoubtedly inspire school leaders at all levels to reflect and 'adjust the sails' as he skillfully couples personal anecdotes with real-world examples. The result is a perfect balance of the theoretical, the ethical and the practical."

~ *Walter Brown (Co-Founder of New York City Department of Education's EDxED Annual Conference and current Assistant Principal at Hudson High School of Learning Technologies in New York City)*

"This book will help many sitting and future education leaders sift through the smoke and mirrors and do what's best for children."

~ *MDonnell Tenner (Current Superintendent and Author of Realistic Strategies that Eradicate the School to Prison Pipeline)*

"Public education is changing rapidly and that change requires a new mindset and skillset from educators. With this text, Dr. Fowler articulates a road map for current and aspiring school leaders to meet these new challenges head-on for the benefit of student learning and growth, and as such, it is a must read for practitioners."

~ *Dr. Justin Geurin (Educational Leadership Consultant and Professor)*

Join the conversation online!
Use #21stCenturyLeader when posting on all social media including Twitter, Instagram, LinkedIn, Facebook, and the like...

Forthcoming books from Dr. Denver J. Fowler

with Tentative Release Dates

Educational Setting

Human Resources: A Practical Guide for School Leaders
by Dr. Denver J. Fowler and Dr. Douglas R. Davis
Due to be released in 2019 from Rowman & Littlefield

A Guide to Educational Technology in the Digital Millennial Age
by Dr. Denver J. Fowler, Dr. Marlena Bravender, and Mr. John Riley
Due to be released in 2020 from ICPEL Publications

Transformative Leadership in Schools
by Dr. Denver J. Fowler and Dr. Sarah Graham
Due to be released in 2021 from Word & Deed Publishing

Thoughts on Race, Class, and Education
by Dr. Denver J. Fowler and Mr. MDonnell Tenner
Due to be released in 2022 from Harvard Education Press

Memoirs

*I'm Your Huckleberry: A Completely True Story of
Perseverance, Resilience, Persistence, and Triumph*
by Dr. Denver J. Fowler
Release date TBA

Two Years in Mississippi
by Dr. Denver J. Fowler
Release date TBA

The 21st Century School Leader:

Leading Schools in Today's World

A ~~Nation~~ Generation at Risk

Dr. Denver J. Fowler

Foreword by
Dr. Todd Whitaker
Best-selling author and leading speaker on Educational Leadership

Afterword by
Dr. Thomas Tucker
Two-time National Superintendent of the Year in the United States

The 21ˢᵗ Century School Leader:
Leading Schools in Today's World

Edited by: Darrin Griffiths, Ed.D.
Book design by: bookdesign.ca

PowerPoint/Prezi Presentations* Designed by Dr. Denver J. Fowler
*free with purchase of the book, download at www.wordanddeedpublishing.com

ISBN 978-0-9918626-6-5

Word & Deed Publishing Incorporated
434-2000 Appleby Line
Burlington, Ontario, Canada, L7L 7H7
(Toll Free) 1-866-601-1213
Visit our website at:
www.WordandDeedPublishing.com

Connect with the author, Dr. Denver J. Fowler via social media:

Twitter: @DenverJFowler
Skype: DenverJFowler
Instagram: drdenverjfowler
Facebook: @denver.j.fowler
LinkedIn: https://www.linkedin.com/in/dr-denver-j-fowler-8798511b/
ResearchGate: https://www.researchgate.net/profile/Denver_Fowler2
Faculty Website: http://www.csus.edu/coe/profiles/fowler-denver.html
WordPress: https://denverfowler.wordpress.com
Booking Inquiries (LaMasters Group, LLC) at: lamastersgroup@gmail.com

Dedication

I would like to dedicate this book to my wife and best friend, Anna Caroline Fowler. Thank you for your unconditional love, unwavering support, and consistently sound advice. "God blessed the broken road that led me straight to you."

To my daughter, Haley Jade Fowler (currently an Early Childhood Education major at The Ohio State University), and my two sons, Beckett Daniel Fowler and Teagan Robertson Fowler. May you forever remain curious and always chase your wildest dreams, whatever they may be.

To my mother, Cathie Jane Fowler, a single parent who worked two and three jobs her entire life to raise my brother and I. Thank you for all of the sacrifices that you made for us. They did not go unnoticed. Thank you for always telling me that I can accomplish anything, to always chase my dreams, and to always focus on what I have, versus what I do not.

To my brother, Levi Hunter Fowler, we've been through it all together, and we still rose from the ashes. Glory be to God!

I would also like to dedicate this book to my late grandpa, 1st Lt. Francis 'Fritz' Moran, an Indian motorcycle dirt track racer and Tank Commander in World War II, fighting in two major campaigns, The Battle of the Bulge and Normandy, later receiving the Purple Heart. My late grandma, Helen Moran, who held a family together years before they began to diagnose our soldiers with post-traumatic stress disorder.

To my late grandpa, George Lee Fowler, who coal mined his entire life in the coal mines of West Virginia, before eventually dying of black lung disease. My late grandma, Mary Katherine Fowler, who was a *Rosie the Riveter* during World War II and successfully raised 13 children on miner's pay.

To my late uncle, Chris Fowler, a Veteran who worked construction and rode Harleys his entire life. You were there for me so many times to offer sound advice. Thank you.

To my late uncle, Patrick Moran, a Vietnam Veteran who never really came home from the Vietnam War.

To all the teachers, coaches, professors, colleagues, friends and family members who have consistently "nudged my boat" over the years. Thank you for believing in me.

Finally, to all the individuals working in the education setting. We have the most important job in the world. Don't ever forget that. Our children's hopes and dreams start and end with you each and every day. Teach them to dream big and be great!

God, Family, Academics, Athletics, the Arts.

Greatest Love of All

I believe the children are our future,
teach them well and let them lead the way,
show them all the beauty they possess inside,
give them a sense of pride, to make it easier,
let the children's laughter, remind us how we used to be.

Everybody is searching for a hero,
people need someone to look up to...

Written by Linda Creed and Michael Masser
Sung by Whitney Houston

Contents

List of Tables

List of Figures

Foreword by Dr. Todd Whitaker

"A must-read for all aspiring and practicing school leaders."

The PreK-12 educational landscape is changing, and changing quickly. Leading schools in today's world, in many ways, is very different than leading schools in the past (even the most recent past). Perhaps the most significant change deals with technology and the fact that our stakeholders, including students, staff, parents, and community members, are what many would classify as "digital natives."  That is, oftentimes they are more well versed in technology (including educational technology) than the very individuals that lead and teach in their schools.

In *The 21st Century School Leader: Leading School's in Today's World*, author Denver Fowler highlights this changing landscape and suggests how school leaders should navigate the new terrain. He shares many innovative insights with regards to school leaders utilizing social media, the importance of branding your school building and/or district, participating in Twitter chats for professional development, using data teams to close the achievement gap, strategies to cultivate a positive school climate and culture, and the importance of maintaining a healthy work-life balance. A former award-winning practitioner, Denver offers proven strategies to successfully implement these items in both your life and school.

In addition, Denver covers school law, school finance, and human resources – all things equally important to leading schools effectively. Having had experience in both the PreK-12 educational setting and higher education, Denver helps bridge the gap by addressing items such as the new standards guiding educational leadership preparation programs across the nation and how they affect school leaders in the PreK-12 educational setting. With a research agenda focused on ethics and leadership, he offers helpful insights on how to lead with integrity. His chapter on the importance of networking and advocacy efforts shines much-needed light on both federal and state advocacy initiatives, and how a school leader might help influence them. Finally, through a social justice lens, Denver makes a strong argument that we have an equity issue in education, not a quality issue. He also makes some innovative suggestions on how we might fix this problem in order to avoid what he describes as "a zip code determining the quality of education a child receives, as well as their future."

The 21st Century School Leader: Leading Schools in Today's World is a must-read for all aspiring and practicing school leaders; this book is filled with helpful insights, proven strategies, and tips for school leaders to effectively lead schools in today's world.

Preface

A few years ago, after a trip to Italy in which I served as the keynote speaker at the International Conference on Interdisciplinary Research in Education, I decided to write *The 21ˢᵗ Century School Leader: Leading Schools in Today's World*. I made this decision after traveling much of the world, visiting schools, and speaking with students, educators, and school leaders across the globe. Through these visits and conversations, one common theme emerged, many of the school leaders were leading schools much like we have in the distant past. Moreover, other common themes emerged. I found that many school leaders were great managers, but much less instructional leaders. I unearthed that many failed to utilize readily accessible and available resources such as student achievement data, social media, and stakeholders. I discovered that school leaders had a lousy work-life balance, failed to understand the importance of fostering a positive school climate and school culture (and the difference between school culture and school climate), undervalued advocacy efforts, and were not well-versed in school law, school finance, and human resources. Furthermore, I found that school leaders were not doing a great job at being life-long learners, did not understand the importance of networking, and the majority were not actively involved with the educational leadership organizations and associations they belonged to. I uncovered that many school leaders were intimidated by technology, mainly due to the fact that their students (and in some cases, teachers) understood it better than them. I realized school leaders did not fully understand the educational leadership standards and where they came from, and how these very standards determined the coursework they completed to become a licensed school leader. Finally, I found that there were some unethical school leaders out there (I know, big surprise), who had no business being in a leadership position in any organization, especially a school. As I thought more and more about these items on my long flight back from Italy to the United States, I kept asking myself ... *What can I do to shed light on these issues?* ... and perhaps more importantly ... *How can I help current and aspiring school leaders prepare to lead schools in today's world?* On that long flight home, it occurred to me that I must write this book to ensure we were leading schools effectively in the 21st Century, where most of our stakeholders are digital natives[1] and have the highest expectations of the individuals responsible for educating and leading their children on a daily basis.

A Unique Perspective

In order for readers to fully understand the content of this book, I believe it would be doing them a disservice not to paint a clear picture of who I am, and furthermore, the mold from which I was cut. Growing up, I was sometimes homeless, lived in a battered women's shelter, and often moved from place to place. My younger brother and I were raised by my single mother who worked two to three jobs her entire life in order to both support and raise us. I attended six different elementary schools in four different states by the time I was in fifth grade. I had my first child at 16 years old. I was the poster child for all of the demographics we researchers and educators mull over; demographics which set most children up for failure, and perhaps even worse, the school to prison pipeline, a topic that has garnered much attention and debate in recent years. Because of these demographics, I am much more like your students, and perhaps much less like you, or the school leaders employed throughout our nation and around the globe. That is, the fact that this is my background, and the fact that I became a school leader (and later a professor), would certainly be the exception, not the rule. Thus, it is my belief that this book will offer a much desirable and dissimilar perspective to both aspiring and practicing school leaders around the globe. A perspective from an individual that, in many ways, shares a similar background with many of the students you will and/or currently serve.

For a moment, let's think about my demographics ... teen parent, high student mobility, single parent household, a witness to severe domestic abuse, and in some cases, a minority in the schools in which I attended, and of course, low socioeconomic status (SES) – this was me, and this is your students. Students that you are expected to lead, teach, and provide

---

1   A digital native is an individual who was born and/or brought up during the age of digital technology and is therefore familiar with computers and the Internet from an early age.

with the best education possible, despite the overwhelming obstacles and conditions they bring from their home lives. Now, we know that statistically speaking, in many ways, students with these demographics do fail, and in some cases, do end up in prison. Furthermore, we know that schools who serve a higher number of such students tend to be the schools that have lower test scores, lower graduation rates, lower numbers of students matriculating into college, and are located in low income communities.

However, let's for a moment think about those schools that get the job done anyway; leaders, that despite these odds, are leading high performing schools. We might turn to the 90/90/90[2] schools in the State of Wisconsin (Reeves, 2003), schools known as "High Poverty but High Performing." One might look to Kannapel, Clements, Taylor, and Hibpshman's (2005) study of elementary schools in the State of Kentucky that continue to have success educating low SES minority students, or David and Talbert's (2012) study of a school district in the State of California, that was once named one of the lowest performing schools in the state, but now has miraculously and consistently been achieving at high levels with regard to student achievement. Dating back to the Coleman Report (1966), as well as Brookover and Lezotte's work (1979), this concept of identifying effective schools that were high achieving regardless of low SES and the like is not new. Therefore, the question about *if* it is possible has long since been answered, and we know that it *is* possible to be a high performing school providing a quality education to students regardless of their SES, ethnicity, or, perhaps more encumbering, their zip code. That is, there are many examples of schools getting the job done regardless of these obstacles both in the United States and elsewhere (Barker, 2006; Black, 2008; Howard, Nitta, & Wrobel, 2010; Martin, Fergus, & Noguera, 2010; Ramalho, Garza, & Merchant, 2010; Rennie Center for Education Research & Policy, 2011). Thus, as school leaders, we must have a "no-excuses mindset" in educating our students. Anything less is unacceptable and miscreant. Furthermore, we might

---

2   90/90/90 schools are schools in which 90 percent of their students are on free and reduced lunch (low socioeconomic status), 90 percent of their students are from ethnic minority groups, and 90 percent of their students are meeting achievement standards reflected in the student achievement data (Reeves, 2003).

identify students who, despite such demographics (such as mine), don't fail, don't end up in prison, and in contrast, become successful adults. I think of individuals like Oprah Winfrey (The Oprah Winfrey Show), Manny Scott (Freedom Writer), Michael Oher (The Blind Side), Andy Andrews (Author), and many others, who all, despite great odds, went on to become successful adults in their own right. Might we learn something from these folks? Might their stories help us better understand and identify how school leaders can "nudge the boat" of such students in order to ensure they become successful adults? I think so, and it is my hope that you do too!

Although this book will be less about *individuals* (particularly PreK-12 students) overcoming monumental odds, it will shed light on how to lead such students and the schools they attend, to success. I will be the first to tell you, that, statistically speaking, I was supposed to fail, and I am here to tell you, my friend, I almost did. In fact, a lot of my childhood friends did just that: failed, ended up in prison, and sadly, some will stay there for the rest of their lives. One might wonder how I overcame such odds, and although it will not be fully discussed in this book (albeit some aspects will be shared as it relates to the content of the book), it will be thoroughly covered in another book that I am writing titled *I'm Your Huckleberry: A Completely True Story of Perseverance, Resilience, Persistence, and Triumph* (publisher and film rights TBD). Throughout my childhood (and like most students with such demographics), school and athletics were the only two constants in my life. That is, no matter where we moved, I always had a school to go to and sports to play, and fortunately, I was a decent athlete. Even today, when I walk into a school building, or onto a playing field, I feel most at home. Unfortunately, as one might imagine, the aforementioned demographics played a large part in my success (or lack thereof) as a student in the PreK-12 educational setting, much as it does for the students in your schools. Nonetheless, if our aim is to help such individuals, then I believe the best place (and most practical place) to start is in our schools, one day at a time, one student at a time. Now, I went on to college (as a first-generation college student), was able to overcome these demographics, and went on to become a successful coach, teacher, athletic director, technology coordinator, school leader, and now a professor. But unfortunately, as I previously mentioned, we know this is the exception and not the rule. Nevertheless, I believe it would be reckless of me not to point out that I had some excellent coaches, teachers, administrators, professors, as well as a loving and supportive mother – all of which nudged my boat along the way.

This book will focus on the latter portions of my life, that is, as it relates to my school leader experience and my experience as a professor preparing future school leaders. Furthermore, this book encompasses and embodies effective school leadership practice—practices that I believe to cover every aspect of what it means to successfully lead a school in today's world. The content focuses on leading school buildings and school districts in the digital age (21st Century) with the knowledge that all stakeholders, including students, teachers, parents, community members, and business owners are digital natives. In addition, the book infuses this approach into all aspects of successfully leading a school building/district, attempting to leave no rock unturned. In making a deeper connection between the content and practice, I have included questions and scenarios (with optional roles and settings) at the end of each chapter for both practicing and aspiring school building/district leaders to consider and mull over as it relates to the content within each chapter.

It is my hope that this book will become a staple in university school leadership programs across the nation (and around the globe) that prepare aspiring school building/district leaders. Additionally, it is my hope that the book will become an excellent source of valuable information for practitioners in the field. Finally, and perhaps most importantly, I hope that you, the reader, enjoy this book and will share your takeaways with individuals who are currently leading schools and/or aspire to lead schools in the 21st Century.

Your Partner in Education,

Dr. Denver J. Fowler – a #21stCenturyLeader

Chapter 1

Leading Schools in Today's World

"There are two types of schools: those that prepare kids for the future, and those that allow adults to live comfortably in the past." ~ Wes Kieschnick

Introduction

"Leadership skills aren't stagnant." I remember reading these words as I skimmed over an article in Forbes (2017) titled *13 Leadership Skills You Didn't Need A Decade Ago That Are Now Essential.* I thought to myself ... these authors are on to something here. It is true, with different generations entering our schools (and others leaving the workplace/retiring), we must begin to identify what it means to be an effective leader in the 21st Century, not only in our schools, but in other settings as well. I have often argued that leadership is leadership, regardless of the setting. Nonetheless, in the same breath, I would argue that there is a certain amount of knowledge base required to lead in a given setting, specific to the setting. Likewise, I would argue that "sitting in all the required seats" on your way up the ladder of success in a given organization is equally important in fully understanding a given organization. For example, in the school setting, this might mean being a student teacher, substitute teacher, coach, teacher, lead teacher, dean of students, assistant principal, principal, district office personnel, assistant superintendent, and associate superintendent, all before becoming a superintendent. Worth noting: my own research has shown the importance of experience as it applies to the ethical leadership perspectives of superintendents (Fowler & Johnson, 2014; Fowler, Edwards, & Hsu, 2018). Nevertheless, I want to share what the 13 professional coaches at Forbes (2017) identify as the 13 leadership skills needed in today's world. As you read through each, think about how they might apply to the education setting. After each skill, I will report the individual who suggested the particular skill, and their affiliation.

13. *Co-Creative Leadership* by Steffan Surdek, Pyxis Technologies
12. *Leadership of Virtual Teams and Independent Contractors* by Shauna C. Bryce, Bryce Legal Career Counsel
11. *Mastery of Crucial Conversations* by Jody Michael, Jody Michael Associates
10. *Authenticity* by Michelle Tillis Lederman, Executive Essentials
9. *Social Media Presence* by John O'Connor, Career Pro Inc.
8. *Emotional Intelligence* by Gia Ganesh, Gia Ganesh Coaching
7. *Collaboration* by Maureen Metcalf, Metcalf & Associates, Inc.
6. *Multigenerational Management* by Linette Montae, Profitable CEO
5. *Hybrid of Skills* by Adrienne Tom, CERM, CPRW, MCRS, Career Impressions
4. *Navigation of Ambiguity* by Rey Castellanos, Feed Your Wolf
3. *Culture Management* by MaryAnne Gillespie, Red Apple Coaching
2. *Resiliency* by Irvine Nugent, Sonos Leadership
1. *Executive Presence* by Leslie Mizerak, Lead Coach Mentor, LLC

As you read through each of the skills listed above, one thing becomes blatantly apparent: leaders in today's world, in any setting, need an array of skills to not only lead, but lead effectively, and furthermore, what was once effective leadership (then) may not be what we consider to be effective leadership in today's world (now).

Then and Now

"In order to change an existing paradigm, you do not need to struggle to try and change the problematic model. You create a new model and make the old one obsolete."
~ *Buckminster Fuller*

What does it mean to lead schools in today's world? It quite simply means that leading schools in the 21st Century is rather different than leading schools in any other day and age throughout history. Today we have to lead schools while being cognizant of, and knowing how to use, a slew of technology at the fingertips of the very stakeholders we serve, including students, staff, parents, community members, and business owners. It necessitates the tradigital[3] approach to school leadership. That is, school leaders must be able to utilize what we know are best practices of traditional school leadership, and somehow combine them with the best practices of school leadership in the digital world, the 21st Century. At perhaps no other time in history, new technology is being created and released at colossal rates. New Apps and educational technology are invented daily, and more innovative and efficient ways of doing things become the norm, and many of these innovations can be utilized by school leaders. To put it in perspective, if you are like me, you are considered to be part of the micro-generation (born between 1977-1983) which had an analogue childhood that morphed into a digital adulthood. Think about our students today ... their entire lives have been all digital. I am sure we all know at least a few two-year-olds who operate technology better than most adults. Folks, the digital natives are here, and they are coming to our school buildings. We had better be ready to lead them, and lead them effectively in the 21st Century and beyond.

> "The finest educators consider it professional malpractice to not change when they learn new and better ways of doing their work."
>
> ~ Casas, Whitaker, and Zoul

School leaders who force themselves to become comfortable with, and use, the latest technology, become models of technology users in schools. This type of principal is an instructional leader who is also a technology leader. Quite contrarily, those school leaders who do not attempt to become comfortable with the latest technology, and refuse to use it,

---

3   Tradigital learning is where teachers keep the best practices of a traditional classroom and combine it with the best practices of a digital classroom (Seymour, 2017).

become a very different model within their schools. They become one who emulates someone who is not a life-long learner, and one who refuses to embrace innovation and utilization of new technologies. In fact, some might argue, this type of school leader is simply ineffective based on this trait alone, especially in the 21st Century. This idea is perhaps best captured in a book titled *Leading the Technology-Powered School* by Marilyn Grady (2011), in which she wrote the following:

> To be a principal in the 21st Century school demands leadership of technology. To be a leader of technology requires a willingness to learn, embrace flexibility, and the capacity to accept change as a constant factor. Adaptability and acceptance of ambiguity are essential. Because technology changes continuously, there is no menu of technology must do's and must haves. Instead, leaders of technology must be lifelong learners and explorers of the new, the exciting, and the useful in technology (p. 3-4).

Although I will thoroughly cover social media in chapter two (it needs its own chapter), in this chapter we will focus on the other Apps and technology that school leaders can utilize and promote the use of by the teachers whom they lead. In keeping with Marilyn's quote shared above, I do not intend to provide the "must do's and must haves," as they constantly change. However, I do intend to provide what I consider to be the current foundational technology that should be utilized by all school leaders. That being said, in order to highlight each, and how each can be used, I have inserted two Tables including the following information with regards to each App and/or technology shared: name, where to find it, how to use it, why use it, and any notes I deem useful. Table 1 is specifically for school leaders. Whereas Table 2 is for your teachers. Table 2 is included because as an instructional leader, you will want to share and support the effective use of technology by your teaching staff. Furthermore, Table 2 highlights many of the new technologies out there to be utilized effectively with classroom instruction. In order to provide you with an excellent starting point without overwhelming you, I have chosen to provide what I consider to be my "top picks" for both school leaders and teachers.

*Table 1: Apps and Technology Recommendations for School
Leaders*

Name	Where to find it	How to use it	Why use it	Notables
Classroom Walk-Through (App)	www. classroomwalk-through.com or App Store	Conduct Classroom Walk-Throughs using the App.	Send walk-through feedback to the teacher via email before you even leave the classroom.	The walk-through form is editable to ensure it aligns with your district's/state's formal walk-through template.
Splashtop	www.splashtop. com or App Store	Access anything via your iPad that exists on your desktop in your office. This process is called mirroring.	iPads do not have Microsoft Office, likewise, you can access teacher folders, etc. when conducting evaluations.	Most states utilize an online data base to upload your formal observations to. This App will ease that process.
Storify	www.storify.com	Celebrate all things happening in your school throughout the week by creating a Storify each Friday and releasing it via social media to your stakeholders.	This gives you the opportunity to celebrate and share all things happening throughout the week in your school. This gives your stakeholders a pulse on your school and helps you brand your school (I will discuss branding your school in chapter two).	Storify is easily shared through social media, thus allowing your stakeholders to easily access it. Think of it like live blogging. Storify supports hashtags and is often used to capture Twitter chats (I will discuss hashtags and Twitter chats in chapter two).

WordPress	www.wordpress.com	Create a blog to celebrate and share important information with your stakeholders and colleagues.	A blog allows you to inform your stakeholders on important issues in education and/or items affecting your school. Likewise, it gives you the opportunity to share best practices (things you have found work) with colleagues (other school leaders) on a global scale.	Blogs are a great resource if used properly. Blogging is an excellent way to tell your school's story, versus allowing others to tell it for you. Note: Readers beware... blogs are not peer-reviewed.
Prezi	www.prezi.com or App Store	Think PowerPoint on steroids. This is a great tool for creating dynamic staff presentations.	It is quite simply, a better way to present and conduct professional development.	Be sure to sign up for the educator account. Be mindful, when presenting a Prezi, you need Internet connection. You can now download Prezi's into PDF's and they have an App.
PollEverywhere	www.polleverywhere.com	Create live polls for your staff. Audience members vote by texting or by accessing a website (connected to your poll).	It is live and the poll results are happening in real time in front of your staff/audience.	Plickers, Quizizz, and Kahoot! can be used in this fashion as well. They are included in Table 2.

Hootsuite	www.hootsuite.com or App Store	Control all of your social media through the use of Hootsuite.	Essentially it acts like a social media dashboard and allows you to access and post on all of your social media from one place (versus logging in and posting from each).	It is a time saver and allows you to schedule posts on your school and personal social media outlets.

Again, Table 2 is provided so that you can share the latest classroom technology with your teaching staff. However, it is important to remember that your teachers will have varying levels of knowledge and comfortability when it comes to technology. As a school leader, it will be your job to identify your teachers' skill level, comfort, and knowledge of technology. In addition, you will need to assess how much time you will set aside for things such as professional development in order to devote time to the technology you believe is most vital for the entire staff to utilize in the classroom. For example, I found Plickers (See Table 2) to be extremely important when I was a practitioner. This was mainly for two reasons: (1) Plickers did not require students to have a smartphone; and (2) we felt formative assessments at the end of each lesson were extremely important in determining what would be taught and re-taught the next school day – intervention and/or enrichment. Thus, we devoted much time to training our staff on how to use Plickers for formative assessment in their classrooms after every lesson taught. This is just one example; you will need to decide what is most vital and important with regards to training your staff in using specific educational technology.

Table 2: Apps and Technology Recommendations for Teachers

Name	Where to find it	How to use it	Why use it	Notables
Edmodo	www.edmodo. com	It is a Learning Management System (LMS) much like your students will use in college (i.e., Blackboard, Carmen, Canvas, eLearning, etc.).	By using a LMS like Edmodo, your teachers can create a digital classroom, while also preparing their students for the higher education setting (a LMS is utilized on every campus around the globe).	Other forms of LMS's exist as well, including Google Classrooms, Moodle, etc. Please note that Edmodo supports Google Docs and Microsoft Office products as well.
Plickers	www.plickers. com or App Store	Teachers can access the App on their smartphones, make the response cards for free (print and laminate), and conduct real-time formative assessments at the end of each lesson without the need for student devices (i.e., smartphones).	Students love using it and it allows teachers to conduct formative assessments to inform instruction for the next school day.	Print the response cards for free (and in varying sizes) via the Plickers website or purchase a set of professionally made cards on Amazon.
AirPlay	Usually built in to Mac devices such as iPads and Macbook Pro. Apps exist for Androids, etc.	Allows teachers to mirror student work in real-time projected on the board with the option of zeroing in on one student (i.e., if call on a particular student).	Teachers can monitor all work in real-time on their projector screen via their classroom desktop. Especially useful in 1:1 districts. Allows all students to see a classmates work on their iPad.	Especially great when utilized in math classes and with any type of group work (i.e., four students to one iPad).

ClassDojo	www.classdojo. com or App Store	Teachers can create a positive classroom environment, engage parents, encourage students, and even be sure not to call on the same students, all via this App.	The App is fully customizable, allowing the teachers to make the App work most efficiently for their particular classroom (i.e., classroom expectations, etc.).	Students can also create Student Stories through student-led digital portfolios and then share it with their parents.
Kahoot!	www.kahoot.it or App Store	Teachers can design and create their own fun learning game in just minutes. Students respond via their smartphones and music plays (and speeds up as the time expires) for each question.	Minimal time to create quizzes and students get competitive as it ranks each student after each question. Think the BW3's trivia game adults play.	Teachers can add images, video, and the like within each question and choose how the students' progress and/ or rank will be revealed.
Skype	www.skype.com or App Store	Teachers can Skype with other classes within the building, district, state, nation, and globe.	Allows teachers to connect with colleagues near and far, with the opportunity to align a particular lesson and interact with another class.	Great way to connect your classroom with other classrooms. It is also a great way to utilize experts around the globe, who many schools cannot afford to bring into the school physically. Thus, alleviating travel costs associated with bringing in experts on particular topics.

Teacher Aide Pro	www.teacheraidepro.com or App Store	Allows teachers to conduct attendance, use gradebook, seating charts, track data, and more.	Teachers can track and store many different types of classroom items easily and efficiently through the use of their smartphone.	No need for a written gradebook, seating chart, or attendance sheet. All of these items can be managed with one App on a smartphone.
Remind 101	www.remind.com or App Store	Allows teachers to send messages in real-time to school, a specific group, or individual. Also sends reminders.	It allows teachers to send quick, simple messages to any device that a parent/student may have.	What I most like about Remind 101 is the ability to include the parent in the learning process…and as we all know, with a busy schedule, parents like a reminder every now and then.
Quizizz	www.quizizz.com	Much like Kahoot! and Plickers, it is a great way to make quizzes more fun.	Teachers can conduct formative assessments in a fun and interactive fashion. Students see (on their devices) the questions in a different order than their classmates.	Works great with Google classroom. Music is included and allows group work up to 12 students. Easily loads quiz data into Excel. Can assign homework based on results and email parents the results at the push of a button.

Below are a few more resources I wanted to share to encourage students to continue their learning over the summer months.

- Free Rice at www.freerice.com
    - Students improve their vocabulary (and more) on the free-to-play website. For each correct answer, 10 grains of rice are raised to help end world hunger through the Word Food Programme.

- Google Story Builder
  - Students can use the App to create dialogue between two or three people with the purpose of studying English (Ferlazzo, 2017).
- Student Designed Summer Projects
  - No technology here, simply have students create a summer project they will complete over the summer months. The key here is to have a general template in place for the project (with rubric), while keeping the template (and rubric) broad enough to allow true student choice with regards to their summer project.

As you can see, there are many different types of Apps and technology that can be utilized by both school leaders and the teachers they lead. This is vital in that our students (and many of our stakeholders) are digital natives, and expect us to utilize the latest and greatest technology in our schools. Furthermore, many of our schools have become 1:1[4] schools, and at the very least, many of our students have some sort of handheld device that they are regularly using from a young age. Thus, in many cases, they are not only familiar with similar technology, they imagine their teachers and school leaders to be familiar with this technology as well. In the 21st Century and beyond, technology in schools, and, more specifically, how it is used effectively with classroom instruction and to improve student learning outcomes, will continue to be at the forefront of much conversation and debate amongst both scholars and practitioners around the globe. Here is a great visual shared by a student on Twitter named Austin Gagnier (follow him @Austin_Gagnier8) of fifteen goals your teachers should set for next academic school year. I believe you will find many of them align with the information shared in Tables 1 and 2 (See Figure 1).

---

4   In the context of education, a 1:1 school is a school that issues an electronic device to each student. Furthermore, this is done so with the thought in mind that students will have access to the Internet, digital course materials, and digital textbooks.

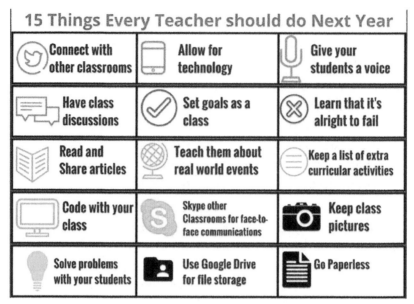

Figure 1: 15 Things Every Teacher should do Next Year

Leading Digital Natives

First and foremost, in order to make sure that you (the reader) and I (the author) are on the same page, we must first define what a digital native is. As defined in the footnote, think of a digital native as an individual who was born and/or brought up during the age of digital technology, and therefore is familiar with computers and the Internet from an early age. For most of you, this is a high percentage of your stakeholders, including students, staff, parents, community members, and business owners. In my experience, I have found that many of these stakeholders are more well-versed and familiar with the latest technology than the school leaders in their schools. Now, some might argue that this is an age thing, and to some extent it is. That is, as the definition implies, if you were brought up and/or born during the digital age, you are much more likely to be comfortable using things like computers, the Internet, and pretty much any type of digital technology out there. If you are someone who feels that you are not literate in digital technology, you might be considered a digital immigrant. This is where intergenerational efforts come into play. We need more of our digital natives to reach out to our digital immigrants. To put this in layperson's terms, we need our younger school leaders to reach out to our older school leaders in an effort to bridge the digital gap (worth noting here, age does not always correlate with digital awareness, this is just an example). On a much broader scale, we need our students to feel comfortable reaching out to their teachers, and our teachers need to feel comfortable reaching out to their school leaders, and so forth – all in an effort to bridge the digital gap. In essence, we need to be willing to learn from each other, and sometimes this means learning from a student or teacher. Perhaps Jeff DeGraff (2014) explains this best in his article on the blog Huffington Post titled *Digital Natives vs. Digital Immigrants*:

> Don't let the word "digital" fool you in all this talk about how difficult it is for digital natives and digital immigrants to communicate. The truth is that this generational gap between the so-called digital natives (the generation of people born during or after the rise of digital technologies) and the digital immigrants (people born before the advent of digital technology) doesn't actually have to do with technology. The real issue is that the two worldviews that they represent are so different. The irony is, eventually, we will come full circle: The children of digital natives will act like digital immigrants. This is just how things work: We see the world differently from the people who came before us. Generations are simply oppositional in nature. But they don't have to be at odds with each other. It's about talking with and learning from people who you normally wouldn't work with, who don't see things the way you do. What will you do to start a dialogue with a generational stranger, your digital other?

I found this blog post somewhat fascinating. It reminded me that we can learn a lot from our students, who in many cases are much younger than we are. I was just listening to the radio on my way into the office the other day and someone called into the station. As he and the radio jockey were discussing technology, he said jokingly, "and if I have a problem with technology or need help with it, I just go consult my ten-year-old." The radio jockey replied, "Me too, I just find my daughter who is in middle school." Personally, I have experienced this myself and I have a technology background as a former computer science teacher, technology coordinator, and a professor who has taught classroom technology courses. The other day, I wanted to mirror a game from my iPhone to our television and was having trouble making it work. My five-year-old came over, grabbed my phone from me, and showed me what I was doing wrong and immediately fixed the problem. My wife and I looked at each other in amazement as he quickly jumped back on his iPad and started playing his Minecraft game. Unfortunately, this is all too common: teenagers (and in some cases, even younger) know how to use the latest technology better than a majority of adults, including educators and school leaders. Nonetheless, they expect us to know it better. In their mind, educators and school leaders are to be the experts at all things. Now, I am not saying that we cannot learn from our students, because we can (and we should – the importance of student voice in schools will be covered later in this book). However, I would liken it to a parent who cannot help their child with their math homework because they just do not have the knowledge to do so. In this case, I see two things happening: (1) the child may begin to believe that this math is not particularly important if their parent does not know how to do it; and (2) the parent loses credibility with their child, as often children believe adults should know more (or at least a little more) about all things, including technology. Now, this particular scenario (a parent unable to help their child with math) should occur much less frequently because of available (and free) resources such as Khan Academy (see: www.khanacademy.org). Nonetheless, this scenario can be dangerous, especially in the education setting where students expect to go to school in order to learn and be pushed to learn more from both their educators and school leaders, who are supposed to be life-long learners, and keep up with the latest trends in education, including all forms of technology.

It is worth noting that this does not only apply to academics, but discipline issues as well. One concern that I found, that has become the new norm, was that in many cases, when dealing with discipline, before I even had a chance to speak with the students concerned, or the teachers who brought/sent the students to the office, their parents would be waiting outside my office or calling the school to ask me about what had happened, when I had not even acquired the full story myself. That is, students would text their parents that they were waiting in the office or on their way to the office because this or that had happened. This would lead to the parent immediately calling the school and/or arriving at the school in order to determine what was going on before I had even spoken with the teacher or students about the incident. This communication from the student to the parent would happen in just seconds, giving school leaders very little time to figure out what happened and how to handle it, before all parents were involved. I found this to be extremely problematic, as now you are trying to wrap your head around what has happened, how to deal with it, and in addition to the students, the parents are present and/or on the phone as well. Certainly, this is not the ideal situation with handling discipline, however, it is the new norm, especially if you as a school leader are going to incorporate things such as Bring Your Own Device (BYOD) and allow the use of cell phones and other handheld devices throughout the school day. In addition, if you do not fully understand the technology that students (and in some cases, teachers) are using, it can be difficult to manage and make informed decisions regarding the technology and incidents that arise and occur from the use of it. With technology such as Snapchat (see: www.snapchat.com) and others, it is important to understand how the technology works – as I have personally experienced many discipline issues that arise from the latest technology including cyber bullying and the like. In my experience, I have found that school leaders who do not fully understand such technology have a difficult time understanding what exactly is going on, and, furthermore, have a hard time making an informed decision with regard to such incidents and how to handle the discipline/consequences aspect of it. Students who understand technology better than the educators and school leaders in their school building (and know it), can be problematic. In fact, some may take pride in the fact that they can get one over on their teachers and principals, and even their superintendents. For example, in one of the school districts in which I served, a student created a fake Twitter (see: www.twitter.com) account for our superintendent. The student proceeded to tweet some pretty witty things, but nonetheless, mostly negative things. This lasted for quite some time, as we were unable to determine who was behind the account. It became extremely problematic, as many students thought they were following the actual superintendent on Twitter, and did not realize it was actually someone else. In fact, the fake account had several hundred more followers than the superintendent's real account. Thus, each tweet was reaching a much wider audience. Things reached a new level when on one snowy morning in the winter months, this student tweeted that school was closed due to weather. Because this fake account had so many followers, word spread quickly and most of the school did not attend school that day. The student was eventually caught and the Twitter account was removed, but not before some major damage had been done. These are just a few examples of how and why it is important for educators and school leaders to fully understand the latest technology as well as the digital natives in our schools and communities. If they do not, it can be extremely dangerous, as educators and school leaders may not fully understand the extent to which damage may be caused by one student to another, or, as in the latter scenario, by one student to a district. Without fully understanding the technology and how it works, both educators and school leaders are at a disadvantage and can easily let such incidents slip through the cracks, and, perhaps more troubling, allow a student to be bullied via such technology, or an entire school district to be affected by one snow day tweet. These scenarios, coupled with other discipline issues that arise from technology, can give educators and school leaders a negative perception of technology use in their schools, which oftentimes leads to schools getting rid of all technology altogether. I do not believe this is the answer; rather, I believe incorporating technology (all forms, including student cell phones and other handheld devices) allows for teachable moments that students will need to learn as future citizens of our society such as "pause before you post" and "face your problems, don't Facebook your problems", and others.

In recent years, we have seen the detrimental effects of social media. Nonetheless, students will benefit from learning such skills now, versus in adulthood when it could cost them a job, an athletic scholarship, and perhaps even worse, get them charged with breaking the law. It is vital to discuss with students the importance of fully understanding their digital footprint,[5] and how it may affect their livelihood. That being said, I believe it is doing a disservice to our students when schools ban all technology in order to make things easier on the educators and school leaders in a school building or district. In my mind, buildings and districts who implement such bans are only focused on the short-term versus the long-term. We must be cognizant that our students are digital natives and as school leaders we must teach them how to be responsible in using technology.

Digital natives are used to accessing information quickly, and literally at the touch of their fingertips. With so many handheld devices available to students, parents, community members, and business owners, a simple Google search can lead to information with the click of a button. It is no wonder parents are much more prepared when it comes to Individualized Education Plan (IEP) meetings, parent-teacher conferences, data meetings, community meetings, and the like. Parents and community members can search Google on a particular topic and can quickly and easily access an array of information on any subject. I believe this is great: it forces our teachers to be prepared to have meaningful and deep conversations regarding curricula, IEP's, and student data, and how it is being used for intervention, enrichment, etc. However, and here is the issue, parents and community members (and even teachers) will sometimes access inaccurate information via the Internet, and refuse to accept it as inaccurate because it was on the Internet. That is, they believe that because it was on the Internet, it is accurate. It reminds me of that quote that you have probably seen circulating the web: "If it is on the Internet, then it must be true, and you can't question it." ~ Abraham Lincoln. Now obviously the irony there is that Abraham Lincoln was not alive when the Internet was invented. Nonetheless, it is a great reminder that the Internet is a place where anyone can post anything, regardless

---

5   The information about a particular person that exists on the Internet as a result of their online activity.

of whether it is true or not. In fact, one of the biggest downfalls of the Internet is the enormous amount of false information that does exist. In a lot of ways, you can think of the Internet like politics, all smoke and mirrors. That is, it is full of obscuring and embellishing of the truth, and has an immense amount of misleading and irrelevant information.

Many years ago, I was in Columbus, Ohio attending a technology conference as, at the time, I was serving as a technology coordinator. I attended a session on Wikipedia (www.wikipedia.org). During this session, the presenter wanted to show us the dangers of using Wikipedia as a sole source of information (i.e., he was making a point that students should find additional sources because so many students were relying on Wikipedia alone for school projects, papers, and the like). Now, Wikipedia has improved their "anyone can edit" approach. However, at the time of this presentation, it was relatively easy to change information on Wikipedia. In fact, the presenter logged in and changed key information about George Washington in real-time, right there during the presentation. I could not believe it, as I was guilty of using Wikipedia every now and then myself (not as a resource, but to settle disputes of historical information amongst friends). Nevertheless, when looking to the Internet for information, it takes any individual quite a bit of time to sift through it all, and determine excellent sources versus just the top results of a search. Unfortunately, as you will find, your parents and community members oftentimes do not take the time to determine what is an excellent source and what is not. Moreover, they are unaware how easy it is to change information on well-known websites such as Wikipedia and the like. This can lead to issues arising during meetings in which the parent is wrongly informed and unwilling to listen to the teacher and/or school leader because they read something on the Internet that says otherwise. Again, this can be a teachable moment for parents and community members who are digital natives, but do not fully understand the amount of inaccurate information on the Internet. Thus, as a former school leader, I expected my teachers to be prepared to deal with such issues as they arose, and I held myself to the same standard. In my mind, we needed to be the experts when it came to such questions and debates, and I felt it was equally important for our parents to know this as well.

When it comes to digital natives, it would be reckless of me not to mention what I deem to be the great divide, that is the digital divide between the haves and the have nots. With most states moving to online standardized testing, I believe we will see a greater achievement gap, at least in the short-term, until technology becomes more affordable, between the students (especially in the early grade levels) that have access to technology and the Internet at an early age and those students who do not. For example, simple things such as knowing how to play a video, operating an online protractor, dragging things with the mouse (and the list goes on), can be challenging for a student who has not had access to both technology and the Internet from a young age. For the time being, I believe we will continue to see the achievement gap widen as we work though this issue. As technology and Internet become cheaper due to supply and demand, I believe things will eventually even out for such students, but not in the short-term. However, some school districts have gotten creative in how they are ensuring students have access to both technology and the Internet. Many of our nation's schools are implementing 1:1 initiatives in which, for example, each student in grades K-6 is issued an iPad (or the like) and each student in grades 7-12 is issued a Macbook Pro (laptop, or the like), thus, allowing each student to have access to technology. Furthermore, in order to combat the Internet issue, many schools have adopted some creative models in ensuring their students have access to the Internet after school hours. For example, many districts have teamed with local businesses in order to offer their students access to the local businesses Wi-Fi[6]. Additionally, some school districts have installed Internet ports in their buses and then park their buses in strategic locations throughout the school district so that students can access the school Internet via the buses that are picking up the Internet from the school. This is certainly creative, and this is how we must think and operate until all students have equal access to such resources. I have always said that Internet companies should offer free Internet to all schools across the globe, and believe me, they could make this happen, and do so without losing money. The Facebook model is a perfect

---

6   Wi-Fi is technology that allows electronic devices to connect wirelessly to an
    Internet network via a wireless local area network (WLAN).

example: Facebook is free, yet they make their money elsewhere. I have tweeted at these Internet companies suggesting this model, to no avail. In fact, I pitched this very idea (offering free Internet) to ViaSat (they use big geostationary satellites to offer Internet) with no response, only to see Airbus months later announce that it will use low earth orbit satellites to offer cheap (not yet free) Internet to the most remote parts of the world. Nonetheless, I predict it will happen someday, and the Internet company that first offers free Internet world-wide will make enormous financial gains while also allowing students from all socioeconomic groups the opportunity to access the same resources as their wealthier classmates. On one hand, I believe it is too early to move to online testing with regards to state achievement tests, in that there is not equal access to technology resources and the Internet by all students. On the other hand, by moving towards this model, I believe it will force school buildings and school districts to get creative in finding new and innovative opportunities for their students to have equal access to such resources, thus working towards closing the opportunity gap, and perhaps in the near future, the achievement gap.

Time to Adjust the Sails

"The pessimist complains about the wind. The optimist expects it to change. The realist adjusts the sails."
~ *William Arthur Ward*

In my experience, when discussing the differences between how school leaders led then versus now, without question the topic most discussed is this notion of the instructional leader versus a managerial leader. In 2014, I conducted a study on all 614 public school district superintendents in the State of Ohio. The data indicated that the number one teaching license held by superintendents in that state was Social Studies, closely followed by Physical Education (Fowler & Johnson, 2014). Now, I theorize that if we conducted the same study in ten years, we would find that this specific outcome would have changed. We are no longer in the days of school leaders being high profile managers, that is, disciplinarians who were often former coaches who hold a Physical Education, History, and/or Social Studies license. In today's world, school leaders are so much more than disciplinarians and managers. School leaders must be instructional leaders and they must surely be able to analyze data and use it to guide decision-making throughout the building and/or district, especially as it relates to classroom instruction (e.g., interventions, enrichment, etc.) and the curriculum. In addition, they must still be able to "manage" the day-to-day tasks as well. This is no easy task in and of itself. Perhaps Midgley, Stringfield, and Wayman (2006) said it best with regards to the changing tides in school leadership, "Principals and other school leaders have been given a difficult charge: take an abundance of student data, mostly in the form of assessments, and turn this data into information to be used in improving instructional practice." In the United States and around the globe, the role of the school leader is changing and the PreK-12 educational setting continues to evolve. This notion of a school leader needing both strong managerial and instructional skills is relatively new in the grand span of time. Nonetheless, this is where we are in today's world.

It is high time to adjust the sails, as the wind in the PreK-12 educational setting has changed direction, and from a larger-scale bird's eye view, the winds of the world have changed. As school leaders, we must constantly reflect upon our practices and identify strategies in order to become more effective. We should do this because it is what is best for students. We must identify innovative strategies to engage all stakeholders in the process of raising student achievement, infusing character education within the curriculum, and we must be intergenerational, that is, be able to relate to the world our current students are growing up in, be willing to learn from it, and stay relevant. A world where our country has been at war for most (if not all) of our students' (and in some cases, teachers') lives. A world where mass shootings, school shootings, police shootings, and terrorist attacks seem to be becoming the norm rather than the exception (and news of these events is very accessible via technology and the Internet). A world where inequality still exists, especially in education. A world where an effective school leader is someone who is single with no children and a dog, versus someone who is married with a family (I will cover work-life balance in chapter eight). A world where we no longer place value on the things that really matter such as family, the time spent outside of work, and being a good person. A world where our schools are constantly compared to other countries and other models where little diversity exists both culturally and economically amongst their much smaller (overall) student populations (e.g., Finland, China, etc.). As school leaders, we must adjust our sails to the realities that exist. We must lead by example in all that we do, not only as a school leader, but as a parent, marital partner, community member; we must appear more human to the stakeholders that we lead. We must fight for what we know is best for our students (see advocacy in chapter 11). We must speak up for our teachers and students, and ensure we are doing what is best for them in the long-term. We must understand that our students are the future, and that it is up to us to educate them and prepare them to be contributing members of a global society. A society where we embrace each others' differences and celebrate them. A society where we care about the well-being of all members. A society where a zip code no longer determines the type of education a child receives, and, in many cases, their future.

Final Thoughts

I recently read an article (Gupta, 2016) about NOKIA being acquired by Microsoft. I felt this article had relevance to serving as a school leader in the 21st Century. The article reported that the CEO of NOKIA was quoted as saying, "We didn't do anything wrong, but somehow, we lost." As he said this, his entire upper level management team nearby began to cry, literally cry. The truth is, maybe NOKIA, the CEO and his management team didn't do anything wrong. However, maybe the world around them changed so rapidly that they missed out on their chance to *adjust the sails*. "They missed out on the learning, they missed out on changing, and they lost their chance of survival" (Gupta, 2016, p. 1). I personally believe change is difficult, but necessary. The one constant in our life is change, and, as we educators know, the one constant in education in change. Nonetheless, many of us are resistant to any form of change and we tend to be set in our ways. Gupta (2016) advises/writes:

The advantage you have yesterday, will be replaced by the trends of tomorrow. You don't have to do anything wrong, as long as your competitors catch the wave and do it RIGHT, you can lose out and fail. Those who refuse to learn and improve, will definitely one day become redundant and not relevant to the industry. They will learn the lesson the hard way (p.1).

With that in mind, what kind of school leader do you want to be? Do you want to be a school leader who refuses to learn and improve, and becomes irrelevant? ... or do you want to be a 21st Century School Leader and be a life-long learner and stay relevant? Be an innovative trailblazer and lead the way? It is my hope you chose the latter. If you did, the task will not be easy, my friend. If it was, we would all be *Superintendent of the Year*, *Principal of the Year*, and *Assistant Principal of the Year* employed at Nationally Ranked Blue Ribbon Schools. The truth is, to be a 21st Century School Leader, you will have to live outside of your comfort zone on a daily basis. There will be fear that you will have to combat with courage, there will be anxiety that you will have to combat with faith, and there will be skeptics that you will have to combat with knowledge and proven best practices. I'm here to tell you it will take cage-busting leadership. You will have to be a change agent and ignore the status quo – and do so while exercising some political sensibility (i.e., keeping your job). The fact is, if we do not become 21st Century School Leaders, we will most certainly have a generation at risk. It is high time we adjust the sails of school leadership, and not fight the direction of the wind, if not for ourselves, for our students.

Reflection

Questions for Practicing and Aspiring School Leaders

1. Of the technology shared in chapter one for school leaders, what technology do you plan to use, and how will you use it?
2. Of the technology shared in chapter one for teachers, what technology do you plan to share with your teachers, and how (and how often) will you expect them to use it?
3. How will you ensure that you are leading schools in such a way that your leadership embraces digital natives as well as technology in schools?
4. How will you be sure that you are "adjusting your sails" and being an instructional leader versus just a managerial leader?
5. How might you embrace and lead your school in our ever-changing global society?

Problem-based Scenario

You Can't Teach an Old Dog New Tricks

As a building (or district) level school leader, you recently received SMART Boards for every classroom in your building (or district) through a grant. In the summer following the first full academic school year with the SMART Boards installed in every classroom in your building (or district), you are walking your school building (or one of the school buildings in your district) and discover that many of the SMART Boards are not being used. In fact, you discover that many are collecting dust. Upon discovering this, you notice one of your superstar teachers in the hallway and stop her to ask if she had noticed that many of the SMART Boards are not being used. She replies, somewhat irritated, "I am the only one is this hallway who uses a SMART Board with my classroom instruction, aside from showing movies", as she heads back into her classroom. Surprised, you wonder how you might motivate and support the use of this wonderful resource the school/district has received. Upon further reflection, you realize that aside from the superstar teacher, every teacher in said hallway is within 2-3 years of retiring. As a school building (or district) leader, how will you effectively plan to solve this problem?

Choose Your School Setting

Choose your role and then choose your school building/district characteristics before you respond to the scenario. As you draft your response, please be cognizant of how your setting might affect how you respond to the scenario. Essentially, based on the characteristics listed below, think about what we generally know about these characteristics, and, furthermore, how they impact schools/districts. How might they affect your decision-making with regards to the scenario, if at all? Be sure to clearly describe your school setting in your response.

Role: Superintendent, Principal, or Assistant Principal
Locale: Urban, Suburban, or Rural
Size: Small District, Medium District, or Large District
Diversity: No Diversity, Some Diversity, or Very Diverse
SES Status: 100% Free and Reduced Lunch (FRL), 50% FRL, or 0% FRL

Chapter 2

Social Media for School Leaders 101

"We don't have a choice on whether we DO social media,
the question is how well we DO it."

~ Erik Qualman

Celebrate and Celebrate Often

In a recent class discussion with my graduate students, of whom all are aspiring school leaders, a debate occurred in which about half the class believed in the use of social media in schools and the other half did not. Worth noting, and perhaps more disturbing, is that almost all students in my class iterated that their school district did not embrace social media use by teachers or administrators, and in many cases discouraged students from using it, especially on school grounds. I must say that this was shocking to hear, especially in the 21st Century. Nonetheless, after hearing both sides of the debate (obviously I was with/for the students who agreed with utilizing social media in schools), I told the class that as school leaders, "you should tell your school's story, don't let other people tell it for you."

Furthermore, I explained that they also needed to tell their own individual story, and not let other people tell it for them. This is where social media comes into play. I always say that school leaders should "celebrate everything and celebrate often." This includes your own achievements as well. There is a quote that I like that says, "I'm not interested in competing with anyone, I hope we all make it." I mention this here because people can see a little shameless self-promotion by an individual on social media as being competitive with others, or, worse, as coming from someone who is full of themselves and lacks the ability to be humble. By contrast, I see it as celebrating your accomplishments with others (not against others). In the school setting, this is key to telling your school's story. Too often, school leaders do a lousy job of celebrating all of the wonderful things happening within their schools/districts on a daily basis. In addition, they do a lousy job celebrating their own achievements. I believe this serves students, staff, parents, community members, and business owners poorly. When school leaders do not highlight and celebrate all of the wonderful things happening in their building/district on a daily basis, stakeholders can only cling to what they hear and do know about the building/district. In many cases, these are negative rumors and state assessment results.

Although student achievement often determines a school's/district's success or failure, it is certainly not the only thing worth celebrating. As school leaders, we must learn to celebrate all things positive happening in a given school building/district. I call this *Branding Your School*. Much like a business would brand itself, it is your job as the school leader to brand your school, and brand yourself.

Branding Your School & Quality Profile Reports

In recent years, many school leaders have gotten creative about branding. For example, in the State of Ohio many school districts provide a Quality Profile Report (QPR) on an annual basis. Although this report does include academics (i.e., student achievement from state assessment results), it also includes everything else, including areas such as the arts, student leadership and activities, fiscal stewardship, parent and community involvement, and student services. Often, the QPR is located and easily accessible on the school district's website. In addition, in more recent years, a statewide template was created. Since then, a majority of districts providing the QPR use the template in some form or variation. This is a great way of showing the community that schools are so much more than just state assessment results, and that although those results are an important indicator, there is much more to celebrate and share with all stakeholders. Essentially, the QPR provides "the rest of the story" of a given school building/district, giving stakeholders a complete and transparent report on how a school/district is performing in all areas. We all know education goes far beyond what is measured on a consistently changing state report card which, more often than not, focuses primarily on the results of standardized tests given to students in certain grades. As school/district leaders, we must do better than that for our stakeholders and for ourselves. Celebrate it ALL! Because it ALL matters! Below I have provided a few links to school districts in the State of Ohio which are implementing a QPR. Don't reinvent the wheel, don't wait on your state, school or district to initiate this process, recreate this template now, and make it part of your school building/district right away!

Below I have provided two links to examples of QPRs that I thought were well constructed and thought out. If the links below no longer work, please just Google "quality profile report" – as when I did, 367,000,000 results appeared. Find a template you like, and then recreate for your school or district. That being said, you will find very few (if any) school building QPRs (versus school district); however, I strongly believe school leaders are missing the boat here. I envision school building websites with both the district QPR and building QPR readily accessible on their school building website in addition to the district QPR on the district website. There is no such thing as over-celebrating all the wonderful things happening in your school/district. Celebrate and celebrate often!

QPR for Upper Arlington Schools, Upper Arlington, Ohio.
https://www.uaschools.org/uploaded/uploaded_documents/ quality_profile/quality_profile_15-16_FINAL.pdf

QPR for New Albany Plain Local Schools, New Albany, Ohio.
http://www.napls.us/cms/lib07/OH01914683/Centricity/ Domain/251/QualityProfile2013- 2014.pdf

Social Media. In addition to the QPR, school leaders around the nation have become extremely strategic in how they incorporate and utilize social media on a daily basis in their respective schools/districts. The most effective school leaders I know today use Facebook, Instagram, Storify, Twitter, LinkedIn, Hootsuite, Voxer, and other social media not only to brand their schools/districts and themselves, but also for free professional development (this will be covered in the next chapter titled

The Importance of Being a Life-Long Learner). In addition, these school leaders utilize hashtags[7] in their schools/districts, creating and using a hashtag that is unique to their own school/district. Significant thought should go into the hashtag that you decide to use in your school/district, not only from the importance of keeping it relatively short (I recommend keeping it under 5 characters), but also by way of preliminary research to ensure the hashtag you want to use is not being used by someone else. If not, you may set yourself up for failure. For example, if I were the super-intendent at Newcomers Local School District (NLSD), I might use the hashtag #NLSD. Another example might be, if I were the principal at Newcomers Middle School (NMS), I might use the hashtag #NMS This would allow me to connect all social media with my district/school hashtag. Thus, parents could easily search these hashtags, and have a good pulse on all things happening with regards to both NLSD and NMS. This is perhaps especially important for school/district leaders serving in districts where both students and community members are from low SES backgrounds. In an article by CNBC titled *For more poor Americans, smartphones are lifelines* (Ungarino, 2015), it was reported that a Pew Research Center study found that when it comes to the poorest members of society in the United States (in the article termed "the working poor or the financially vulnerable or unstable"), these individuals check their smartphones dozens more times in a single day than the average user. In particular, three groups were found to be "heavy smartphone users." These groups included individuals with extremely low incomes and edu-cation levels, nonwhites, and young adults. That being said, I believe it shows a clear trend for individuals who belong to these subgroups, and I believe it does them a disservice if school leaders do not communicate

---

7   A hashtag is a type of label or metadata tag used on social networks and microblogging services which makes it easier for users to find messages with a specific theme or content. School leaders can create and use hashtags by placing the hash character (or pound sign) # (also known as a number sign or octothorpe) in front of a word or unspaced phrase, either in the main text or at the end. Thus, when stakeholders search for that hashtag, it will yield each message that has been tagged with it. A hashtag archive is consequently collected into a single stream under the same hashtag (Chang & Iyer, 2012).

with such stakeholders in a way that is easily accessible for these individuals, their students, and their families.

Posting on the school district/building website is not enough, as the article further states that the majority of smartphone users do not have any other form of Internet access. Thus, social media Apps may be the best way to communicate with all stakeholders, regardless of their demographics. Nevertheless, in addition to social media communication, it is vital for school leaders to communicate in several other different formats as well, including the school/district website (make sure it is mobile friendly), hard copy of newsletters mailed out and available for pick-up in the main office, a downloadable version in several formats on the school/district website, and of course by phone via a school notification software/system that easily allows schools to deliver phone calls, emergency texts, and email reminders to parents and students within seconds.

It is important to note here that no one way of communication is more important or better than another; they all should be implemented by school leaders in order to ensure that all stakeholders are communicated with in an easily accessible format in a timely fashion. There is no such thing as over-communicating. Communicate and communicate often! I have highlighted some strategies for using social media as a school leader at both the district level and building level (See Table 3).

Table 3: Communicating with Stakeholders via Social Media

Social Media Type	District Use	Building Use	Notables
Facebook www.facebook.com or App store	Create a school district Facebook page and post district information daily. You can post photos, video, and plain text. In addition, you can post live links to items you would like stakeholders to access.	Create a school building Facebook page and post building and district information daily. You can post photos, video, and plain text. In addition, you can post live links to items you would like stakeholders to access.	Get the lingo right, ask stakeholders to "Like" your Facebook page. Easily connect Twitter and Instagram accounts to your Facebook page. This will eliminate the need for you to post in all three places. Although Facebook hashtags are somewhat meaningless in the context of proper hashtag use, they are still helpful in promoting your district/building hashtags. You can tag people in your posts, but I would be careful, especially when it comes to students.
Instagram App store (however, Instagram now has a website for viewing purposes ONLY: www.instagram.com)	Create a school district Instagram feed to post photos and videos.	Create a school district Instagram feed to post photos and videos.	Use frame Apps (I like the Frametastic App and it is free) and built in filters to spice up images, add text, etc. In addition, I like to use the Squaready App and Repost App with Instagram. Instagram does use hashtags, so be sure to incorporate them with posts. Instagram allows photos and videos to displayed as Instgram Stories as well. Get the lingo right, ask stakeholders to "Follow" your school district/building Instagram feed.
Storify www.storify.com	Celebrate all things happening in your district throughout the week by creating a Storify each Friday and releasing it via Social Media to your stakeholders.	Celebrate all things happening in your school throughout the week by creating a Storify each Friday and releasing it via Social Media to your stakeholders.	This is a great way to highlight all the wonderful things happening in your school district/building on a weekly basis. In a way, it serves as a weekly recap of all things good from the school week. Hashtags are supported by Storify, so be sure to incorporate them with your post.

Twitter www.twitter. com or App store	Create a school district Twitter account. Tweet everything from snow days to scores of the high school football game each quarter.	Create a school building Twitter account. Tweet everything, from a teacher being named teacher of the week, to classroom visits, to retweeting the snow day tweet from the district Twitter account.	Get the lingo right, ask stakeholders to "follow" your school district/building Twitter feed by sharing your "Twitter handle" (i.e., your Twitter name, for example @DenverJFowler is my Twitter handle). Twitter utilizes hashtags, so be sure to include them with all of your tweets.
Hootsuite www.hootsuite. com or App store	Control all of your school district social media through the use of Hootsuite.	Control all of your school building social media through the use of Hootsuite.	It is a time saver and allows you to schedule posts on your school district/building as well as your personal social media outlets. Essentially it acts like a social media dashboard and allows you to access and post on all of your social media from one place (versus logging in and posting from each).
LinkedIn www.linkedin. com or App store	Create a LinkedIn group for your school district. Alumni on LinkedIn can easily join via their LinkedIn account.	Create a LinkedIn group for your school building. Parents and alumni (of your school building) on LinkedIn can easily join via their LinkedIn account.	Ensure you visit the group settings to allow LinkedIn members to easily join your groups or pre-approve group members. Worth noting, a common mistake I see on LinkedIn is that the logo or picture associated with a school district/building often needs updating. For example, many of your district employees may want to have their current employer on their LinkedIn page. Thus, when they add this information, it automatically populates the picture associated with a given organization (in this case a school district/building). This photo will appear everywhere a district is listed on LinkedIn, be it education experience or work experience. So be sure your district logo is correct. If not, you may have a picture of a high school football player making a play on Friday night as your logo (I have personally experienced this one).

| Voxer
www.voxer.com or App store	Voxer is a great way to connect all of your administrative staff throughout a school district.	Voxer is a great way to connect all of your teaching staff throughout a school building as well as a separate Voxer for the school building administration team.	Voxer is live and recorded audio, text, photos. It is a Walkie Talkie-like functionality on a smart device. This App allows users to access messages later, if they are not available right away. Voxer users within (a) chat(s) can see who has viewed the audio, text, and photos, and who has yet to view/access them. I could see this as replacing and/or a backup to Walkie-Talkies used during emergency drills in a school building or throughout a school district if utilized properly. Next time your school district/building is up for new Walkie-Talkies, consider this as a cheaper alternative. Plus, unlike the Walkie-Talkies, Voxer has no limited range. Thus, it may be safer to use in particular emergency situations that could occur in the school setting.

Note. Include social media icons on district/building websites so that all stakeholders can easily access the school district/building social media sites.

To give you an idea, I have provided examples of items I would post on social media below. These are mere examples, but it should give you some ideas on how to start incorporating social media into your daily routine, to give your stakeholders a good pulse on each school day. In addition, in some ways, it validates all that you do as a school leader. That is, the amount of time you dedicate to your school from the beginning of the school day until the last after-school event. Although I have personally never implemented such posts for these reasons, it could certainly be argued that they could be used in such a manner. Nonetheless, provided below are a wide variety and uses of posts I would include on social media associated with the school district/building. As previously mentioned, be sure to include your school district/building hashtag with all of your posts.

- Live updates from after-school events such as athletic games (i.e., scores at the end of each quarter), concerts, plays, clubs, parent meetings, etc.
- Classroom visits, observations and walk-throughs.
- Birthdays of staff and students.

- Awards received by staff and students.
- Snow days, fog delays, and one/two hour delays.
- Academic achievements by staff and students.
- Town hall meetings and school board meetings.
- School district/building needs in conjunction with an upcoming levy.
- New hires and teacher spotlights, in order to help the community get to know your staff.
- Selfies with all stakeholders (some superintendents and principals even use the selfie stick[8]).
- School/district emergencies.

Here are a few helpful tips with regards to the information above. Years ago, my wife and I were in Rome visiting Vatican City. As we were waiting to tour the Vatican, individuals were selling these strange looking sticks to all of the tourists. This was the first time I ever saw a selfie stick. I turned to my wife and said, "Who would ever buy that?" She responded, "Apparently everyone in this line, they are selling like hotcakes." As we stood in line, they were doing exactly that, selling like hotcakes. I will note here that we did not purchase one, but I certainly thought about it. That all being said, I never thought I would say/write this, but a selfie stick can make photos at all school related events extra cool and give you the ability to take photos of large crowds, such as the student section at a high school football game or the like. It has become quite the rage. An item often used with the selfie stick is the GoPro[9]. These small, almost indestructible cameras can be used to shoot videos and take photos. Additionally, the images and video can easily be uploaded and/or downloaded to post on your

---

8   A selfie stick is a monopod used to take selfie photographs by positioning a smartphone or camera beyond the normal range of the arm (Martinez-Carter, 2014). The metal sticks are typically extensible, with a handle on one end and an adjustable clamp on the other end to hold a phone in place while you take a picture from the handle, usually using a small button that connects to your smartphone via the selfie stick (Kosoff, 2014).

9   GoPro is actually the name of a company, however, it is a term often used to describe portable cameras designed by the company, known as HERO cameras. The cameras are almost indestructible and take excellent photos and videos that are easily downloaded and uploaded to computers and all social media.

school district/building social media pages. In addition, if your school is so lucky to have a jumbotron (a large video screen) associated with their athletic fields, you can connect the GoPro to the screen and stream for instance, the student section at a high school football game. The students love this and it further builds school community and in a way, student voice. Nevertheless, both the selfie stick and the GoPro are great additions in utilizing social media as a school district/building leader.

One last tip: it is vital that your school district/building adopt policy (district level) and procedures (building level) with regards to including students on social media used by school employees as well as students. I believe the essential piece to the policy is that some sort of waiver exist for parents to either approve (or disapprove) the use of images of their child on school district/building social media, websites, and the like. For example, when I was a school administrator, we implemented a simple waiver that went home at the beginning of each school year (with all of the other beginning of the year paperwork), and once completed and signed by a parent was kept on file in the office. My secretary was in charge of filing these forms and accessing them as needed. For example, I would often take photos during classroom visits and walk-throughs. Usually, I would take a picture of the teacher teaching (and try to avoid having students in the pictures). However, in some cases, the students would be in the photos as well. Thus, before posting said pictures on social media, I would have my secretary check to ensure that none of the students that appeared in the photo were on our social media blacklist – that is, our list of students whose parents did not approve use of their images on our social media sites. That being said, I would estimate that over 90% of our students were allowed to appear on our social media pages and websites. Nonetheless, you want to ensure you do not post pics of students whose parents do not want their images on school district/building social media and websites. In addition, I would reach out to your staff about posting images of them as well. It is rare, but I have had some staff members ask that we not use their images on our school district/building social media, and I was always respectful of their requests. Edutopia, in collaboration with Facebook, has created an excellent resource for school district/building leaders titled *How to Create Social Media Guidelines for Your*

School (Anderson, 2016). It can be found here: https://www.edutopia. org/pdfs/edutopia-anderson-social-media-guidelines.pdf

> "Technology use is established. School leadership needs to model that approach. Enact rituals and practices designed to reinforce it, and lend a coherent voice leading the entire community in a fashion consistent with its vision to improve the lives of young people." ~ Heard on BamRadioNetwork.com

School leaders/districts who do not embrace social media are not only behind the times, they are missing out on valuable teaching moments for their students (and in some cases, their staff, parents, community members, and business owners). A simple Google search will show you the destruction that can be caused by social media posts, and it can be costly. For example, jobs are lost, internships are lost, and athletic scholarships are lost, all due to what many would perceive as derogatory social media posts. I will share a few real-life stories to drive this point home. Recently, a lineman at the University of Mississippi lost an estimated $7-12 million dollars (DeShazo, 2016) after a video of him smoking marijuana through a gas mask bong appeared just minutes before the NFL draft had started. He was originally projected to be drafted 6th in the first round and ended up falling to the 13th pick. In another case, I used to work at a gym in downtown Columbus, Ohio where I served as a personal trainer. This was the MySpace era of social media. One of my clients had shared the news with me that she had recently obtained an internship in Washington, D.C. and would be leaving that Friday. Much to my surprise, she showed up at the gym the following Monday evening. Essentially, on Monday morning when her internship was supposed to start, she was called into a room where printed pictures from her MySpace account of her beer bonging a beer were shared with her, along with the news that she had lost her internship. She was flown home that same day. Siemer (2013) estimates that 56% of adults do not actively think about the consequences of their online activities. If 56% of adults don't actively think about what they post on social media, then what do you think is the percentage of PreK-20 students who do actively think about what they post on social media. Probably a much lower percentage as you could imagine. In the same article, it is further reported that 21% of adults have lost a job, 16% lost out on getting a job, 16% lost their health insurance, 15% were turned down for a mortgage they wanted, and, perhaps most relevant to school district/building leaders, 14% lost out on the college they wanted to attend (Siemer, 2013). Thus, I contend that it is our job to teach students and staff how to be digitally responsible and be cognizant of their social media presence and digital footprint. In addition, we can be examples to all stakeholders, including parents and community members. Herein lies the valuable teaching moment: excluding all social media and technology is not only behind the times, it can be perilous. It might be that you are setting your students (and staff) up for failure in the 21st Century, in the digital world in which they will work and become global citizens.

As school leaders, we must embrace technology, and more specifically, social media, in order to use it as a teaching tool, in addition to all its other advantages. This is where, as previously reported, we can teach our students and staff to "pause before they post" and "face their problems, don't Facebook their problems," all in an effort to help them understand the importance of their presence on social media and other online outlets as well.

Finally, please note that although I have mentioned the current and latest social media being used as I write this book, the landscape is constantly changing. This became clear to me when I attended my daughter's freshmen orientation at The Ohio State University a few years ago. The new president of the university was speaking to both the parents and incoming freshmen. He asked, "How many of you use Facebook as your main source of communication on social media?" Surprisingly, all of the parents raised their hands and almost none of the students raised theirs. Then he asked, "How many of you use Twitter as your main source of communication on social media?" Much to my surprise, almost all of the students raised their hands, while hardly any of the parents raised theirs. You see, technology trends change and change fast, much like the educational landscape. As a school leader, you must be a life-long learner and keep up with these changes. It was not too long ago (2005-2009) that MySpace was the largest social media networking site in the world and even had more visitors than Google (Cashmore, 2006; Olsen, 2006). However, in more recent years, the number of MySpace users has steadily declined despite a barrage of several redesigns and a guerilla marketing campaigns to try and get MySpace back where it once was. The point is, as a school leader, you must stay relevant. You must know what it is your students, parents, staff, community members, and business owners are interacting with in regards to social media, and tap into the resource with your own school district/building social media.

Communications

Perhaps worth mentioning is a new trend I have seen in several school districts across the nation: the newly created district office level position of *Communications Director* or *Director of Communications* or *Public Information Officer*. In many ways, this individual not only handles all social media for your school district (while also monitoring building-level social media throughout the district), but is also responsible for building relationships with all media outlets in the community, including (but not limited to) local and state newspapers, professional education organizations at the local, state, and federal levels, and key community members such as the mayor. In a quick review of several job postings for such a position, I found that the job functions and responsibilities vary widely depending on the school district and its needs as they relate to communications as a whole. In addition, several consulting companies have outsourced all things social media (and the like) for many school districts across the nation. This is especially apparent in the large school districts where, because of sheer numbers, it can be overwhelming for school district/building leaders to keep up with and celebrate all that is going on in a given school district/building. In my discussions with school leaders who use said consulting companies, they simply like it because in many ways it shifts a lot of responsibility to the consulting company with regards to all things social media. I don't necessarily agree with that, as I have always said, "As school leaders you can delegate tasks, but you cannot delegate responsibility." Nonetheless, I am reporting what I have heard and discussed with school leaders of large school districts where, for example, four high schools, five middle schools, and fifteen elementary schools might exist within one district. Building further on this point, while attending the National Conference on Education organized each year by the American Association of School Administrators (AASA), I was having dinner with twelve or so superintendents in Scottsdale, Arizona. In addition, a few consultants from a group which does social media consulting joined us. Through my discussions at dinner, I quickly determined that every superintendent at the table used this consulting company to handle their social media, to the tune of over six figures per academic school year per school district. In fact, at least one superintendent shared with me that he was paying over $200k per academic year for their services. That being said, it should be mentioned that said consulting group was handling many other items for this particular superintendent's school district in addition to the district/building social media. Nonetheless, as more and more social media and Apps are developed, I envision some school leaders will look to other resources to handle social media in their respective school districts/buildings.

Social Media Policy

"Overly restrictive social media policies can present complex issues under the First Amendment and other federal and state laws."
~ *Joel D. Buckman*

Finally, as previously mentioned, it is a good idea to have general policies in place regarding social media use by students and staff. However, the policies should not be overly restrictive. In fact, if they are, you may be violating individuals' First Amendment rights as well as other federal and state laws. When creating such policies, you want to ensure your school district is FERPA (The Family Educational Rights and Privacy Act[10]) compliant. That is, ensure the use of social media is FERPA compliant and that the policies adopted do not lead to FERPA violations and liabilities. Essentially, as a district, you are going to need

10 The Family Educational Rights and Privacy Act (FERPA) is a federal privacy law that gives parents certain protections with regard to their children's education records, such as report cards, transcripts, disciplinary records, contact and family information, and class schedules.

to decide on what limits should and should not be placed on your staff in terms of what they say and don't say on social media (Gilsbach, 2017). As always, all policies should be created and adopted with the mindset of doing what is the best for your students and staff. Nevertheless, you do not want to set yourself up for a lawsuit either. In addition, because technology changes so rapidly, and as previously mentioned, new Apps and forms of social media and the like are created on a daily basis, you must be flexible in your approach to such policies. That is, be willing to amend current policies and change as needed. For example, when electronic cigarettes came out, I was serving as a school administrator in a middle school in the State of Ohio. We had to add electronic cigarettes to our school district policies and the electronic version of our student handbook in the middle of the school year. Much like the case with the electronic cigarettes, social media policy can (and most likely will) change from year to year. Thus, it is important for school leaders to stay abreast of the latest technology, Apps, and social media available to their students and staff, and plan accordingly. Nonetheless, when creating and adopting such policies, I would do so with the following thoughts in mind: (1) what is best for all stakeholders involved, including students, staff, parents, community members, and business owners; (2) how might such policies encumber the learning process – essentially deciding if the risk of allowing such social media is worth it given the opportunities to utilize said social media with classroom instruction and the like (a great example of this is Internet filters); and (3) is the policy FERPA compliant. These three items will be an excellent source to reference when initiating conversations on what policies need to be created and adopted in a given school district with regards to social media and the like.

Reflection

Questions for Practicing and Aspiring School Leaders

1. As a school district/building leader, how will you celebrate, and celebrate often, through the use of social media?
2. As a school district/building leader, how will you brand your school?
3. As a school district/building leader, how will you communicate with all stakeholders on a daily basis in real-time?
4. Of the social media shared in chapter two, what do you believe will be most effective for your school setting and why?
5. As a school district/building leader, how will you attempt to teach both your students and staff to be responsible when it comes to posts on social media?

Problem-based Scenario

Teachers on Facebook

As a building (or district) level school leader, a parent has voiced a complaint that teachers in your building (or district) have been posting and liking things on Facebook during and throughout the school day. Although you have recently supported the use of social media by your staff, you have determined that many of these "likes" and "posts" are not school related. Furthermore, after a more careful investigation, you realize that the time and date stamp of such posts are during the school day, when said teachers have students in their respective classrooms. You want to be a 21st Century School Leader and support the use of social media by your staff in your building (or district). However, you agree with the parent, in that staff should not be posting and liking things that are not school related, especially during class time. As a school building (or district) leader, how will you plan to effectively solve this problem?

Choose Your School Setting

Choose your role and then choose your school building/district characteristics before you respond to the scenario above. As you draft your response, please be cognizant of how your setting might affect how you respond to the scenario. Essentially, based on the characteristics listed below, think about what we generally know about these characteristics, and, furthermore, how they impact schools/districts. How might they affect your decision-making with regards to the scenario, if at all? Be sure to clearly describe your school setting in your response.

Role: Superintendent, Principal, or Assistant Principal
Locale: Urban, Suburban, or Rural
Size: Small District, Medium District, or Large District
Diversity: No Diversity, Some Diversity, or Very Diverse
SES Status: 100% Free and Reduced Lunch (FRL), 50% FRL, or 0% FRL

Chapter 3

The Importance of Being a Life-long Learner

"We now accept the fact that learning is a lifelong process of keeping abreast of change. And the most pressing task is to teach people how to learn."

~ *Peter Drucker*

Introduction

Life-long learning is the "ongoing, voluntary, and self-motivated" pursuit of knowledge for either personal or professional reasons (Department of Education & Science, 2000). Due to what many would categorize as an overwhelming schedule of long hours which turn into long weeks and long years, school leaders both at the district and building levels need professional development that is delivered quickly and efficiently. In my experience, there is little professional development built in for school leaders. However, we are in charge of both organizing and producing meaningful professional development for our staff. Contradictory though that may be, it is the environment in which school leaders often work. Thus, it is vital that school leaders continually seek ways to be life-long learners through professional development that is easily accessible and meaningful to their cause: leading schools effectively. In this chapter, I have highlighted some innovative strategies to assist school leaders in both participating in free professional development and leading professional development in a given school building/district.

Professional Development

Again, I have approached this section from two angles: (1) professional development as it applies to you, the school leader; and (2) leading professional development for your staff. I have outlined some innovative possibilities for both participating in and leading professional development in the 21st Century. This includes Twitter chats, EdCamps, webinars, conferences, digital badging, MOOCs, TEDxTalks, and teacher-led professional development. The focus here is the idea of personalized, differentiated, and individualized professional development versus the normal "catch-all" whole-group professional development we see in almost all schools today. Essentially, my aim is for you to seek out professional development that meets your own needs (through the resources shared within this chapter) and lead professional development that meets the needs of your staff members (by utilizing the resources shared in this chapter and/or pointing staff to such resources).

Twitter chats. "Today, more and more school leaders and educators are creating Twitter accounts in order to access the overwhelming amount of free professional development that Twitter has to offer." (Fowler & Riley, 2015, p. 1). My colleague John and I wrote that sentence almost three years ago to the day I am writing this current sentence. It appeared in an article we wrote titled *How to Build Your PLN* that appeared in *THE Journal: Transforming Education through Technology*. It is still true today; most of my friends and colleagues in PreK-12 school leadership positions around the globe are involved, in some way, shape or form, with a Twitter chat on a regular weekly basis. As shared within our original article, Morris (2011) suggests that Twitter is an excellent way to access individuals around the world with rich backgrounds and experiences that can contribute to your own professional growth. Furthermore, Leishman (2012), a former MIT social media strategist, suggests there are four main benefits from Twitter chats: (1) Learning; (2) Networking; (3) Visibility; and (4) Reputation. For the purposes of this chapter we will focus on the learning, however it goes without saying that there certainly may be benefits to be gained from networking, visibility, and reputation as well.

When it comes to professional development as we generally know it (or have experienced it), especially in the PreK-12 educational setting, certain characteristics emerge. Oftentimes, time and resources are wasted, and the professional development is not specific with regards to the learning outcomes needed at the individual level. Snow (2014) best describes the norm with regards to professional development practices when she writes:

> Typically designed and delivered school-level professional development is largely a waste of time and money. Professional development focused on specific learning/teaching challenges tied to specific curricular efforts, rather than on general pedagogical principles, is much more likely to be effective (p. 465).

This is perhaps why, in recent years, we have seen a shift to the need for differentiated professional development. However, the sad reality is that most school leaders cannot get professional development right, differentiated or not. Thus, I share this resource (Twitter chats) with the best of intentions, because it is perhaps the easiest and most accessible way to stay relevant in the education field, or any field for that matter, regardless if you are a teacher, school building leader, or school district leader. As a school district/building leader, by being a life-long learner, and staying abreast of the current trends and best practices in education, I would argue that this knowledge would naturally spill over into the professional development that you provide for your district and/or building staff. Keeping with this theme, one might argue that as the superintendent/principal goes, so goes the district/building. As Todd Whitaker says, "When the principal sneezes, the whole school catches a cold." Might we also say that when the superintendent sneezes, the whole district catches a cold? Furthermore, might we say when the principal/superintendent is a life-long learner, the whole building/district becomes life-long learners? I think so. Nevertheless, the amount of learning that takes place in an hour-long Twitter chat once per week is hard to measure. In my experience, it is information overload, and I mean this in a good way. I have been part of professional development (either as a participant or facilitator) all around the world. There are times I have learned more in a Twitter chat than I have learned in an entire semester of coursework in college. This is by no means an exaggeration; I highly recommend you experience it for yourself. Here is your mission: I challenge you to get involved with at least one Twitter chat that meets the needs of your current position and job responsibilities. Below I have carefully provided (in layman terms) a step-by-step guide to: (1) creating your Twitter account; (2) building your Professional Learning Network (PLN); (3) locating Twitter chats that are relevant to you and what you do; and (4) how a Twitter chat works, as well as how to immediately get involved with a Twitter chat.

Step 1. Create a free Twitter account. Visit www.twitter.com and sign up for a free account. Please exercise thought about the Twitter handle that you choose. For example, my Twitter handle is @DenverJFowler. You don't want a weird Twitter handle any more than you want a weird email address. I do not believe I need to provide "weird" examples of Twitter handles and emails; keep it simple and professional. This would also be a great time to go ahead and add a profile picture, header photo, screen name, bio, location, and website (see edit profile). You can also add your birthday and change the theme color of your Twitter profile if you so choose (also see edit profile). Now you are ready to start building your PLN.

Step 2. Build your PLN[11]. In order to start building your PLN, I suggest a two-step process: (1) Follow all of your friends, family, celebrities, professional athletes, and the like. This will allow others to see you are on Twitter and will most likely allow you to gain some followers as well; and (2) Search a hashtag that is relevant to your job as a school leader. For a school district leader, you might search #UrbanSuptsAcademy – this is a Twitter chat that AASA sponsors for superintendents. For a school building leader, you might search #LeadUpChat – a chat for school leaders. For assistant principals/vice principals, you might search #APChat

---

11 Your Professional Learning Network (PLN) on Twitter applies to the individuals you follow on Twitter and the individuals that follow you. Essentially, in simplest terms, your PLN is the network of folks you interact with on Twitter (Fowler & Riley, 2015).

– a chat specifically for assistant principals sponsored by NASSP. By searching these hashtags on your Twitter account, you will begin to see who is using these hashtags on a regular basis. You will want to follow the individuals who are using these hashtags, as they are individuals who are participating in these Twitter chats and most likely will be part of *your tribe* (see chapter nine). Other chats and hashtags worth checking out are #SATChat, #CPChat, #SuptChat, #EdLeadership, #EdAdmin, #EdLeader21, #Leadership, #LeadwithGiants, #ChristianEducators and #LeadFromWithin – to name a few. Please note you will need to have at least 10 followers on Twitter before you can take part in Twitter chats. This is a way that Twitter protects against spam. Thus, start building your PLN right away! Now it is time to find a Twitter chat that is right for you.

Step 3. Locating a Twitter chat that is right for you. You will want to decide what Twitter chats are most relevant for you and what you do. You will also want to be cognizant of when the Twitter chats are held (i.e., what day/time of the week is going to be most appropriate for your schedule). Often, Twitter chats are held once a week, on the same day of the week, at the same time. Most Twitter chats are an hour long. For a complete and comprehensive list of Twitter chats visit: https://sites. google.com/site/twittereducationchats/education-chat-calendar. This list (chat calendar) is updated on a regular basis, and allows one to easily navigate all of the different education related chats. You can even select your time zone, as well as select a Week, Month, or Agenda view of the chats. Each listing includes the name of the chat, hashtag of the chat, and when you click on the title of a chat, *when* and *description* are provided as well. This will give you the opportunity to research and decide the chat that is right for you with regards to your current position, whether you are an aspiring school leader (great way to network) or a current assistant principal, principal, or superintendent. There is a chat for most anything related to education. Thus, the options and subject matter of the chats are endless. You will need to spend time deciding which chat is right for you. Now it is time to get involved with your first Twitter chat. Before doing so, I highly suggest watching this entertaining video titled *You're*

Doing Twitter Wrong. It is very insightful with regards to Twitter etiquette. Visit: https://www.youtube.com/watch?v=7wGhiEfq0Ks.

Step 4. How a Twitter chat works. In order to participate in a Twitter chat, all you have to do is login to your Twitter account, search the hashtag of the Twitter chat you wish to join (I prefer to search the hashtag in the Twitter search bar and then stay in the "All Tweets" side of the search). By sliding down with your finger on your smartphone, it will refresh the search and allow you to see the most recent tweets using the hashtag you searched. You will want to search the hashtag of the Twitter chat you want to participate in around 5-10 minutes before it is supposed to start. During this time, counting down to start time, often the moderator(s) (individual[s] leading the chat) will ask all participants to introduce themselves (i.e., name, district, song of the day, etc.). Shortly thereafter, the topic for the chat will be introduced and the first question will be asked. Both the moderators and participants in the chat will use the Q1:A1 format, where Q1 is question 1 and A1 is answer 1 to question 1, and so forth. Most, if not all, Twitter chats follow this format. During the chat, it can sometimes be hard to keep up with all of the tweets at first. Nonetheless, this will become easier the more you actively participate. In addition, many Twitter chats utilize a Storify to curate a summary of the chat that you can access after the chat concludes. Essentially, it will replay the entire chat so that you can take it all in and review as needed. For an excellent article on Twitter chats (with screen shots included), visit: https://thejournal.com/Articles/2015/09/11/How-to-Build-Your-PLN-on-Twitter.aspx?Page=1.

You can locate a Twitter chat for just about anything. For example, my buddy is a high school football coach, so he is involved with a Texas high school football coach Twitter chat #TXHSFBChat. My wife is a fashion designer, so she might get involved with the fashion designer Twitter Chat Style Chat #StyleChat, to keep up with current fashion and beauty trends. I like to do triathlons (and hope to complete an Ironman someday), so I might get involved with the Endurance Nation triathlon chat #ENTriChat. You see, there are Twitter chats for everything, I highly suggest that you get involved with a Twitter chat or two that you might be interested in (perhaps one personal and one professional). On that note, and also worth mentioning, you might at some point experience what I call "meeting one of your cyber friends in person." I have experienced this several times at conferences I have presented at, or attended, across the nation and around the globe. Someone will say, "Hey, I follow you on Twitter" or "I participate in #LLWorldChat each week with you." I always enjoy these moments, as it allows me to put a name with a face and make a deeper connection. It is certainly a great way to network (see Leishman's [2012] list, number two), and that is why it is important to remember Leishman's (2012) four main benefits previously mentioned, as number four (reputation) is extremely important. How you act, interact, and what you post online will become your reputation (and part of your digital footprint). Be cognizant of this, as you will end up meeting the individuals you interact with online someday in person, when you least expect it (e.g., in elevators, airplanes, rental car lines, bathrooms, conference rooms with 500+ attendees and they are sitting right beside you, etc.). So be sure to always "Pause before you post."

Although I highly suggest using Twitter chats to access free professional development in this day and age, it would be thoughtless of me not to mention other free professional development opportunities that exist for school leaders. Below I have highlighted a few other resources for free professional development for school leaders.

EdCamps. The EdCamp model provides educators with sustainable models for learning, growing, connecting, and sharing. EdCamps require school leaders to get together and meet somewhere (preferably with whiteboards). Everyone's expertise is honored, and specific, concrete strategies are exchanged. When professional development is created "for teachers (for school leaders) by teachers (by school leaders)," everyone wins (Swanson, 2016). EdCamps are free and are often organized by school leaders (or teachers) in districts that are nearby and held at school buildings, coffee shops, and the like. More recently, EdCamps have appeared in conjunction with several national and international education conferences. These EdCamps are often included in the conference fee as a free event, and are certainly worth attending. If you are interested in planning an EdCamp, I would highly recommend you reach out to the EdCamp guru himself, Dr. Joe Mazza at the University of Pennsylvania. Tell him I sent you!

Webinars[12]. Most professional organizations provide free (with membership dues) webinars for their members. Much to my surprise, members often do not participate in such webinars. I personally have found such webinars to very insightful, especially as it applies to policy and advocacy efforts (advocacy will be discussed in greater detail within chapter 11), as well as how such policy will/does affect what we are doing as school leaders. Professional organizations such as ASCD, AASA, and NASSP all do a great job of providing free webinars to their active members. Although they are advertised as free, obviously, in most cases, you must be an active member of said organization to access the webinars. Nevertheless, if you plan to join or currently belong to a professional education organization, I suggest determining if they offer free webinars in the form of professional development for their members, and participate when you can. Due to the highly interactive capabilities a webinar affords, I have found them to be worthwhile and very informative. Likewise, you can create your own webinars for your school or district. This can easily be achieved with a smartphone and YouTube channel (www.youtube.com).

Conferences. Not necessarily a new trend, but a trend that has certainly become more efficient, is professional organizations creating a series of professional development opportunities in conjunction with their annual conferences. Again, an additional fee can be involved, especially as continuing education units (CEUs) can be obtained (you'll want these, as this is how you will keep your teaching, principal, and superintendent license renewed). I personally recommend the AASA conference for superintendents, NASSP/NAESP conference for principals/assistant principals, and ICPEL, AERA (Division A), and UCEA for professors of educational leadership. Other conferences worth mentioning include

---

12 A webinar is a web-based seminar. Essentially, it is a presentation, lecture, workshop, or seminar that is transmitted over the Internet using video conferencing software. A key feature of a webinar is the interactive capabilities that include the ability to give, receive, and discuss information in real-time with others (Molay, 2007).

ASCD, AMLE, and EDxEDNYC. Conferences are also a great place to network (see chapter nine).

Digital Badging. When considering how we might offer a more individualized professional development to all involved within the education setting, from custodians to superintendents, digital badging may be the answer. We have all sat through a professional development session that was not meaningful to us simply because we already knew what they were presenting on/providing professional development for. As we know, this is a complete waste of our time and district resources. I believe the answer to individualized professional development may be this concept of digital badging. District/school leaders can organize their own training sessions and create digital badges for individuals upon completion of said sessions. Digital badging is relatively new in the grand scheme of things. In Muilenburg and Berge's (2016) book titled *Digital Badges in Education: Trends, Issues, and Cases,* they define digital badging as:

> A credible means through which learners can establish portfolios and articulate knowledge and skills for both academic and professional settings ... a digital badge is an online based visual representation that uses detailed metadata to signify learner's specific achievements and credentials in a variety of subjects across K-12 classrooms, higher education, and workplace learning (p. 2).

Essentially, participants complete trainings and the like, usually followed by a test, in order to receive a digital badge for completion of the training. Many workplace settings have used a similar process for items such as *Preventing Employment Discrimination,* and *Preventing Sexual Harassment* trainings for years. Just as with these processes, participants receive a certificate of completion, or, in this case, a digital badge (record of completion exists online). In digital badge systems, learning is the ultimate goal. Gibson, Ostashewski, Flintoff, Grant, and Knight (2013) contend that the three main goals of digital badge systems are: (1) to map progress and foster discovery; (2) to signal reputation beyond the community where it was earned; and (3) to incentivize learners to engage in pro-social behaviors. Essentially, badges are awarded for the completion of tasks, whatever they may be. Due to the array of technology growing in this arena, I envision that school leaders will be able to design and create trainings specific to a teacher's evaluations and the feedback provided. The options here are endless. With the implementation of digital badging techniques, I imagine professional development days where a school/district leader kicks off the day with the necessary agenda items, followed by individualized professional development where teachers go to their computers and complete trainings based on what they would like or need to learn about, or in some cases, what a school leader's evaluation has suggested they should learn more about. This is certainly a more personal approach to professional development than the normal "catch-all" whole-group approach we have often seen in schools.

Teacher-led. Some of the best professional development I have ever been part of as a teacher (participated in) and school administrator (led) were teacher-led. The best teacher-led professional development I ever organized was completed in true education conference-like fashion. Essentially, I used a Google Form to gather ideas and submissions from my staff over several days. Much like a conference, they submitted "proposals" (i.e., completed the Google Form) to present and share their ideas and best practices. Then, using a Google Doc, I allowed the staff to serve as the reviewers (a blind review) and select which presentations they wanted to have at our upcoming professional development day. Thus, by the time a teacher was selected, they had gone through a true "light" peer-review process, much as they would when submitting a proposal to present at an education conference. Once we had our selections, each presentation was to be presented three times in a row – over a four-hour period. This allowed teachers to attend any and all sessions they wanted to, without having to choose one over another. We gave participants ample time between sessions, had snacks and drinks in the library, lunch on their own, and truly ran it like a conference. The feedback was great! Looking back, the only thing I wish we had done differently was to have lunch together, with "ignite" session presentations in order to allow those not selected to present in a shorter session, a "lightning round." For the past couple of years, I have attended and presented at EDxEDNYC in New York City, New York (see: http://www.edxednyc.com/) and they do a great job of incorporating these ignite sessions during the lunch hour (they call them *Lunch Table 5-Minute Lightning Sessions*).

Do not be afraid to allow your teachers to lead professional development. In my experience, it has been some of the best professional development I have been part of. Likewise, as you can imagine, it was well-received by staff as it was teachers presenting to teachers. Much like the EDxEDNYC motto, *For Educators by Educators*, allowing teachers to share best classroom practices with one another builds a sense of collaboration and teamwork in your building/district. Thus, one could argue that teacher-led professional development is also conducive to a positive school climate and culture.

MOOCs. Another way to access educational content is through the use of Massive Open Online Courses (MOOCs). If you have an Internet connection, you have access to these free online courses, which have been described as "free, open educational content, personalized learning systems" (Muilenburg & Berge, 2016, p. 7). Although, many MOOCs are introductory courses such as *Learn to Program, Introduction to Mathematical Thinking,* and *Introduction to Philosophy,* I do believe we can find ways to incorporate them into our professional development, not only for ourselves, but for our teachers and students as well. Some of the nation's most prestigious colleges and universities now offer MOOCs, including Stanford, Penn, Harvard, MIT, Yale, Duke, Ohio State, and many others. On the *Online Course Report* website, they have ranked *The 50 Most Popular MOOCs of All Time* (2017). You can check them out here: http://www.onlinecoursereport.com/the-50-most-popular-moocs-of-all-time/. Enjoy!

TEDxTalk. TEDxTalks have become a great resource in the educational setting, and elsewhere, as the talks are not limited to education. I regularly use them, coupled with course content and a Learning Management System (LMS) such as Blackboard or Canvas, with my aspiring school leaders and doctoral students in the higher education setting. This is a great way to show my students an idea worth spreading, without the loss of valuable class time. Much like a flipped classroom model[13], my students will watch these videos on their own, post in the LMS's Discussion Board, and interact with their classmates there, all before discussing the video during our next class session. Essentially, school leaders and teachers can use TEDxTalks in the same manner. As a former school leader, I would use them to kick off the school year, or brighten up a staff meeting, or the like. For example, when the late Rita F. Pierson's *Every Kid Needs A Champion* came out, I showed it to my staff at the beginning of the year. It was so compelling that I still run into former staff members who will reference that school year. They will say, "that video you showed, it set the tone for the entire school year." I consider a TEDxTalk a great way to share a perspective, or an idea other than your own, from other educators and school leaders from around the globe. Again, as with similar resources, the great challenge is to know exactly what TEDxTalk your staff needs to see and hear. Given the demographics of our students in that particular school building, I knew the Pierson TEDxTalk was what my staff needed to hear at the beginning of that school year. You will need to decide what TEDxTalk (if any) makes sense for your particular school setting and/or professional development goals. You can see Pierson's talk here: https://www.ted.com/talks/rita_pierson_every_kid_needs_a_champion. Additionally, you can access and easily search thousands of TEDxTalks here: https://www.ted.com/talks.

In my experience, there are two types of school leaders. Those who are life-long learners, who consistently find ways to access free professional development in order to stay abreast of current trends and best practices in education, and those who are not and do not. Let me ask you, which one are you? Furthermore, which one would you want leading the school your child attends? It is never too late to start being a life-long learner - you can start right now, and you can do so for free! Make the time … remember, action reveals commitment.

---

13 The flipped classroom is a pedagogical model in which the typical lecture and homework elements of a course are reversed. Short video lectures are viewed by students at home before the class session, while in-class time is devoted to exercises, projects, or discussions.

Just as important is the ability to lead professional development effectively. This takes strategic thinking on the part of the school/district leader. School leaders must be able to identify what their staff needs the most when it comes to professional development, both as a whole and on an individualized level. In doing so, I ask that you please be mindful of the ideas I have shared in this chapter. That is, this idea of moving towards a personalized, individualized, and differentiated professional development. After all, I doubt your 35-year veteran teacher needs the exact same professional development as your first year teacher hired directly out of college. Do you agree? The truth is, they both probably need something (we all have room for improvement), but the traditional "catch-all" whole-group professional development is going to leave one of them bored out of their mind, and completely waste their time and your school/district resources. Teachers should look forward to your professional development days and not dread coming to them. It is my contention that the more individualized the professional development is, the better the experience that will be had, and the more learning that will take place, because it is meaningful on an individual level.

Read, Read, and Read Some More

Not long ago I had the opportunity to speak on Capitol Hill in order to advocate for educators and school leaders. Afterwards, my wife and I had the opportunity to meet with several senators, congressmen/women, and the like. In between visits, my wife and I decided to head over to the Library of Congress, as I wanted to see/visit the Rare Books and Special Collections (RBSC). During our visit I had the opportunity to meet the curator at the RBSC, and he showed us Abraham Lincoln's personal bible. What made this experience extra special was the fact that it also happened to be the 150th anniversary of Lincoln's inauguration (for which he requested that his personal bible be used– the one I was now holding in my hands). As we were discussing the book, the gentlemen explained that he, along with his staff, had recently completed Thomas Jefferson's personal library and that it was on display. Upon hearing this news, we headed directly over to see the exhibit before they closed. After taking in this vast collection of books, I turned to my wife and said, "Was it that Thomas Jefferson was a genius, or was it the fact that he had access to more books and information than any other human being in North America during his lifetime?" It certainly is a question to be pondered. He did in fact own the largest collection of books in the United States in 1814 (Library of Congress, 2016). This is a long way around to supporting what it is I am really trying to get at here, the importance of making time to read, especially as it applies to your profession.

Much like the book you are currently reading, there are millions of books on school leadership. In addition, there is an abundance of both peer-reviewed and non-refereed journals, both in hard print and on-line, on a variety of education topics, most of which are easily accessible. Several organizations, as part of your membership, will send you books, magazines, and journals. ASCD used to send our school building (we had a building membership) so many books that I could hardly keep up with the reading. Organizations such as AASA and NASSP release monthly magazines such as *School Administrator* and *Principal Leadership*. Publishing groups such as Word & Deed Publishing, Harvard Education Press, Corwin, Rowman & Littlefield, SAGE Publications, Routledge, and McGraw Hill consistently publish books on school leadership and other related topics in education. If you want to be an excellent school leader, you have to make time to read. If you don't, you'll fall behind. There is one individual that produces book notes that I particularly enjoy reading, and I will often access these notes for sake of time. His name is Jim Mahoney, and he is the former Executive Director of Battelle for Kids. You can access his book notes here: http://hosted. vresp.com/1820435/57201e377b/TEST/TEST/. That being said, he recently retired, and I am not sure whether he intends to continue releasing his book notes as he has done in the past.

I suggest that you make time for leisurely reading as well. I will normally have two books going at once; one education related, and one I consider more leisurely reading (although I find this book is often related to education as well). In addition, I read several magazines and journals each month including the *Smithsonian, School Administrator, Principal Leadership, Review of Educational Research, Educational Researcher,*

Rotarian, and *Outside,* to name a few. I also enjoy reading the newspaper each morning. No matter where we live, I usually subscribe (either electronically or in hard-copy format) to *The New York Times, USA Today, Columbus Dispatch* (we are Ohioans) and *Los Angeles Times.* I repeat, make time to read - it is vital to being a great school leader. I have worked with great school leaders, and I have also worked with not so great school leaders. The key is, I learned from them both, the good ones and the bad ones. I could easily categorize them into two categories, those who read regularly, and those who do not read. I am sure you can guess which type of school leader falls into the "those who read regularly" category. That is the category you want to be in. That is, those who read regularly. I have yet to meet or work with an effective school leader who does not read on a regular basis. Likewise, I have yet to work with or meet an effective professor who does not read on a regular basis. I strongly believe there is a trend here. Now, was Thomas Jefferson a genius? Maybe, but I can tell you one thing, he read (and owned) a large number of books. In fact, he owned 6,487 volumes at the time the Library of Congress purchased his collection. This count may be low, as it is reported that Jefferson's personal collection had suffered two fires, one in 1770 and later in 1851 (Library of Congress, 2016). Nonetheless, the guy read books, and a lot of them. In chapter 14, I have provided a list of recommended books, journals, magazines, blogs, podcasts, and other great resources.

Stay Curious, Stay Cautious

I have seen two common mistakes from school district/building leaders when it comes to reading, and reading some more: (1) much like a fart in a skillet, they want to jump around quickly, constantly rolling out new initiatives to their staff after reading said book with some new awesome flawless practice (on that note, beware of said new awesome flawless practice); and (2) they incorrectly believe that an initiative that worked in one school building/district will automatically work in their setting. These two mistakes can have severe consequences for both the school leader and their staff. In these instances, usually one of two things ends up happening: (1) the school leader eventually loses his/her job; and/or

(2) the staff never buy-in to any new initiative the school leader rolls out because said initiatives are constantly changing, with no follow-through on any of them – leading to burnout. There is no magic bullet for a given school district/building. That being said, I have certainly had success using portions of initiatives that worked in other school buildings/districts. However, it worked because I made decisive adjustments to how it would be implemented in my setting, being cognizant of how it would best work for my students and staff. Likewise, I did not roll out something new every staff meeting. I was patient and followed through on anything and everything I rolled out. As a school leader, if you do not follow through on the initiatives you set forth, your staff will begin to not trust you or your leadership. I am a strong believer that the worst phrase in any organization, including schools is, "we have always done it this way." Thus, it is extremely vital for school leaders at both the district and building levels to stay curious, while exercising some caution. If not, the consequences could be detrimental.

Finally, since I have included "stay cautious" in this section, I felt compelled to discuss the idea of blogs[14] in this section. As you may be aware, several school leaders have become bloggers[15] and taken to blogging[16]. Although I do believe a blog is a great way to share personal thoughts and essentially maintain an on-line journal or diary, I have found it can also be a place for propagating misleading and inaccurate information. There are some great blogs out there (I share some I recommend in chapter 14), however, reader beware, as there are strong opinions and mis-information in many of the blogs I have encountered. Remember the fake quote by Abraham Lincoln I shared with you in chapter one? Just because it is on the Internet does not mean it is factual. To put it in perspective, blogs are usually a place for someone to express personal ideas and opinions regarding a particular topic. In this context, it may serve as a place to discuss all things school leadership. Nonetheless, do your research and be wary of non-refereed sources such as blogs and the like.

---

14 A journal or diary that is on the Internet.

15 A person who keeps a blog.

16 The action of writing a blog.

Reflection

Questions for Practicing and Aspiring School Leaders

1. Why is it vital to be a life-long learner as a school leader?
2. What types of free professional development exist for school leaders?
3. What are a few examples of reading resources shared in this chapter for school leaders?
4. Why is it important to "stay curious, stay cautious" as a school leader?
5. How will you make time to be a life-long learner? That is, how will you make time to participate in free professional development such as Twitter chats, EdCamps, Webinars, and to read?
6. As a school/district leader, how will you ensure the professional development you lead is worthwhile, meaningful, personalized, differentiated, and individualized for your staff?

Problem-based Scenario(s)

Choose one (or more) scenario(s) to respond to...

Scenario 1. *You Make the Time to do What is Important to You*

As a school district/building leader, you are having a difficult time making room in your schedule to participate in professional development such as the aforementioned Twitter chats, EdCamps, and webinars. In addition, you have found it difficult to carve out any time in your schedule to read. You know it is important for you to stay abreast of current trends and best practices both as it applies to teaching and school leadership. Thus, you are determined to make time to be a school leader who is a life-long learner. In what ways will you strategically create time in your schedule while maintaining an excellent work-life balance (discussed in greater detail in chapter nine)?

Scenario 2. *Teacher Burnout*

You were recently named the new principal (or superintendent) at your school building (or school district). You are excited to roll out a two-part initiative that you believe will get the school (or district) moving in the right direction with regards to both academic achievement and the current negative culture/climate that exists. However, the principal (or superintendent) before you was known for rolling out new initiatives every few weeks, with absolutely no follow-through. Thus, the staff have experienced burnout with all of the constant initiatives given to them. This burnout has also affected the school culture/climate in your building (or district). You know your initiative is going to improve things. How will you get everyone on board with your new plan? How will you create buy-in? How will you ensure your staff is implementing this new two-part initiative? How will you follow-through with regards to whether or not the new initiative is working?

Scenario 3. *Planning Professional Development*
It is late July and you are in charge of planning and leading the upcoming professional development day in your school/district. You want to ensure that the professional development is meaningful and worthwhile for your staff. That is, personalized, differentiated, and individualized to meet the needs of every teacher/administrator in your building/district. How will you go about planning this professional development day? How will you know what each teacher needs in the form of professional development? In detail, please create/include a tentative schedule for your professional development day, and explain your reasoning for this schedule? Remember, 21st Century School Leaders do not lead "catch-all" professional development.

Choose Your School Setting
Choose your role and then choose your school building/district characteristics before you respond to the scenarios. As you draft your response, please be cognizant of how your setting might affect how you respond to the scenarios. Essentially, based on the characteristics listed, think about what we generally know about these characteristics, and, furthermore, how they impact schools/districts. How might they affect your

decision-making with regards to the scenarios, if at all? Be sure to clearly describe your school setting in your response.

Role: Superintendent, Principal, or Assistant Principal
Locale: Urban, Suburban, or Rural
Size: Small District, Medium District, or Large District
Diversity: No Diversity, Some Diversity, or Very Diverse
SES Status: 100% Free and Reduced Lunch (FRL), 50% FRL, or 0% FRL

Chapter 4

Closing the Achievement Gap

"Poverty is not a learning disability."
~ Dr. Pedro Noguera

Introduction

Before we begin this chapter, I want to pass on something that was shared with me by my colleague Dwight Carter, a high school principal in the State of Ohio. Below is a bullet point list of *My Beliefs About Students* (Carter, 2016):

- I believe all students can and will learn.
- I believe students are the reason why we are here and we have our jobs.
- I believe engaged students will exceed our expectations.
- I believe the more we know about our students, the better we will be able to create the conditions for them to demonstrate growth.
- I believe in the development of the whole child: intellectually, emotionally, socially, physically, and spiritually.
- I believe student voice and student choice lead to more engaged, active learners and leaders.
- I believe successful schools promote the 7 A's: *Academics, Attendance,* positive *Attitude,* the *Arts, Athletics, Acts of Service,* and *Activities* (clubs). This creates a sense of belonging for every student.

I believe that this must be the mindset of all stakeholders involved in educating children. If you want your students to achieve, anything less would be preposterous. As Carter (2016) shared, we must believe all students can and will learn. I strongly believe this is the very foundation and core of being an educator, and school building/district leader. We must first believe that all students are capable, and then we must figure out how to tap into that capability in a way that is best for students, which may be less convenient for us as both teachers and school building/district leaders. As school leaders, we must ensure these beliefs about students are shared by all stakeholders involved in the process of educating our students. Once this foundation is set and established (along with a positive school climate and school culture, see chapter seven), only then can we begin to move on to the larger order at hand, closing the achievement gap. To do this, we must first fully understand exactly what closing the achievement gap means. In layman's terms, as a school building/district leader, it means ensuring that all students in your building/district are achieving at close to[17] the same level, regardless of student demographics such as race, gender, and socioeconomic status (SES). The achievement gap is the difference in performance (i.e., test scores) between one group of students compared to another. Essentially, it is what occurs when one group of students (such as students grouped by race, gender, SES, etc.) outperforms another group of students, and the difference in the average score is statistically significant (NAEP, 2015). Closing the achievement gap is no easy task. A simple Google search of "achievement gap" will provide over 13 million results in 0.58 seconds. The extant literature is full of methods and suggestions on how to close the achievement gap (Beecher & Sweeny, 2008). However, the fact is the achievement gap still remains, and even with this bulk of research, extant literature, and the like, some researchers argue it has worsened over recent years (Harris & Herrington, 2006). The strategies I used and implemented in my school building worked for me, and I would argue they might work elsewhere, in a different setting: in your setting. Nonetheless, as stated in chapter three, "stay curious, stay cautious" - there is no such thing as a magic bullet to close the achievement gap and/or to raise student achievement in a given school building/district. Your plan must be personalized to

---

17 I use "close to" because there will always be variances in how students are achieving. The key here is to ensure those variances are not in great disparity, and, perhaps especially important, not correlated with the demographics such as race, gender, and socioeconomic status of the students that you serve.

both you and your stakeholders. There is certainly nothing wrong with reading about and identifying how others have accomplished certain initiatives in their school buildings/districts. That said, it is up to you to decide what is going to (or not going to) work for your current school setting. A perfect example is a school building/district mission and vision statement. All too often, you will see cases where some school buildings/districts have copied and pasted a building/district vision and mission statement from elsewhere, and taken it as their own. In this scenario your vision and mission statement might read and sound great, but at the end of the day, you need to ask yourself, *"Does it really describe the vision and mission needed for my particular school building/district?"* Probably not. I have yet to be in a school building or district that has the exact same needs and goals as another building/district. Similar, yes; exact, no. That is why your vision and mission statement should be a collaborative effort involving all stakeholders, including students, staff, parents, community members, and business owners. You cannot just copy and paste the vision and mission statements of the number one school district in your state or nation, and adopt them as yours. The same goes for your school turnaround initiative. How could you possibly know everything you need to include in your plan without including as many of your stakeholders as possible? The truth is, if you come up with it in your office one night by yourself, not only is it not going to work, but you are probably not going to meet the true needs of the students in your school building/district. If you want your plan to work well, I strongly suggest you include as many stakeholders as possible. Only then can you come up with a school turnaround plan that meets the needs of your students, staff, parents, community members, and business owners. Only then will you have complete buy-in from everyone involved. It is as Jason Isbell's daddy said, "the right thing is always the hardest thing to do." There are no shortcuts to being an excellent school leader and leading a school turnaround initiative. Now, that all being said, let me share with you how I turned around my school. A school in which we would eventually receive all A's on our state report card, raised our *Gap Closing/AMO* grade from a D to an A, and received the highest *Performance Index Score* in the history of the school building. In addition, we had a student in our school building score the highest in the state on the math state assessment. As you read though my story, think about what takeaways may apply to your current school building/district. There is no need to reinvent the wheel, use the portions of my story that you believe will work in your school building/district and get to work!

My School Turnaround Story

First and foremost, it would be doing a disservice to the reader not to report that abridged versions of my school turnaround story have been shared and are in print within both national and international journals and books. If you would like to read a more concise version of my story, you could locate it via one of the references provided below. This is the first time I have had the opportunity to include the entire unabridged version. Enjoy!

Chapter in Book:

Fowler, D. (2017). Leading for school improvement: Collecting, analyzing, and disseminating achievement data to guide instructional practices in schools. In D. Griffiths & S. Lowery (Eds.). *The Principal Reader: Narratives of Experience.* Ontario, Canada. Word & Deed Publishing.

Journals:

Brown, K., & Fowler, D. (2018). Data driven decision: Using equity theory to highlight implications for underserved students. *AASA Journal of Scholarship & Practice.*

Fowler, D. (2016). Using data to close the achievement gap: The secret to success in data deployment is the data team. *Principal Leadership 16*(7), 52-57.

Fowler, D. (2015). Using data in urban schools to close the achievement gap. *The GAP E- Magazine: America's Elite Diverse Education Forum 1*(1), 28-36.

My Story (Unabridged)

My story reflects the changing landscape in the PreK-12 educational setting. Gone are the days of school leaders being great managers. In the 21st Century, school leaders must be instructional leaders, and in the United States, the role of a school leader in the PreK-12 educational setting continues to evolve (Hallinger, 1992). Just one of the many evolutions is the expectation that school administrators will have the ability to effectively analyze student achievement data and use it to guide instructional practices in their school building. "Principals and other school leaders have been given a difficult charge: take an abundance of student data, mostly in the form of assessments, and turn this data into information to be used in improving instructional practice" (Midgley, Stringfield, & Wayman, 2006). As the role of school leaders continues to change, one thing is for certain: school administrators must be data-driven instructional leaders, and exercise data-based decision-making (Blink, 2007; Midgley, Stringfield, & Wayman, 2006). Blink (2007) wrote, "The increased attention and focus of legislators at all levels on public education provides the impetus for building and implementing a data-driven instructional system that will ensure improvements in student achievement while closing identified achievement gaps" (p. xv).

School leaders across the nation continue to seek ways to effectively plan for improved student achievement based on an array of assessments being administered to students nationwide. "Although the research and literature provides numerous case studies on individual schools or educators that have successfully used data to improve student achievement, Stringfeld, Reynolds, and Schaffer (2001) found the use of data at the school level to be an incredibly difficult task because school personnel often lack proper systematic supports for data use" (Midgley, Stringfield, & Wayman, 2006). However, many school leaders (including myself) have implemented successful data use through the creation of data teams. With the increased pressure to improve student achievement in the PreK-12 educational setting at both the national and state levels in the United States, the creation of data teams in school buildings across America is on the rise. According to Midgley, Stringfield, & Wayman (2006), data teams are created "to support educators in conducting inquiry into practice, and make this inquiry efficient and fruitful" (p. 2).

In this chapter, I will share with you my personal success story in creating a data team and how we used it to close the achievement gap within our school building. As previously mentioned, there is no magic bullet for turning around a school. With that in mind, take from my story practices and aspects that would apply to your school setting. A data team can be implemented in any school building/district. At the very least, it will support a culture in a given building/district that values data, and regularly collects and analyzes data. That is the easy part; the hard part is using data to guide key decisions with regards to instructional practices throughout a given school building/district. But first, get the easy part down: implement benchmark tests, formative assessments, summative assessments, common assessments, and the like. Then you'll have the data to collect and prepare for analysis. After you get this realized, you can begin to use said data to drive instruction. You will become a data-driven school building/district! Let's continue with my story and see how it might work for you in your school setting.

Creating a Data Team

It was summer and I had just accepted a new position as the Assistant Principal at a middle school located in the Midwest. Having already completed some surface level research on the building data for the interview process, I was aware of the report card and the areas that needed attention. During my first week on the job, I met with the principal and proposed the idea of creating and leading a data team within our school building. To my delight, my colleague was very receptive of my idea. I envisioned the data team would consist of as many stakeholders as possible. In the end, it would consist of school administrators, teachers, intervention specialists, gifted coordinators, and instructional coaches. The objective was to provide as much data to the staff as possible in order to inform targeted interventions with all students, close achievement gaps, and inform instructional practices across the entire school building within all three grade levels (6-8). In August, I sent an email to all staff members asking if anyone was interested in serving on our data team. The response was overwhelming, and in the end we had 13 committed staff members on the team to start the school year.

Analysis of Data

Shortly after the academic school year began, we held our first data team meeting. After we agreed on our goals, objectives, mission and vision for the team, the first step was to carefully analyze our most recent state report card. For the most recent academic school year, our middle school had received all A's and B's in every component of the state report card except for the *Gap Closing/Annual Measurable Objectives (AMO)* component. In *Gap Closing/AMO*, we had received a D (66.7%). This component would immediately become an area of focus as, in our state, the *Gap Closing/AMO* grade indicates how well students are doing in math and reading. It answers the question, "Is every student succeeding, regardless of income, race, culture or disability?" (Ohio Department of Education, 2012). Additionally, we decided to focus our efforts on our overall *Achievement (Performance Index and Indicators Met)* component. In the *Achievement* component, we had received a B, but regardless, we felt this measure remained important because this grade combines two results for students who took the tests. The first result, *Performance Index,* answers the question "How many students passed the state test?" and the second result, *Indicators Met,* answers the question "How well did students do on the state test?" (Ohio Department of Education, 2012). We also decided to focus on the *Progress (Value-Added)* component. More specifically, we focused on the *Lowest 20% in Achievement* measure, as we had received a B in this area. This particular component measures "the progress for students identified as the lowest 20% state-wide in both reading and math achievement" (Ohio Department of Education, 2012). Because the Progress component measures how much students grow each school year, we felt it was an important component to focus on, along with the others. In addition to the focus areas on our state report card, we made it a goal to promote and support the regular analysis of more recent student data such as various benchmark reading assessments and teacher-developed formative assessments – basically any assessment data we could get our hands on. Finally, we decided that we would share as much data with staff as possible, provide detailed methods on how to use the data, and conduct professional development with both the data team and staff when possible.

The next step was to collect and disseminate the data. The team would use *Education Value-Added Assessment System*[18] *(EVAAS)* to collect student data from the state assessments. If you do not have access to EVAAS, don't fret, you should have some sort of access to your state assessment results. Whatever program you use to access this information most likely works in a similar fashion to EVAAS.

Collecting and Disseminating the Data

Below is a shortened list of data sets (as an example) that we gathered through the use of EVAAS. Each data set was shared with staff throughout our school building with the inclusion of a detailed description of what each data set represented, how to use the data to guide targeted interventions, and how to use the data to drive instructional practices within the classroom and grade levels. This data was shared using Microsoft Excel in order to keep it organized, readily accessible, and easily shared. In the district I served in, we had Google emails in addition to our Outlook emails. Thus, I shared the Excel sheet within Google Drive so that it was accessible to all staff members via their Gmail. I personally like using Google Drive when it comes to a large number of individuals accessing content simultaneously. In addition, any changes made to the document are saved automatically, in real-time.

Data Set 1. This data set included students who were considered *Not Likely To Be Proficient (NLTBP)* in Math and Reading (grades 6-8) and Science (grade 8) on the upcoming state assessments, based on their previous performances on such assessments.

Data Set 2. This data set included students who were identified to be in three or more subgroups (e.g., Individualized Education Plan [IEP], Socio Economic Status [SES], Race, Gifted, Limited English Proficiency,

---

18 Education Value-Added Assessment System "provides valuable diagnostic information about past practices and reports on students' predicted success probabilities at numerous academic milestones" (SAS EVAAS for K-12, 2015).

Free & Reduced Lunch, etc.) in grades 6-8. These students could really hurt (or help) our school building report card data, based on their performance on the upcoming state assessments. Essentially, because these students fell under several different subgroups, they could be in multiple relevant subgroups for measures such as Value-Added. For example, a student who is identified as gifted in Math and on an IEP would be in the Gifted-Value-Added measure and that same student would also be included in the Students with Disabilities Value-Added grade. Essentially, their performance on the state assessments carried "more weight," so to speak, in either direction with regards to how well they performed.

Data Set 3. This data set included students who were both NLTBP and in three or more subgroups (i.e., Individualized Education Plan [IEP], Socio Economic Status [SES], Race, Gifted, Limited English Proficiency, Free & Reduced Lunch, etc.) in Math and Reading (grades 6-8) and Science (grade 8).

Data Set 4. This data set included students who were *Not Growing* year-to-year in Math and Reading in grades 6-8. Within this data set, we also included what subgroups these students belonged to.

In addition to the four data set examples listed above, we also collected and analyzed data from benchmark assessments via STAR[19], BAS[20] and teacher-developed formative assessments throughout the academic school year. We also provided several professional development opportunities outside of the school day and within staff meetings for both data team members and whole staff. For example, we shared how to analyze and use STAR data to set up interventions and goals for students, how to interpret the scores, shared examples of student growth versus non-growth, presented how to use the student diagnostic report and instructional reading level (IRL) effectively with classroom instruction, shared

---

19 STAR Enterprise "assessments offer expanded skills-based testing, providing even more information to help you better understand student performance and improve instruction" (Renaissance Learning, Inc., 2009).

20 "The Fountas & Pinnell (F&P) Benchmark Assessment System (BAS) seamlessly links assessment to instruction along The Continuum of Literacy Learning. This comprehensive system for one-on-one assessment reliably and systematically matches students' instructional and independent reading abilities to the F&P Text Level Gradient" (Heinmann, 2015).

how to interpret the growth proficiency chart, and how to use the built-in interventions within the STAR software. We also emphasized the importance of discussing STAR data with students and explaining their scores to them in a way that allowed for them to clearly understand their own data, how we used it, and why it was so important for them to do their best on each assessment. Finally, we discussed an aspect of STAR that is often overlooked - how the normal curve equivalent is constantly affected by students taking the STAR test nationwide. This is just one example of professional development that the data team presented to our staff throughout the school year, however our focus was to provide meaningful professional development that could be utilized with classroom instruction.

Using the Data to Guide Instructional Practices

Perhaps the most important element of forming a data team is ensuring that the data collected, analyzed, and shared, is put to use by your staff. The data from the state assessments (i.e., Data Sets 1-4) was used to create initial intervention groups. This data was also useful in creating a snapshot of our school building and each grade level as it pertains to state achievement. Our staff also found this data helpful, as they were able to reference the data sets (list of names) in order to ensure the students in their respective classrooms were growing throughout the year, and, if they were not, to provide necessary intervention/enrichment as needed. The STAR and BAS scores were used in several different formats as well. For example, our staff used this data to determine instructional and independent reading levels for each student. Because the STAR and BAS assessments are administered throughout the school year, it allowed the data team and staff to identify trends in student growth. English Language Arts (ELA) teachers used the data to form *Zone Intervention*[21] groups. The focus of this intervention was to close students' reading gaps. Content teachers used the data to determine the reading levels and

---

21 Zone Intervention is one class period a day set aside for each grade level to pull students for pure intervention (remedial or enrichment) during the school day. Not to be confused with Study Hall, as students still have Study Hall for one period each school day as well. Study Hall is used more for things such as homework, make-up work, testing, and re-testing, but it also can be used for intervention and enrichment as needed.

abilities of their students, which allowed them to differentiate articles and assignments. The data also allowed us to determine which seventh grade students would benefit from taking eighth grade *Academic Connections*[22]. Our Science teachers used the data to level articles being used within their instructional units. That is, all students receive articles covering the same content; however, articles can be leveled so that the content is more accessible to students. Our Social Studies teachers used the data to place students into ability groups for instructional units, especially for the *We The People*[23] unit. Each group of students was given a textbook that more closely reflected their reading levels. Our Health teachers used the data to determine appropriate leveled articles as well. Overall, by using the data to be aware of students' reading and performance levels, our teachers were able to locate articles and books that make content more accessible to all of our students.

Results

In the end, we received all A's on our report card. We raised our *Gap Closing/AMO* grade from a D to an A, the highest in our school district (of 11 school buildings). Additionally, we raised our *Performance Index Score* from 101.5 (84.6%) to 102.4 (85.4%), the highest in the history of our school building. Finally, we raised our *Lowest 20% in Achievement* from a B to an A. In addition, we were the only school building in our district (and within Central Ohio) with all A's on our state report card, and one of only a few with an A in the *Gifted Measure*. As previously mentioned, we had a student in our school building score the highest in the state on the eighth grade Math state assessment. These outcomes were certainly an area of satisfaction for all stakeholders involved including students, staff, parents, community members, and business owners. But

---

22 Academic Connections was an ungraded class that appears on a student's schedule outside of Study Hall and Zone Intervention. This class time is used in its entirety for intensive intervention purposes and for closing achievement gaps.

23 "The We The People: The Citizen and the Constitution Program promotes civic competence and responsibility among the nation's upper elementary and secondary students" (Center for Civic Education, 2015). We were the only middle school in the State of Ohio to send a We The People team to the national competition each year in Washington, D.C., where our students participated and competed in simulated congressional hearings.

perhaps one of the most important results is unquantifiable: I felt our data team and staff became better at analyzing and using data to drive instructional practices in our school building across all three grade levels (6-8).

The addition of the data team proved to be extremely beneficial to our school building, and in the following school year there was even more interest from our staff in serving on the team. Thus, we were able to be more cognizant and strategic as to who was on our data team. We added several more members, and we were even granted several professional development days by district office in order to allow our data team to meet during the school day (versus before or after). For example, our district purchased new performance tracking software called PerformancePlus[24]. We spent professional development time teaching the data team how to run reports (create data sets) and share them with their colleagues. We also challenged the data team members to be the "data leaders" in our school building. There were also perks to serving on the data team. For example, district office granted all team members special access to student data district-wide (versus only the students in their respective classrooms). In addition, the success we experienced with our data team was contagious, as several other school buildings within our district (as well as other surrounding school districts) created data teams the following school year and modeled their teams after ours.

Keeping It Real

Although leading for inclusiveness will be discussed in chapter 10, it is worth mentioning some tough conversations that we had as a data team with regards to our school building data. As a staff and data team, we had to ask ourselves why certain gender and/or ethnic groups were not excelling in our school building. That is, after our initial analysis of the trend data, it was identified that certain subgroups of students were struggling academically, and perhaps most importantly, some were growing year-to-year (in grades PreK-5) until they walked through our school doors (in grades 6-8) at the middle school. Thus, we had to have conversations about why certain subgroups of students were traditionally not growing

---

24 PerformancePLUS "provides educators a single point of contact to easily access state, national, and local assessment data" (PerformancePLUS, 2015).

year-to-year in our school building. That is, the trend data suggested that overall, certain subgroups stopped growing when they left our doors and matriculated to high school. For example, in analyzing the data, it became apparent that our African-American students were not growing in math during their time with us at the middle school. This particular outcome led to meaningful discussions amongst the data team/staff aimed at identifying the root cause. Furthermore, such conversations led to our data team/staff discussing and thinking about possible implicit bias and preconceived notions our staff may have had with regards to how certain subgroups of students would perform with regards to a given subject area, such as math. Although it is hard to measure how much such conversations affected our school turnaround story, it certainly got us thinking about our perceptions as a staff as well as ensuring we had the same expectations for all students regardless of race, gender, SES, etc. Thus, I strongly believe the process of having such conversations were beneficial to our data team and staff as a whole.

General Tips

The process of creating a data team can be overwhelming when added to the many other responsibilities that school administrators have. That being said, I can speak from experience in that it is well worth your time and energy, as we all know that student achievement, more often than not, determines the success (or failure) of a school building/district. Below are some general tips from my experience in creating and implementing a data team.

- If you are in a union strong state, as I was, you will need to be cognizant of when the data team meets. That is, participation must be on a volunteer basis, and meetings will often need to be held before or after the school day, after the school year begins, etc. Our school district union president was also a teacher in my school building, so I was very cognizant of this as we mapped out our yearly meeting schedule. In the second year, we were very fortunate in that our district saw the benefit of our data team and we were granted several professional days and provided substitute teachers in order for our data team members to meet during the school day.

- When deciding what data to focus on, be sure to select specific areas and be very clear as to why these areas are important for your students, data team and school building. When we were deciding focus areas, it was somewhat easier for us to determine where our focus would be because they stood out. However, this may not be the case in all school buildings. You may be low- or high-performing in all areas, thus you may need to dig a little deeper into the data to determine where your focus will be. For us, we went into our second meeting with the plan that we would focus on three main areas (which we did) while being cognizant that all areas (components/measures) of the report card were important to our school building. We had the mindset that we would analyze and share as much data as possible, as well as share how they relate to each area of the component/measure of the report card.

- The professional development aspect is an important component of a successful data team. It is extremely important that everyone on the data team clearly understands the data, how to analyze it, how to share it, and how to explain it. Also, if you don't know it well enough to teach, then find someone who does. For example, a teacher in our building was very well-versed in STAR testing and STAR data. Thus, I included her in the process of conducting the professional development on the STAR testing and data.

- If you have the luxury of carefully selecting your data team members, you should be cognizant of who you have on your team. For us, the first year I took whomever was willing to be on it, as we had less interest. For the second year, we had so much interest that I was able to be more strategic in selecting members for our team. For example, the second year I felt it was important to include at least two members from each grade level (preferably one Math and one ELA teacher – state tested subject areas), a Science teacher, instructional coaches, gifted coordinators, intervention specialists, and individuals that we felt were capable of being data leaders within their respective grade levels (i.e., lead the charge, run data, share data, explain it, and be the "go to" for questions from their grade level team). We were very fortunate to be able to be selective the second year; however, when you are first creating your data team, you may need to take anyone willing to volunteer.

- Encourage your staff to discuss data with students. We found this to be very meaningful and helpful. For example, as I mentioned earlier, we encouraged our teachers to discuss STAR data and individual scores with their students. This allowed our students to more clearly understand their data, why it was important for them to do their best each time they were being assessed, and how the data was used to inform instructional practices. By doing this, we felt that they began to take the assessments more seriously after they fully understood the intentions behind them.

- Be careful when determining how to measure the success (or failure) of your data team. Too often, I have heard stories from other school leaders who have created data teams in which they believed their data teams were a failure because their student achievement or report card did not improve right away, or in the areas they focused on. Be sure to hang in there for the long haul, and remember, the fact that you are making data important (and a focus) in your school building, as well as helping your staff carefully and effectively analyze, share, explain and understand data is a success in its own right.

- As my colleague Dr. Bobby Moore says, "old data is cold data." As much as I hate to admit it, he is right! Although trend data is certainly important and allows you to see certain trends with regards to your district/building student achievement (usually in the form of state assessments), it is vital that you are collecting more recent data from formative assessments, benchmark assessments, quizzes, pre/post tests, common assessments, etc. This data (versus year old state assessment data) is much more telling and indicative of how your students are doing right now, and therefore, I would argue, is much more meaningful for driving instructional practices as well as intervention/enrichment.

- Although we did not, some schools have utilized data walls. I must say that I was somewhat skeptical about this process at first, but after visiting a few schools who utilize them, I have found that it: (1) creates some friendly competition amongst the teachers; and

(2) reminds staff on a daily basis that data matters. A data wall is essentially just that, a wall full of data (often in chart form) usually located in the back office or teachers' lounge, that depicts how well students are doing within each class on common assessments. In my experience, the data walls are updated on a regular basis (either by the teachers themselves or by an administrator) in an effort to both keep the data as accurate as possible, while making it a priority day in and day out.

■ With almost all states moving to online state testing, or in the process of shifting to this practice (that is, students complete their state assessments on computers), it is important that you plan accordingly. Before sharing how we did this, let me say that I believe this is where we are going to initially see the largest disparity between the "have's" and "have not's" with regards to state assessments. Again, my thought is, children who have technology throughout early adolescence will have a head start with regard to key computer operations such as clicking and dragging objects with a mouse, video play/pause/stop operation, and all mouse operation/use in general, compared to their lower SES peers. More specifically, I believe we will see this disparity more in the lower elementary grades. Nevertheless, as technology continues to become increasingly affordable (and maybe we are almost there), I believe the disparity will eventually phase out. Nonetheless, there are some great resources online to help students' general computer skills, much like the operations I highlighted. For example, for the online math assessment, it is vital that students be able to operate an online protractor, or easily go back and find a particular part in a narrative or video: this all takes prior knowledge of some basic computer skills. There are several free online resources for students to develop these skills. A simple Google search will lead you to these websites, and many are broken down into grade levels. Thus, I suggest spending some time with your staff in order to identify the best resource available that meets the needs of both your students and staff.

■ I should also mention that we utilized the Lucy Calkins workshop model throughout our school building. Our district allowed us to send some of our intervention specialists to Columbia University to be professionally trained using this model, so that they could come back and train our teachers on how to use it. You can learn more about this model at: http://readingandwritingproject.org/about. I believe this model worked exceptionally well in our school building because both our teachers and intervention specialists were dedicated to making it work.

■ Finally, use these five C's to build your world-class data team:
  - Collaboratively create a clear vision and set goals for your data team.
  - Collectively analyze the data, discuss it, and decide what to do with it.
  - Check to ensure teachers are using the shared data as well as collecting their own data to effectively drive their instructional practices in the classroom and with individual students.
  - Constantly reanalyze the most current data collected to ensure you are working toward your goals, and adjust goals as needed.
  - Create a school climate/culture that values data.

No Magic Here
Again, I do not believe there is any magic bullet to turning around a given school building/district. However, I do believe there are several aspects from my school turn-around story that could be implemented in any given school building/district across the nation, and around the globe for that matter. Furthermore, I believe the addition of a data team is beneficial in and of itself. Once you have made the decision to create a data team consisting of staff members and other stakeholders interested in helping collect, analyze, and disseminate student achievement data in a way that is readily available and accessible to your staff, you as a school leader have taken an important stand that your building/district will value data and be data driven. This alone, I believe, will be beneficial to your building/district. Making data a priority will most certainly lead to everything else that you would hope will happen, and thus, I would argue, is a worthwhile endeavor.

Efficient Analysis is Key

I suppose it would be advantageous to include some recommendations with regards to books I believe would be beneficial to your school turn-around efforts. Below, in no particular order, I have provided a few books I believe would be helpful in efficiently and effectively analyzing/understanding the data. Please note these books are also reported in chapter 14 in my list of book recommendations for school leaders.

Recommended Resources

Everything School Leaders Need to Know About Assessment by W. James Popham

Answers to Essential Questions About Standards, Assessments, Grading, & Reporting by Thomas R. Guskey and Lee Ann Jung

Schools and Data: The Educator's Guide for Using Data to Improve Decision Making by Theodore B. Creighton

Educational Research: Planning, Conducting, and Evaluating Quantitative and Qualitative Data by John W. Creswell

Quantitative Data Analysis Using Microsoft Excel by Gerard Babo and Leonard H. Elovitz (Please note: The authors have created two editions, a PC edition and a Mac edition. The Blue cover is for PC users, whereas Red cover is for Mac users)

An Administrators Guide to Student Achievement & Higher Test Scores by Marcia Kalb Knoll

Quantitative Research in Education by Wayne K. Hoy

Qualitative Research in Practice by Sharan B. Merriam

The School Leader's Guide to Formative Assessment by Todd Stanley and Jana Alig

Reflection

Questions for Practicing and Aspiring School Leaders

1. What steps will you take in order to start closing the achievement gap in your school building/district?
2. What beliefs do you have about students? How do they differ from the list (see Carter's [2016] list at the beginning of the chapter) shared in this chapter? How are they similar to the list shared in this chapter? Why is this important?
3. As a school district/building leader, how will go about creating a data team? Furthermore, what assessments might you implement in your school building/district in addition to the state assessments? Finally, with regards to your current school building/district, what data do you believe needs to be collected, analyzed and discussed on a regular basis? Why?
4. As a school district/building leader, what obstacles and potential setbacks do you foresee in creating a data team? Please share how you might strategically plan for such possible obstacles and setbacks.
5. As a school district/building leader, how might you incorporate the five C's to build your world-class data team?

Problem-based Scenario

The Third C is the Hardest Part

As a building (or district) school leader, you have created a data team in your building (or district). So far the process has been going great! You have your team up and running, data is being collected, analyzed, and shared with all staff (and/or administrators). However, in accordance with the five C's, you have decided to "check to ensure teachers (and/or administrators) are using the shared data as well as collecting their own data to effectively drive their instructional practices in the classroom (or building[s]) and with individual students (or teachers and administrators)." In doing so, you have discovered that only the members of the data team are participating in using the data to drive instructional practices in their respective classrooms (and/or administrators in their respective school buildings). You do note that for the most part, all staff (and/or administrators) are collecting data. Unfortunately, they are not doing anything with the data. How will you take the necessary steps to: (1) ensure the data being shared is being used by all staff (and/or administrators) effectively with classroom instruction (and/or instructional leadership) as well as to drive other instructional practices such as delivery methods, differentiated instruction, small groups, interventions, and enrichment?; and (2) how will you provide the necessary professional development to ensure your staff (and/or administrators) know how to use the data effectively with classroom instruction (as it very well may be the case that they don't know what to do with it, and worth mentioning, perhaps you don't know what to do with it)? What will you do?

Choose Your School Setting

Choose your role and then choose your school building/district characteristics before you respond to the scenario above. As you draft your response, please be cognizant of how your setting might affect how you respond to the scenario. Essentially, based on the characteristics listed below, think about what we generally know about these characteristics, and, furthermore, how they impact schools/districts. How might they affect your decision-making with regards to the scenario, if at all? Be sure to clearly describe your school setting in your response.

Role: Superintendent, Principal, or Assistant Principal
Locale: Urban, Suburban, or Rural
Size: Small District, Medium District, or Large District
Diversity: No Diversity, Some Diversity, or Very Diverse
SES Status: 100% Free and Reduced Lunch (FRL), 50% FRL, or 0% FRL

Chapter 5

Ethics and Leadership

"Ethics is knowing the difference between what you have a right to do and what is right to do."

~ *Potter Stewart*

Introduction

The goal of this chapter is to: (1) introduce ethics in general; (2) to highlight the need for more research on ethics and leadership, in particular, school leadership; (3) to highlight the need for ethics course work and training to be an integral aspect of both educational leadership programs (preparing aspiring school building/district leaders) and professional development for practicing school leaders; (4) to give you, the reader, a snapshot of my research on ethics and leadership as it applies to superintendency and principalship; and (5) to provide an opportunity for you to conduct a self-analysis with regard to your own self-awareness, ethical leadership perspectives, and social desirability. Finally, you will have the opportunity to test your ethics quotient and complete an ethical leadership self-assessment tool. Given that ethics and school leadership is my research focus, I could write a book on ethics and school leadership alone (and plan to, someday). Being cognizant that this book is not solely focused on this topic, I will instead aim to give you a snapshot of ethics and my research as it applies to ethics and school leadership, namely as it applies to superintendency and principalship.

In general, there are three underlying theories regarding ethics (Dreisbach, 2009); (1) consequentialism; (2) regularianism; and (3) deontology. Below I have provided a definition for each (C. Dreisbach, personal communication, October 6, 2017):

Consequentialism: An act is morally good if its consequences are good and bad if its consequences are bad.

Regularianism: An act is morally good if it obeys a rule or rules, and morally bad if it violates a rule or rules.

Deontology: An act is morally good if it is done from duty and morally bad otherwise.

The longstanding debate is as to which theory is most applicable to a given situation. Virtue ethics, developed by Aristotle and other ancient Greeks, emphasizes an individual's character as the key element of ethical thinking versus doing one's duty (deontology), obeying rules (regularianism) or acting in such a way to bring about good consequences (consequentialism). In addition to the three underlying theories regarding ethics, there are 12 theories of leadership relevant to both justice and ethics (C. Dreisbach, personal communication, October 6, 2017):

(1) the great man;
(2) traits;
(3) skills (technical, people, and conceptual);
(4) styles (autocratic, democratic, laissez-faire);
(5) situational;
(6) contingency;
(7) competency;
(8) transactional (extrinsic motivators);
(9) transformational (intrinsic motivators);
(10) leader-member exchange;
(11) servant; and
(12) adaptive.

What is important for you, the reader, is to understand the differences of each of the 12 theories, and perhaps more importantly, to know which is the correct theory of justice? Of ethics? Of leadership? ... in contemplating which of the 12 are the correct theory, might we as school leaders instead focus on virtue? What is virtue? Essentially, good character is virtue, whereas bad character is vice. In essence, Aristotle might argue that virtue ethics is the ability to, as a habit, know the good and do the good (Aristotle, *Nicomachean Ethics*) (worth noting here, habit, in Greek means *ethos* and in Latin means *mos*. From *ethos* we get the words *ethics* and *ethical* in English. From *mos* we get the words *moral, morals,* and *morality* in English). Furthermore, here, we might want to consider the cardinal virtues as they apply to school leadership; (1) courage (fortitude); (2) temperance (temperantia); (3) prudence (pridentia); and (4) justice (Iustitia) (Plato, *Republic*). Below I have provided a brief description of each. As you read through each description, please begin to think about how the cardinal virtues might be applied to school leadership.

Courage: fortitude, forbearance, strength, endurance, ability to confront fear, uncertainty, and intimidation...

Temperance: restraint, self-control, abstention, discretion...

Prudence: wisdom, the ability to judge between actions with regard to appropriate actions at a given time...

Justice: fairness, perhaps the most extensive and most important virtue, the Greek word also having the meaning righteousness.

Again, one could easily imagine how each of the 12 cardinal virtues could apply to school leadership, and leadership in general. That said, as you read through the remaining content within this chapter, be sure to think back to the cardinal virtues and how they might apply. Finally, before we delve further into this chapter, I leave you with one last thought to consider, might it really be that in order to lead with integrity, one must integrate each of the cardinal virtues into one's life – and leadership? I think so and I hope you do, too!

Ethics and School Leadership

Since as far back as 300 B.C., the subject of ethics has been examined by some of the most well-known ancient philosophers, including Plato, Aristotle, and Socrates. In fact, in one of Aristotle's best-known work on ethics (*Nicomachean Ethics*), *Book I* is dedicated to *Who should study ethics, and how*. Nonetheless, the study of ethics is difficult, to say the least. That is, there are several moving parts and societal influences that must be taken into account, perhaps especially as it applies to school leadership, where social and cultural norms can heavily influence the decision-making of a given school leader, in a particular school building/district. In short, it is hard to account for all of that grey area. Laws may be black and white, but we all know you can be unethical without breaking the law. Furthermore, we know that laws themselves differ from state to state, country to country, etc. So it may be that looking to laws to guide ethical practices is not enough. Ethical scandals continue to occur today, and researchers know "little about the ethical dimension of leadership" (Brown, Harrison, & Trevino, 2005, p. 117). Moreover, more research is needed in this arena. Ciulla (2004) wrote "it's remarkable that there has been little in the way of sustained and systematic treatment of the subject of ethical leadership by scholars" (p. 3). Although some literature does exist with regards to ethical leadership[25], much of it is written from a philosophical and theoretical perspective, proposing how leaders should lead. There is no doubt that "a more descriptive and predictive social scientific approach to ethics and leadership has remained underdeveloped and fragmented, leaving both scholars and practitioners with few answers to even the most fundamental questions, such as "What is ethical leadership?" (Brown, Harrison, & Trevino, 2005, p. 395). If ethics are truly "the heart of leadership" (Ciulla, 2004), then interventions are warranted for this group (school leaders) - but not the traditional ones. It is my hope that through my research, as well as others', we can begin to shed light on what it means to be an ethical school leader, how we can better cultivate ethical school leadership for practicing school leaders, how we can better prepare aspiring school leaders to lead ethically, and how school leader demographics and school district characteristics affect the ethical leadership perspectives of school leaders, namely superintendents and principals. After all, as you will read in chapter six, all of the standards written and adopted on how school leaders should lead, and content (aligned with the standards) that should be taught in educational leadership programs, include ethics/ethical leadership. So then, one may argue that ethics and school leadership should be a major focus of both scholars and researchers alike. Moreover, one might argue that ethics and school leadership should be a fundamental aspect of programs

---

25 Ethical Leadership refers to the observable behavior rather than a theoretical perception of what ethical leadership is (Brown, Harrison, & Trevino, 2005). Essentially, it is the act of doing what is right versus doing what is wrong. It is the demonstration of normatively appropriate conduct through behavior (Brown, Harrison, & Trevino, 2005). The action after the thought.

preparing aspiring school leaders. Finally, one might also argue that ethics training should be intentionally integrated into continuing education and professional development for both practicing building-level (principals) and district-level (superintendents) school leaders. As we continue to see ethical misconduct in the educational setting as well as in other organizational settings, I strongly believe ethics will someday be at the forefront of all leadership preparation, regardless of the setting. Although I will cover the standards (and the like) in depth within chapter six, here, I wanted to share the *Code of Ethics* released from the American Association of School Administrators (also known as the The School Superintendents Association). See: http://www.aasa.org/content.aspx?id=1390. I find this code of ethics to serve as a great reminder that "an educational leader's professional conduct must conform to an ethical code of behavior, and the code must set high standards for all educational leaders" (American Association of School Administrators, 2017). That is, a code of ethical guidance for school leaders. If I were you, I would print these out and have/hang them in your principal/superintendent office where you can easily access them and/or see them.

Finally, it would be doing the reader a disservice not to at least share with you some of my research as it relates to ethics and school leadership, if for no other reason than that I believe it will be interesting to you. However, I want to do so in a manner that is conducive to the practitioner, as I believe my audience for this text may differ from that of peer-reviewed journal publications (although I would strongly argue both audiences should be keen to utilize both types of media [and others] in an ongoing effort to bridge the gap between the PreK-12 educational setting and Higher Education).

To date I have launched three major research projects focused on the ethical leadership perspectives[26] of state and district superintendents in the United States, and how those perspectives vary according

---

26 Ethical Leadership Perspectives are defined as how individuals (in this case, school leaders) perceive or view their own ethical leadership perspectives as well as what they consider to be ethical conduct versus what is not. Essentially, it is what individuals theoretically believe is ethical leadership and normatively appropriate conduct (Brown, Harrison, & Trevino, 2005). The thought (before the action).

to school leader demographics[27] and school district characteristics[28] (Fowler, Edwards, & Hsu, 2018; Fowler & Johnson, 2014). In addition, I have two more that will be launched in the near future, one of which will be focused on principalship. Additionally, I am currently working on a 1.4 million dollar grant to develop a new ethical leadership scale in the educational setting. That all being said, I have decided to dedicate my life's work to ethics and school leadership, and leadership in general.

In one study, I surveyed every school district superintendent in the State of Ohio, and also interviewed a handful of them. In another, I surveyed every state superintendent (or the equivalent – as some share other/similar titles) in the United States, District of Columbia, and Department of Defense. In yet another study, I surveyed every district superintendent in the State of Mississippi, and interviewed some. In order to be succinct, I will briefly highlight the results in layman's terms as they relate to all three studies. The Mississippi study is yet to be published, although it should be out by the time you read this book. Before reporting the results, it should be noted that a survey (created in Qualtrics) was used to collect both quantitative and qualitative information about superintendents in all three studies. In addition, in the Ohio and Mississippi studies, subsequent interviews were conducted both one-on-one and in small focus groups. Within the surveys and interviews, the ethical leadership perspectives of superintendents were collected by administering the Ethical Leadership Scale (ELS) (you will learn more about this scale later in this chapter when you complete it yourself). Also within the surveys and interviews, the Social Desirability Scale (SDS) was administered to superintendents (you will learn more about this scale later, also). Finally,

---

27 Gender, Age, Highest Educational Degree, Ethical Leadership Coursework Completed, Superintendent License Mentoring Program Completed, Superintendent License Ethics Training Completed, Years of Experience as a Superintendent, Years of Experience as a School Administrator, Institution where Superintendent License was Completed, Professional Organizations Actively Involved, Subject and Grade Levels Licensed to Teach

28 Total Student Enrollment, Total Number of Administrators, Total Annual Budget, Student Achievement, District Locale

all data collected was downloaded into SPSS[29] for analysis, including a multiple regression analysis and/or correlational analysis. For the purposes of this text, I will not delve any deeper into the research methods and design. Nonetheless, if you are interested, please use the references to locate the published versions of the aforementioned studies. Much like the research methods and design, I aim to give you (the reader) a snapshot of my research findings. Essentially, when conducting this research, my aim was to answer three questions: (1) What are the ethical leadership perspectives of state/district superintendents?; (2) To what extent do the ethical leadership perspectives of superintendents vary according to state education/school district characteristics?; and (3) To what extent do the ethical leadership perspectives of superintendents vary according to state/school leader demographics? Below, I have included each question and a snapshot of my findings.

Question 1. *What are the ethical leadership perspectives of state/district superintendents?*

Overall, I found that both state and district superintendents had positively strong ethical leadership perspectives. Nonetheless, there were differences in the three studies. Ethical leadership perspectives were judged on a 5-point Likert scale (1 = *negative ethical leadership perspectives* or *low ethical leadership perspectives* and 5 = *positive ethical leadership perspectives* or *high ethical leadership perspectives*). For example, of the three studies, state superintendents had the lowest mean ($M = 3.8$), while superintendents in the Ohio study ($M = 4.57$) and Mississippi study ($M = 4.65$) were somewhat higher. Perhaps worth noting here, since the SDS was used in all three studies in conjunction with the ELS to control for any socially desirable response tendencies of the participants in the studies (because superintendents rate themselves on the ELS), the SDS was not correlated with the ELS in the Ohio study, however, in the Mississippi and United States studies, the SDS was correlated with the ELS.

---

29 SPSS Statistics is a software package used for logical batched and non-batched statistical analysis.

Question 2. *To what extent do the ethical leadership perspectives of super-intendents vary according to state education/school district characteristics?*

I found that certain state education/school district characteristics were statistically correlated with the ethical leadership perspectives of superintendents in the studies. Perhaps most significant to the study as a whole, I found that superintendents who had stronger ethical leadership perspectives also led school districts with higher student achievement ($p = .012$). In addition, superintendents responsible for larger annual budgets had stronger ethical leadership perspectives than those superintendents responsible for smaller annual budgets. In all three studies, super-intendents did not believe state education/school district characteristics affected their ethical leadership perspectives.

Question 3. *To what extent do the ethical leadership perspectives of super-intendents vary according to state/school leader demographics?*

With regards to question three, I concluded that certain state/school leader demographics were in fact statistically correlated with the ethical leadership perspectives of superintendents in the studies. The older (age) a superintendent was; the stronger their ethical leadership perspectives were ($p = .020$). Female superintendents had slightly stronger ethical leadership perspectives than males ($p = .044$). Superintendents who held a doctoral degree had stronger ethical leadership perspectives than super-intendents who held a Master and/or Bachelor degree ($p = .026$). Those superintendents in the study who had more overall education experience (i.e., as a teacher, principal, superintendent, etc.), had stronger ethical leadership perspectives ($p = .016$). However, superintendents who had more superintendent experience had weaker ethical leadership perspec-tives. In all three studies, superintendents did indicate that they believe variables such as age and experience may affect their ethical leadership perspectives. Coupled with the ELS scores, superintendents who did believe their ethical leadership perspectives were affected by their demo-graphics had lower ethical leadership perspectives.

Finally, the most significant aspect of all three studies was the demo-graphic information collected on superintendents within each study, and perhaps most significantly, the information collected on state superintendents in the United States. This information is not readily available or accessible anywhere else. That is, all three studies paint a relatively clear picture of who is serving as state superintendents in the United States, State of Ohio, and State of Mississippi. Upcoming research projects include the State of California and District of Columbia. In addition, at some point, I would like to begin to research unethical leadership (i.e., the behavior and decision-making) of school building/district leaders. That is, research individuals in school leadership positions that have made unethical decisions or exhibited unethical behavior that has led to termination, suspension, resignation, or the like. As stated, my research up to this point has been focused on ethical leadership perspectives (i.e., the perspectives not the actual act) in an attempt to determine the strengths (and weaknesses) of those perspectives of school leaders. Thus, a study (or several studies) on ethical leadership alone (or in conjunction with ethical leadership perspectives) could prove to be a meaningful contribution to the extant literature.

The aforementioned results serve only as a snapshot of my research and the results thus far. Additional information such as implications derived from the results, accompanying statistics connected to the results, and recommendations for future studies and my personal thoughts with regards to the results have been excluded from this text. Please reference the peer-reviewed journal article publications (Fowler, Edwards, & Hsu, 2018; Fowler & Johnson, 2014) from each study for additional information.

Self-Awareness

"When I do good, I feel good. When I do bad, I feel bad. That's my religion."   *~ Unknown*

The more I research ethics and school leadership, the more I believe self-awareness is a vital aspect of ethical school leadership. According to the Center for Creative Leadership (2017), self-awareness can be challenging to develop. Nonetheless, it is the foundation for strengthening all of your other leadership skills (Center for Creative Leadership, 2017). The Center for Creative School Leadership (2017) suggests there are four facets of self-awareness including: (1) leadership wisdom; (2) leadership identity; (3) leadership reputation; and (4) leadership brand. Below I have defined each (Center for Creative School Leadership, 2017).

Leadership Wisdom. Insights drawn from reflection on your experience.

Leadership Identity. Who you are, including natural traits, chosen traits, and core values.

Leadership Reputation. How others perceive you as a leader based on your behavior.

Leadership Brand. How you would like to be perceived, based on aspirational traits.

After reading through the definitions above, please begin to reflect on your own leadership. *What insights have you drawn from your experiences? What natural traits do you have? What about your chosen ones? What are your core values? How do you believe others perceive you as a leader, based on your behavior? How would you like to be perceived, based on aspirational traits?* Self-reflection is key to leadership growth (and personal growth in general). I would liken it to an artists working on a sculpture. As leaders we should continually be adding to, chipping away at, chiseling, and sharpening all of our edges - with growth mindset of constantly molding ourselves into who we want to become as a leader (and a person). Thus, I have focused the remaining sections of this chapter on you. That is, I have included several exercises for you to complete with an overlying theme focused on self-reflection. In keeping with the theme of this chapter, I have included an ethical leadership scale and an opportunity to test your ethics quotient. Finally, a social desirability scale is included as well. Explanations on how to complete each exercise and understand your results have also been included. Remember, as you complete the exercises, be honest with yourself and your responses. Enjoy!

Self-Awareness Exercise

> *"Experience is a great teacher, but only if you invest the time*
> *to reflect on it. Experience without reflection = no growth."*
> ~ *Tim Kight*

For this exercise, you will simply answer the questions (preferably in bullet-point format) on the right side of the table (See Table 4). If you need more space, pull out a piece of paper and complete the exercise there (I would suggest doing this anyway, perhaps keep it in a notebook. I personally like the MOLESKINE collection, see: http://www.moleskine.com/us/collections/model/evernote-journals). My suggestion is to complete this self-awareness exercise every school year - before the school year, during winter break, during spring break, and at the end of the school year. Lastly, pay particularly close attention to the *Leadership Reputation* category. Some of my own most insightful self-reflection and personal growth has come from asking myself *How do I believe others perceive me, based on my behavior?* Again, be honest in your self-evaluation so that you truly know what you need to work on. After all, we all have room for improvement. Yes, even Jon Gordon, John C. Maxwell, Seth Godin, Tony Robbins, and Gary Vaynerchuk have room to improve. We all do!

Table 4: Self-Awareness Exercise

Questions	Responses
Leadership Wisdom *What insights have you drawn from your experiences?*	
Leadership Identity *Who are you? What natural traits do you have? What about your chosen ones? What are your core values?*	
Leadership Reputation *How do you believe others perceive you as a leader, based on your behavior?*	
Leadership Brand *How would you like to be perceived, based on aspirational traits?*	

It is my hope that upon completing the self-awareness exercise you begin to strengthen your self-awareness. This is a simple little exercise that can be extremely beneficial to any school leader, especially if completed year in and year out. If you are willing to complete this exercise several times throughout each school year, I believe two things will most certainly happen: (1) you will become more self-aware in all that you do (and by becoming so, be able to utilize this self-awareness to reflect and make key decisions to improve yourself as a leader [and a person]); and (2) you will be surprised by the difference between where you start and where you end up. That is, if you do this over several years, I believe you will be pleasantly surprised in the amount of growth you personally experience from your first self-awareness exercise to your most recent. One last thing, if you have a good friend (preferably in school leadership) willing to complete this self-awareness exercise with you each year, this will allow you to learn and grow together. Although I am honest with myself, I have found that sometimes I am perceived differently than I believe I am, or my decision-making and behavior does not align with my core values. By having someone (preferably someone who knows you fairly well) complete this exercise with you each year, I believe it lends itself to even more growth and at a much faster rate. Think of all your friends and family. Then ask yourself, which one of those individuals will be brutally honest with you? That is the person you should choose to complete this exercise with. If they are a school leader, well, that is just icing on the cake.

Ethical Leadership Scale

In this section, you will have the opportunity to complete the ELS created by Brown, Harrison, and Trevino (2005). By completing this scale, we can determine your ethical leadership perspectives. The ELS is a validated 10-item scale and utilizes a Likert scale response. Each individual who completes the ELS will receive a score between 1-5. Additional information about the ELS is provided with the directions, including how to complete the scale, calculate your score, and interpret your score. Remember, the scale is meant to be completed in a timely fashion, thus, do not mull over any one item/statement, go with your first gut instinct, and then move directly to the next item/statement (See Table 5).

Directions. For the following items (See Table 5), please respond by indicating the degree to which the statement reflects your own leadership. Please circle only one of the five options (i.e., Strongly Disagree – Strongly Agree) in the Likert scale for each item.

Table 5: Ethical Leadership Scale

Items	Strongly Disagree	Disagree	Neither Agree nor Disagree	Agree	Strongly Agree	Item Scores
1. Listens to what employees have to say.	Strongly Disagree	Disagree	Neither Agree nor Disagree	Agree	Strongly Agree	
2. Disciplines employees who violate ethical standards.	Strongly Disagree	Disagree	Neither Agree nor Disagree	Agree	Strongly Agree	
3. Conducts his/her personal life in an ethical manner.	Strongly Disagree	Disagree	Neither Agree nor Disagree	Agree	Strongly Agree	
4. Has the best interests of employees in mind.	Strongly Disagree	Disagree	Neither Agree nor Disagree	Agree	Strongly Agree	
5. Makes fair and balanced decisions.	Strongly Disagree	Disagree	Neither Agree nor Disagree	Agree	Strongly Agree	
6. Can be trusted.	Strongly Disagree	Disagree	Neither Agree nor Disagree	Agree	Strongly Agree	
7. Discusses ethics or values with employees.	Strongly Disagree	Disagree	Neither Agree nor Disagree	Agree	Strongly Agree	
8. Sets an example of how to do things the right way in terms of ethics.	Strongly Disagree	Disagree	Neither Agree nor Disagree	Agree	Strongly Agree	
9. Defines success not just by results, but also the way that they are obtained.	Strongly Disagree	Disagree	Neither Agree nor Disagree	Agree	Strongly Agree	
10. When making decisions, asks "What is the right thing to do?"	Strongly Disagree	Disagree	Neither Agree nor Disagree	Agree	Strongly Agree	
					Final Score:	
					Ethical Leadership Scale Score:	

Calculating Your Score. Below are the three steps to calculate your score.

Step 1. Calculate *Item Scores*:
Give yourself *Item Scores* for each item on the scale. *Strongly Disagree =
1 Disagree = 2 Neither Agree nor Disagree = 3 Agree = 4 Strongly Agree
= 5.* Place the corresponding number (score) under the *Item Scores*
column to the far right for each item on the scale.

Step 2. Calculate *Final Score*:
Add up all of your *Item Scores* and place this number next to the *Final
Score* column.

Step 3. Calculate *Ethical Leadership Scale Score*:
Take your *Final Score* and divide it by 10. This will give you a number
between 1 and 5. This number is your *Ethical Leadership Scale Score.*

Interpreting Your Score. Below are the score interpretations.

Low Scorers (0-2)
Such respondents would be considered to have strongly negative ethical
leadership perspectives.

Average Scorers (2-3)
Such respondents would be considered to have average ethical leadership perspectives. That is, these respondents have neither strongly
positive nor strongly negative ethical leadership perspectives, but somewhere in between.

High Scorers (4-5)
These respondents would be considered to have strongly positive ethical
leadership perspectives.

Let's reflect for a moment. *What was your score? Do you believe it is
accurate? Why? Why not?* As previously reported, this is the same scale I
use when conducting my research. Is it perfect? Certainly not. That is why
I am working to validate a new ethical leadership scale in the educational
setting. Nonetheless, it gives us a starting point. I have had graduate and

doctoral students complete this scale and score as high as 5.0 and as low as 1.0. Nevertheless, in my experience, most individuals will fall into the *High Scorers (4-5)* category. I might argue that this is because individuals completing the scale are rating themselves/their own ethical leadership perspectives. Thus, I have attempted to control for this potential socially desirable response tendency by including the SDS in all of my studies. That is what you will be completing next. Now, let's see who is answering in a socially desirable fashion. Please keep these thoughts in mind and/or note down to reference when responding to the questions in the *Reflection* section at the end of this chapter.

Social Desirability Scale

In this section, you will have the opportunity to complete the SDS created by Gerbasi and Strahan (1972). By completing this scale, we can determine your social desirability. The SDS is a validated 10-item scale and utilizes a true/false keyed response. Each individual who completes the SDS will receive a score between 0-10. Additional information about the SDS is provided with the directions, including how to complete the scale, calculate your score, and interpret your score. Remember, the scale is meant to be completed in a timely fashion, thus, do not mull over any one item/statement, go with your first gut instinct and then move directly to the next item/statement (See Table 6).

Directions. Listed are a number of statements concerning personal attitudes and traits. Read each statement and decide whether the statement is *True* or *False* as it pertains to you personally. It's best to go with your first judgment and not spend too long mulling over any one question. Please circle *True* or *False* for each item on the scale.

Table 6: Social Desirability Scale

Items	True	False	Item Scores
1. I like to gossip at times.	True	False	
2. There have been occasions when I took advantage of someone.	True	False	
3. I'm always willing to admit it when I make a mistake.	True	False	
4. I always try to practice what I preach.	True	False	
5. I sometimes try to get even rather than forgive and forget.	True	False	
6. At times I have really insisted on having things my own way.	True	False	
7. There have been occasions when I felt like smashing things.	True	False	
8. I never resent being asked to return a favor.	True	False	
9. I have never been irked when people expressed ideas very different from my own.	True	False	
10. I have never deliberately said something that hurt someone's feelings.	True	False	
		Social Desirability Scale Score:	

Step 1. Calculate Item Scores:

Give yourself Item Scores for each item on the scale. Add 1 point if you answered "True" to items 3, 4, 8, 9, and 10. Add 0 points to the score for each "False" response to these statements. Add 1 point if you answered "False" to items 1, 2, 5, 6, and 7. Add 0 points for each "True" response to these statements. Place the corresponding number (score) under the Item Scores column to the far right for each item on the scale.

Step 2. Calculate Social Desirability Scale Score:
Take your Final Score and place it in the column next to the Social Desirability Scale Score column. This will give you a number between 1 and 10. This number is your Social Desirability Scale Score.

Interpreting Your Score. Below are the score interpretations (Crowne & Marlowe, 1960).

Low Scorers (0–3)
Such respondents answered in a socially undesirable direction much of the time. It may be that they are more willing than most people to respond to tests truthfully, even when their answers might be met with social disapproval.

Average Scorers (4–7)
Such respondents tend to show an average degree of concern for the social desirability of their responses, and it may be that their general behavior represents an average degree of conformity to social rules and conventions.

High Scorers (8–10)
These respondents may be highly concerned about social approval and respond to test items in such a way as to avoid the disapproval of people who may read their responses. Their general behavior may show high conformity to social rules and conventions.

Let's reflect for a moment. *What was your score? Do you believe it is accurate? Why? Why not?* As previously reported, this is the same scale I use when conducting my research in an attempt to help control for any socially desirable response tendencies from the participants in my studies. Is it perfect? Certainly not. Nonetheless, it gives us a starting point. I have had graduate and doctoral students complete this scale and score as high as 10.0 and as low as 0. In my own research, scores have ranged from 0-10 with variations in the mean score. Please keep these thoughts in mind and/or note down to reference when responding to the questions in the *Reflection* section at the end of this chapter.

Leading with Integrity

"Image promises much, but produces little. Integrity never disappoints."

~ John C. Maxwell

In this last section, you have the opportunity to *Test Your Ethics Quotient* (Oliver, 2015). I utilize this test with my students when teaching the school law course (i.e., *Law and Ethics in Education* course). It is "an excellent way to conduct a self-examination on personal ethics" (Oliver, 2015, p. 135). I personally like it because it gives my students an opportunity to discuss realistic scenarios with their classmates. Each of the scenarios poses an ethical dilemma for school building/district leaders. As you will find, some of the scenarios are more cut and dried, while others are more difficult with regards to determining the best (and most ethical) decision. In fact, in some cases I do not agree with some of the "answers," and I often challenge my students to think more deeply about each of the possible responses (even if they are not listed in the responses provided). This usually leads to a meaningful class discussion. Nonetheless, for the purposes of this activity, please put a check mark beside your selected response for each scenario. Please note, some scenarios do have a response such as *None of the above, but rather...* - which would allow you to elaborate in written or verbal format. Please also note that the directions and the answer key are provided. The test (i.e., scenarios) are pulled directly from the book titled *An Administrator's Guide - Leading with Integrity: Reflections on Legal, Moral, and Ethical Issues in School Administration* (Oliver, 2015, p. 135-145):

Directions. Choose one of the responses listed following each scenario as the decision you personally would most likely make if faced with that issue. After considering each scenario, and making a personal choice on the "what to do," compare your responses with the "recommended responses" that are listed and explained at the end of this activity. Scenarios are similar to the Dexheimer and Fenstermaker studies, with preferred decisions based on standards outlined in the AASA *Code of Ethics*, and reflecting opinions of experienced administrators.

Scenario 1. You are attending, at school district expense, a major national conference of school administrators (such as the AASA convention). While there, you meet a group of friends in the hotel lobby. After a few moments your group is approached by the sales representative of a product used by all of your schools. He mingles with the group and before long insists that all of you accompany him to dinner at one of the city's better restaurants, at his company's expense. How do you respond to the invitation?

__ A. Accept with thanks.

__ B. Try to get the salesman aside, indicating that you would enjoy having dinner with him privately sometime.

__ C. Decline the invitation, claiming you have another commitment, even though this is not really the case.

__ D. Accept the invitation, but only if you are allowed to pay for your own meal.

__ E. None of the above, but rather ...

Scenario 2. Your school district is a rural one and quite homogenous in its population. The teaching staff reflects this homogeneity. That is, they are mostly white, middle-class, and Protestant. In your search for new staff members, an excellent candidate with extremely promising credentials appears. The interview turns up the additional fact that this candidate belongs to a racial or ethnic group not generally found in your area (imagine any if you wish). The board has made it clear in the past that all hiring is entirely in your hands; they'll ratify any recommendation you make to them. How will you proceed?

__ A. You turn to other candidates, not out of prejudice, but as a form of protection for this applicant, who would clearly be in a lonely and vulnerable position if hired.

__ B. Hire the minority candidate on your own authority or allow the board to hear the facts and decide for itself.

__ C. Although other candidates are clearly inferior, you hire one of them as the best course of action for this particular community at this particular time.

___ D. You do not hire the candidate yourself, but you do make efforts to seek placement for him in the form of contacts you have in other districts.

___ E. None of the above, but rather...

Scenario 3. The parents of a good student and generally responsible youngster have come to you with complaints about the teaching style of a social studies teacher. They claim he is using biased materials and slanted opinions in his classes. Further, they claim that when their son tried to question these approaches, he was greeted with sarcasm and thinly veiled threats to have his grades lowered. The father is well known for his involvement in civic and community affairs, and he demands evidence of your immediate action. What is your response?

___ A. Agree with the parents that the teacher is in the wrong, and indicate that censure will be applied in some form.

___ B. Have the boy transferred to another classroom with a teacher whose techniques and methods are well known to you and which you know will placate these irate parents.

___ C. Call the most immediate supervisor of the teacher and ask for some corroboration of the incidents; then proceed with action.

___ D. Indicate to the parents that you will take the matter up with the teacher and his supervisors, but that no direct action will be taken until both sides of the controversy have been aired.

___ E. None of the above, but rather...

Scenario 4. A local service organization, of which you are a member, puts on an impressive talent show annually to raise funds. This year they have designated the proceeds to help the AFS Exchange Student Program in your school. All rehearsals and the final show will be in the high school auditorium. The chair of the talent show has come to you to ask for a reduction in the normal rates charge by the school for the use of the facilities, so that a maximum profit may be realized. As superintendent, and a member of the organization, how do you respond?

_ A. You recommend to the board that the request be granted.

_ B. Refuse the request, point out the policy as it stands, and note that other equally deserving groups use the auditorium during the year.

_ C. Since the request will mean more benefits to the district's AFS program, you grant it as an administrative action.

_ D. You give no definite answer, but urge the chair to state his or her case before the board, with your support guaranteed.

_ E. None of the above, but rather...

Scenario 5. You and others see that your supervisor is showing favoritism to an employee. The favored employee is allowed to adjust his time schedule to accommodate some personal needs. Other employees in the department have asked to adjust their time schedules, but are not given this opportunity. What should you do?

_ A. Talk to your supervisor about the situation.

_ B. Ignore the situation. That's just the way some supervisors are and nothing can be done to change the situation.

_ C. Take the issue to higher level (to the assistant superintendent or superintendent of schools).

_ D. None of the above, but rather...

Scenario 6. You, as a night plant operations department supervisor, suspect that a co-worker has been drinking alcohol on the job. What should you do?

_ A. Notify your immediate supervisor/administrator of your suspicions.

_ B. Approach the co-worker and discuss the situation.

_ C. Ignore the situation. It's a personal issue.

_ D. None of the above, but rather...

Scenario 7. You recently were promoted to a senior administrative position in the school system and received a Corporate American Express

Card. Since employees are responsible for paying his/her bills, you used the corporate credit card to pay for a recent meal for your wife and some friends when the group dined at a nice restaurant. Can you use the school card for such "personal expenses"? Possible answers.

    __ A. Not sure. Ask another administrator.

    __ B. Contact the American Express office.

    __ C. Yes. Since the employee is personally responsible for paying the bill each month, it should be allowable to charge personal expenses.

    __ D. No. It is against school district policy.

    __ E. None of the above, but rather...

Scenario 8. You are an assistant principal. While in the school district administrative center, you witness a supervisor sign the name of an assistant superintendent on an important document that must be submitted to the Board of Education for review and action. The administrator tells you he has authority to sign for the assistant superintendent, but you have reason to doubt that administrator's word. What action should you take?

    __ A. Do nothing, because you know that central office administrator can make your life miserable if you challenge him.

    __ B. Suggest that the supervisor telephone the assistant superintendent to inform him/her that he is signing his/her name to the document.

    __ C. Make the assistant superintendent or superintendent aware of the situation.

    __ D. None of the above, but rather...

Scenario 9. On a recent business trip you stayed at a hotel that provided a free breakfast. You accepted the free breakfast each morning of your stay. You believe it is okay to submit an expense reimbursement for a set amount for breakfast each morning since it is your understanding that the school district allows you a certain dollar amount for breakfast. Is that okay? Possible answers.

___ A. No. An employee should be sure that the reimbursement claim is accurate and complete.

___ B. Yes. You are aware that others in the school system have done the same thing.

___ C. None of the above, but rather...

Scenario 10. You decide to rent a car for an out-of-town school business trip instead of driving your own car and requesting reimbursement for mileage and related expenses. While preparing your reimbursement claim, you determine that you could receive extra money if you claimed the mileage for your personal car instead of the costs related to the rental car. What should you do?

___ A. Claim the mileage reimbursement. You deserve a little extra for traveling out of town.

___ B. File the claim for the cost of the rental car only.

___ C. None of the above, but rather...

Answers. The possible answers and rationale provided below are based on "review by several experienced administrators, applying individual interpretations of the *AASA Code of Ethics* and arriving at consensus opinions, the following responses are considered the most appropriate action for each scenario" (Oliver, 2015, p. 142).

Scenario 1. D
Rationale: Avoiding a situation that might leave one with a feeling of an "obligation" to a company or sales representative is important for future business transactions. The reason could be quietly explained to the sales representative in a one-to-one discussion.

Scenario 2. B
Rationale: The best-qualified candidate available should be employed. The applicant probably should be made aware of the community demographics as he/she considers accepting an offered contract.

Scenario 3. D

Rationale: Fairness, loyalty and respect of all people are basic convictions of a good leader. Careful "listening" to all parties and a study of both sides of an issue are critical steps in reaching a wise decision.

Scenario 4. B

Rationale: School district policies should be applied in a consistent manner, even when there is a personal preference to grant an exception. Granting a policy waiver for one organization would prompt others to seek similar privilege.

Scenario 5. C Rationale: Since the supervisor is allowing only one employee the opportunity to adjust his time schedule, it would be best to make a higher-level administrator aware of the issue.

Scenario 6. A

Rationale: Reporting this situation to senior management as soon as possible is important, not only for concerns about safety of students and staff, but also to avoid personal injury to the individual or damage to school property. Approaching the co-worker on a personal level may be an option and would give him or her the opportunity to take care of the problem through some employee assistance program.

Scenario 7. D

Rationale: Personal use of a school credit card is inappropriate, and may lead to cancellation of the card as well as disciplinary action. Normally, such cards may be used to cover such expenses as airfare, lodging, rental cars, meals while at a conference, other business-related travel expenses. A corporate card is provided as a tool to more efficiently cover business-related expenses.

Scenario 8. B or C

Rationale: If you believe the actions are improper, you should speak up and address the matter.

Scenario 9. A

Rationale: Employees should only submit a reimbursement request for expenses they actually incur. If an employee accepts the free breakfast offered at a hotel, the employee should not submit a charge for the breakfast. If the employee ate breakfast elsewhere and paid, then it is an appropriate expense.

Scenario 10. B
Rationale: Employees should only submit claims for expenses they actually incur.

> Score ___ /10

Let's reflect for a moment. *How did you do? How many did you get right? How many did you get wrong? Do you believe it is accurate portrayal of your personal ethics? Why? Why not?* As previously reported, this is the same scale I have used with my graduate students when teaching the school law course. Is it perfect? Certainly not. Nonetheless, it gives us a starting point. I have had graduate and doctoral students complete this test and some get all 10 scenarios correct, while others do not answer any of the scenarios correctly. Nonetheless, when implemented in the classroom setting, it allows us to have meaningful conversations about each scenario, possible additional responses (i.e., the *None of the above, but rather...*), and a way to dissect possible scenarios my students will face as a building/district leaders "on the practice field." That is, before they are out there in the field. Please keep these thoughts in mind and/or note down to reference when responding to the questions in the *Reflection* section at the end of this chapter. Furthermore, please remember that the "right" answer is sometimes a matter of debate.

Recommended Books on Ethics and Leadership

The Ethics of School Administration by Kenneth A. Strike, Emil J. Haller, and Jonas F. Soltis

Leading with Integrity by Clarence G. Oliver, Jr

The Ethics of Educational Leadership by Ronald W. Rebore

Ethics for Educational Leaders by Weldon Beckner

Ethical Leadership in Schools by Kenneth A. Strike

Ethics in a New Millennium by Dalai Lama

A Guide for Teaching Ethics to School Leaders (forthcoming) by Dr. Denver J. Fowler

Reflection

Questions for Practicing and Aspiring School Leaders

1. Where do you look for ethical guidance? Please review the *AASA Code of Ethics* shared in this chapter and describe how you might use this code of ethics as a source of ethical guidance.

2. As a school district/building leader, why is self-awareness/self-reflection vital to improving your leadership over the years? Why might it be advantageous to conduct the self-awareness exercise shared in this chapter with a colleague, spouse, friend, family member, or the like?

3. What do you believe your score on the Ethical Leadership Scale says about your ethical leadership perspectives? Do you believe it is an accurate portrayal? Why? Why not?

4. What do you believe your score on the Social Desirability Scale says about your social desirability? Do you believe it is an accurate portrayal? Why? Why not?

5. What do you believe your score on the Ethics Quotient test says about your personal ethics? Do you believe it is an accurate portrayal? Why? Why not?

Problem-based Scenario

The Ethical Leader

> *"If ethics are poor at the top, that behavior is copied down through the organization."*
>
> ~ *Robert Noyce*

As a building (or district) school leader, you have been asked by your direct supervisor (superintendent [if building school leader] or school board president [if district school leader]) to change the completed evaluation of a teacher (or principal). You have been asked to change their final summative evaluation rating from *Accomplished* (the highest rating) to *Ineffective* (the lowest rating). You know that this is a personal attack that you are being asked to carry out by your direct supervisor due to their differences with the individual. Furthermore, the evaluation has already been uploaded to the online database your state utilizes to audit and store such evaluations. Thus, as part of carrying out this task (if you choose to do so), you will have to log into this state database and edit your evaluation (under your username), which may, in and of itself, have implications as well. Lastly, you have already met with this individual (the teacher or principal evaluated) in a post-conference formal evaluation meeting. At this meeting, you indicated that their final summative rating was *Accomplished*. You are new to the building (or district) and in the second year of a two-year contract that will be up for renewal at the upcoming board meeting in month. Moreover, you have yet to meet with your direct supervisor regarding your own final evaluation. What will you do? Please explain in detail how you would respond to this particular scenario. In doing so, be sure to be cognizant of what is considered to be ethical.

Choose Your School Setting

Choose your role and then choose your school building/district setting before you respond to the scenario above. As you draft your response, please be cognizant of how your setting might affect how you respond to the scenario. Essentially, based on the characteristics listed below, think about what we generally know about these characteristics, and, furthermore, how they impact schools/districts. How might they affect your decision-making with regards to the scenario, if at all? Be sure to clearly describe your school setting in your response.

Role: Superintendent, Principal, or Assistant Principal
Locale: Urban, Suburban, or Rural
Size: Small District, Medium District, or Large District
Diversity: No Diversity, Some Diversity, or Very Diverse
SES Status: 100% Free and Reduced Lunch (FRL), 50% FRL, or 0% FRL

Chapter 6

Professional Standards for Educational Leaders

"The quality of a leader is reflected in the <u>standards</u> they set for themselves."

~ *Ray Kroc*

Introduction

I felt compelled to include this chapter as I have found that outside the realm of the higher education setting, most readers are not familiar with the standards to which all educational leadership programs are aligned throughout the nation. Likewise, this chapter aims to highlight how many states operate somewhat differently with regards to licensure, programs, and the like. I hope that this chapter will serve as a brief history of such standards and how they affect educational leadership programs that prepare our future (and practicing) school leaders. In addition, it may allow the reader to become familiar with the governing body and national organizations charged with developing such standards. Finally, it is my hope that this chapter will encourage the reader to become more interested in learning about the educational leadership standards with regards to both administrative licensure and educational leadership programs in a particular state as these standards drive all of the content in the courses used to prepare our nation's (and your state's) future school leaders.

After reading this chapter, please take a moment to review the educational leadership standards (for aspiring and practicing school leaders) and licensure requirements and structure (policies and procedures) in your particular state. After review, if you believe something needs to be changed for the better, might you make time to advocate for such change? In my experience, it is aspiring school leaders and practicing school leaders that often lead the charge with regards to such effective change. Furthermore, I would argue that this is because those who work in the trenches truly know how such standards, policies and procedures affect the work you do on a daily basis with all stakeholders; students, staff, parents, community members, and business owners. Thus, I would contend that it is vital for you as an aspiring or practicing school leader to be well-versed in the current standards, policies, and procedures affecting your work.

The Standards

In almost every credential-granting and accredited educational leadership program in the United States, national standards directly influence both the content and coursework required for aspiring school leaders. Typically, these national standards drive national accreditation. Currently, the national accreditation governing body is the Council for the Accreditation of Educator Preparation (CAEP), formerly known as the National Council for Accreditation of Teacher Education (NCATE). In addition, individual state standards exist that are often derived from, and aligned with, the national standards. For example, in the State of California (where I currently reside), the Commission on Teacher Credentialing (CTC) is the accreditation governing body. For each type of professional credential in education offered in the State of California, the CTC has developed and adopted standards for programs leading to such credentials. Essentially, the CTC "enforces its standards by evaluating approved programs across California" (CTC, 2017). This is not unlike most states in the United States. In fact, most, if not all, have state standards driving the accreditation of their educator preparation programs, including school leadership preparation programs. An array of standards has been developed over the years, at both the federal and state levels. The standards serve as a guide for practicing school leaders (building and district levels), educational leadership preparation programs (principalship and superintendency), and state and national accreditation. Due to the numerous national educational leadership standards developed, reformed, renamed, and acquired over the years, it can be extremely hard to keep up with all the changes regarding the standards themselves. In addition, many states throughout the U.S., including the State of California, have revised their state educational leadership standards in recent years. Finally, several states operate their licensure differently with regards to principalship and superintendency. In fact, some states, such as the State of Mississippi (where I spent time as a professor at The University of Mississippi [UM]), do not have a license delineating between principal and superintendent, rather they have what I like to call a "catch-all" administrative license. That is, once you have your administrative license, you can become anything from an assistant principal to a superintendent immediately after completing your school leadership program. This is troubling indeed, as during my tenure at UM, it was shared with me that several of our students had graduated from our program and became superintendents (often elected – elected superintendents is a practice widely used in the State of Mississippi) with only teaching experience prior to such appointments. This was certainly a concern for me, as our program at UM was meant to prepare aspiring school leaders to be building level school leaders, and as one might suspect, building level leadership can be quite different from district level leadership in schools. Thus, during my time in the State of Mississippi, I advocated for changes to licensure for administrators throughout the state, as well as several other policies affecting school leaders throughout the state.

It is worth highlighting how states differ with regards to such things. For example, in the State of Ohio, I completed a principal license program focused on building level leadership. Upon completing the principal license program, I was able to obtain my principal license. I also completed a superintendent license program focused on district level leadership, but upon completing this program, I was not permitted to apply for/obtain my superintendent license until I had three years of proven successful experience as a school administrator. Upon completing my third year as a school administrator, only then was able to apply for and obtain my superintendent license in the State of Ohio (even though

I had completed the programs several years prior). Perhaps also worth noting, I had to have five years of proven successful teaching experience before I entered the principal license program. In layman's terms, I would contend that there need to be some checks and balances to ensure school leaders are assuming jobs they are adequately prepared and qualified for. We owe it to our students and teachers to ensure competent school leaders are at the helm. Otherwise, we will have individuals in these positions who are underprepared and may do more damage to a school building/district than good.

A Brief History of the Educational Leadership Standards in the United States

In the United States, the Professional Standards for Educational Leaders (PSEL), formerly known as the Interstate School Leaders Licensure Consortium (ISLLC) standards, were acquired by the National Policy Board for Education Administration (NPBEA) in 2015 (National Policy Board for Education Administration, 2016). The NPBEA is a national consortium of major organizations interested in the advancement of school and school-system leadership. Essentially, member organizations collaborate to represent the educational administration profession and improve the preparation and practice of educational leaders at all levels. Member organizations include: the American Association of Colleges for Teacher Education (AACTE), the School Superintendents Association (AASA), the Council for the Accreditation of Educator Preparation (CAEP), the Council of Chief State School Officers (CCSSO), the National Association of Elementary School Principals (NAESP), the National Association of Secondary School Principals (NASSP), the International Council of Professors of Educational Leadership (ICPEL), and the University Council for Educational Administration (UCEA) (National Policy Board for Education Administration, 2016). The recent acquisition by NPBEA from the Council of Chief State School Officers (CCSSO) was decided in 2015. The current PSEL standards serve as an updated version of the ISLLC standards (the first update of the standards since 1998), and are considered to be professional standards.

That is, "they are created for and by the profession to guide professional practice" (National Policy Board for Education Administration, 2015, p. 2). Subsequently, the National Educational Leadership Preparation Standards (NELP) were developed to align with the newly adopted PSEL standards. The NELP standards, formerly known as the Educational Leadership Constituent Council (ELCC) standards, were approved by the NPBEA and will guide educational leadership program design, accreditation review, and state program approval (NELP Standards Overview, 2016). The PSEL standards and NELP standards serve different purposes and should be differentiated from each other.

> While aligned to the PSEL standards, the NELP standards serve a different purpose and provide greater specificity around performance expectations for beginning level building and district leaders. Whereas the PSEL standards define educational leadership broadly, the NELP standards specify what novice leaders and program graduates should know and be able to do as a result of their completion of a high quality educational leadership preparation program (NELP Standards Overview, 2016, p. 1).

Essentially, the NELP standards will focus on what individuals in school leadership programs should know and be able to do upon graduating from their respective school leadership programs. To be clear, the NELP standards are national, whereas several states have created and adopted their own state standards with regards to their respective educational leadership programs. To highlight this phenomenon and drive this point further home, let's look at the standards that currently exist in the State of California. As you will see, most state standards are aligned with the national standards in some way.

A Brief History of the Educational Leadership Standards in the State of California

In the State of California, educational leadership programs are aligned with the California Professional Standards for Education Leaders (CPSEL). CPSEL has been implemented as part of the Administrative Services Credentials (ASC) and educational leadership preparation programs in the State of California since 2001, and was most recently updated in 2014. The CPSEL standards are based on the aforementioned Professional Standards for Education Leaders (PSEL) developed by the National Policy Board for Educational Administration. The aim of the CPSEL standards is to "identify what an administrator must know and be able to do in order to move into sustainable, effective practice" (Commission on Teacher Credentialing, 2014, p. 1). Essentially, the CPSEL standards serve as the foundation of educational leadership preparation in the State of California. Thus, all Commission-approved programs (preliminary and clear) continue to be framed around the CPSEL standards. The CPSEL standards aim to "describe critical areas of leadership for administrators and offer a structure for developing and supporting leaders throughout their careers" (Commission on Teacher Credentialing, 2014, p. 1). In addition to the CPSEL standards, the California Administrator Performance Expectations (CAPEs) were developed in 2013. The CAPEs standards "describe the set of knowledge, skills and abilities that *beginning* education administrators should have and be able to demonstrate" (Commission on Teacher Credentialing, 2017, p. 11). Today, there are two types of programs for aspiring educational leaders in the State of California that lead to ASC credentials: (1) preliminary administrative services programs (Tier I); and (2) the clear credential programs (Tier II). While the CAPE standards drive the preliminary administrative services program, the CPSEL standards drive the clear credential program (see Figure 1). Both programs and the new structure were "designed to provide the best career preparation and experiences for effective leadership in California's 21st Century schools" (Commission on Teacher Credentialing, 2017, p. 8).

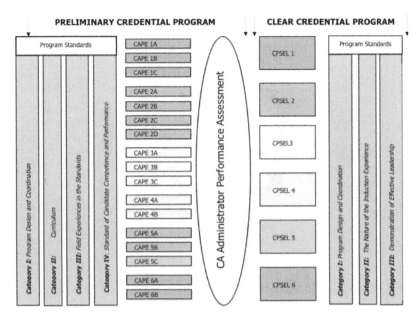

Figure 2: Standards and Performance Measures for the ASC Credentials (Commission on Teacher Credentialing, 2017, p. 12).

In addition, in 2013 CTC amended the requirements for those individuals aiming to earn a preliminary administrative services credential in the State of California to include the California Administrator Performance Assessment (CalAPA). "The CalAPA is structured around three full leadership cycles of *investigate, plan, act,* and *reflect.*" (California Performance Assessments for Teachers and Leaders, 2017). With rubrics designed to address a range of the CAPEs, each of the leadership cycles include the four steps (see Figure 2). CTC is aiming to implement this new addition starting sometime in 2018-2019, and several educational leadership programs are already piloting CalAPA. You can learn more about CalAPA and review the tentative timeline and CalAPA Draft Design here: http://ctcpa.nesinc.com/about_calapa.asp.

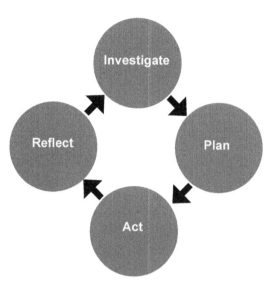

Figure 3: California Administrator Performance Assessment Four Steps (California Performance Assessments for Teachers and Leaders, 2017)

As you can see, the State of California has those "checks and balances" in place that I recommended with regards to state standards and administrative licensure. This model is consistent with ensuring that aspiring school leaders in the State of California are adequately prepared and competent to lead a school building/district. Unfortunately, as previously reported, not every state has such checks and balances in place, and in those that do not, it is certainly a disservice to the stakeholders, including students, teachers, parents, community members and business owners. It is my hope that someday all states will adopt a model similar to that of California and Ohio, to ensure all school leaders are prepared for both building level leadership and district level leadership. I challenge you to take the time to research your own state standards and policies with regards to the standards driving educational leadership programs in your state, as well as the policies regarding administrative licensure in your state. In addition, I challenge you to keep up with the changes to such standards and be active in some (or all) of the organizations creating such standards.

Other Standards for School Leaders

In addition to the aforementioned national and state standards, several national school leadership associations and organizations throughout the United States have additional standards for practicing school leaders. For example, The American Association of School Administrators (AASA), also known as The School Superintendents Association, first released the Professional Standards for the Superintendency (PSPs) in 1993. The PSPs were released by the AASA Commission on Standards for the Superintendency. Essentially, these standards were developed and designed to "ensure excellence in the American school superintendency" (American Association of School Administrators, 2017). Superintendents can actually obtain a copy of the PSPs in book/ebook form, as AASA teamed with Rowman & Littlefield to produce a book focused solely on these standards. See: https://rowman.com/ISBN/0876522029#. On the Rowman & Littlefield site, the book and the PSPs are summarized as follows (R&L Education, 2017 [Summary]):

> School superintendents provide leadership and inspiration in school districts across the country. They must be skilled collaborators who can rally resources to support better education for all children living in our multicultural society. Professional standards will help to ensure excellence in the American school superintendency. Developed by a special AASA Commission on Standards for the Superintendency and reviewed by a national 'Jury of 100' business and education leaders, these eight standards combine administrative knowledge with research on performance goals, competencies and skills in the following areas: leadership and district culture; policy and governance; communications and community relations; organizational management; curriculum planning and development; instructional management; human resources management; and the values and ethics of leadership.

In addition to the PSPs, as previously mentioned in chapter five, AASA also has released a *Code of Ethics*. See: http://www.aasa.org/content.aspx?id=1390. This *Code of Ethics*, coupled with the PSPs, serves as additional guidance for practicing (and aspiring) superintendents. That is, long after a superintendent has completed his/her superintendent license program, he/she can use the PSPs and *Code of Ethics* to guide their district leadership. Both the PSPs and the *Code of Ethics* serve as excellent resources.

In addition to the PSPs and *Code of Ethics* released by AASA, most (if not all) states have standards in place for practicing principals and superintendents that often align with the evaluation processes and models for both. For example, let's take a look at the State of Ohio. In the State of Ohio, five standards (and several accompanying elements for each) exist for practicing school principals. These standards are closely aligned with the evaluation system in place for school leaders in the State of Ohio known as the Ohio Principal Evaluation System (OPES).

You can peruse the State of Ohio Principal Standards here (Ohio Department of Education, 2017): https://education.ohio.gov/getattachment/Topics/Teaching/Educator-Equity/Ohio-s-Educator-Standards/StandardsforEducators_revaug10.pdf.aspx (see pages 40-59).

Additionally, you can access the OPES model here (Ohio Department of Education, 2017): https://education.ohio.gov/getattachment/Topics/Teaching/Educator-Evaluation-System/Ohio-Principal-Evaluation-System-OPES/Principal-Performance-Ratings/OPES-Model-111715.pdf.aspx.

In addition to the Ohio Principal Standards and the OPES model, the State of Ohio also has standards for practicing superintendents. Again, there are five standards with several accompanying elements. You can access the Ohio Standards for Superintendents here (Ohio Department of Education, 2017): https://education.ohio.gov/getattachment/Topics/Teaching/Educator-Equity/Ohio-s-Educator-Standards/Standards-for-Superintendentsfinal_nov2008.pdf.aspx.

Much as with the State of Ohio principal standards, the Ohio Standards for Superintendents are closely aligned with the Ohio Superintendent Evaluation System (OSES). You can access the OSES model here (Ohio Department of Education, 2017):

http://education.ohio.gov/getattachment/Topics/Teaching/Educator-Evaluation-System/Ohio-s-Superintendent-Evaluation-System/reducODE2009-SES-FULLv3.pdf.aspx.

Although I have only highlighted one U.S. state (State of Ohio) here as an example, it is my hope that you can use this information to determine: (1) if your State has similar constructs in place; and (2) if not, why not? Thus, you may find this information to be insightful on many levels, and I hope that it will encourage advocacy efforts on your part to encourage your state policy makers to adopt something similar as I believe the State of Ohio offers an excellent example of the standards that exist for practicing principals and superintendents, and furthermore, how those standards are aligned with the evaluation of school leaders throughout a given academic school year.

Reciprocity

Since this chapter discusses licensure and how licensure differs from state-to-state, I felt it would be useful to include a discussion (albeit small in scope) on reciprocity[30] and how it differs around the globe, across the nation, state to state. Many states in the U.S. have varying levels of requirements, policies, and procedures regarding reciprocity. For example, in some U.S. states, it is relatively easy to obtain what is considered to be the equivalent of a license you hold in another state. In other states, it may be more difficult. This also holds true for the international arena, that is, licensure held in other countries and how it might transfer to the United States. However, here I will focus on state-to-state reciprocity. For example, let's say you completed a school leadership program (or programs) in the State of Ohio and obtained your principal and superintendent license. Then, years later you move to the west coast and decide you would like to obtain your principal and superintendent license (the

---

30 Reciprocity, in layperson's terms, as it is related to the educational setting, deals with the policies and procedures in a state (or nation) for an individual who would like to obtain licensure in said state (or nation), who has already completed the requirements and obtained an equivalent license in another state (or nation). Essentially, it deals with how a license is transferred to new territories (both within the United States and around the globe).

equivalent) in the State of California. This is where reciprocity comes into play. The State of California clearly outlines the policies and procedures that are required for reciprocity on their state department of education website, and this is true of most states. For an example, you can review what the State of California requires for reciprocity here: https://www.ctc.ca.gov/credentials/out-of-state-admin. This is usually fairly cut and dried. However, it is surprising how much states differ with regards to reciprocity, and how differing processes have unintended outcomes that affect (both negatively and positively, depending on the state) their PreK-12 educational setting. For example, let's look at Mississippi. The State of Mississippi opted to have the highest cut score[31] on the School Leadership Licensure Assessment (SLLA). This was aimed at ensuring that only the most adequately prepared and knowledgeable school leaders would be leading their schools. Makes sense, right? However, due to reciprocity policies and procedures, the policy is futile. As a former professor at UM, I witnessed first-hand how the reciprocity procedures and policies created a sort of loop-hole for those aspiring school leaders who did not score high enough on the SLLA. Due to the reciprocity policies and procedures in the State of Mississippi, these individuals could take those scores one state over (Arkansas), obtain their administrative license there (Arkansas had a lower cut score and utilize the same test [SLLA]), and then re-enter the State of Mississippi and obtain their administrative license through the process of reciprocity (they held the equivalent license in a nearby state). So, as you can see in this example, reciprocity policies and procedures should be well thought out in order to ensure no loop-holes exist. This is just one example to highlight the importance of reciprocity procedures and policies state-to-state. It certainly shines light on how such things are interconnected and how noble policies (in this case, the State of Mississippi adopting the highest cut score of all states utilizing the SLLA) can have unintended outcomes and create unforeseen loop holes if the reciprocity procedures and policies are not well thought out and aligned with other initiatives (in this case, an attempt

---

31 The term cut-off score refers to the lowest possible score on an exam, standardized test, high-stakes test, or other form of assessment that a student must earn to either "pass" or be considered "proficient."

through policy to ensure only the most adequately prepared and knowledgeable school leaders would be leading Mississippi schools). Each U.S. state differs in varying degrees with regards to their reciprocity policies and procedures. Much like with any state education information, you can easily access this type of information via the state department of education websites. Nonetheless, I felt compelled to include it here within this chapter in order to highlight reciprocity as it applies to licensure in the educational setting. It is my hope that by sharing this example, as aspiring school leaders and practicing school leaders, we begin to be and will be mindful of such interconnectedness as it applies not only to reciprocity and licensure requirements at the state level, but also how such policies (adopted at the district level – school board/superintendent) and procedures (adopted at building level – principal/staff) are interconnected and how they affect all of your stakeholders. That is, be aware of the possibility for unintended outcomes of such policies and procedures, and perhaps most importantly, be prepared to advocate for and implement swift changes upon discovering those unintended outcomes. Finally, with the anticipated teacher (and administrator) shortage in the United States, reciprocity will most certainly need to change both nation-to-nation, and state-to-state.

It is my hope that this chapter allowed you, the reader, to further understand the development, adoption, and the need for educational leadership standards and what they mean for all stakeholders involved, from the professors teaching in the educational leadership programs, to the students (aspiring school leaders) completing such programs, and further on to the current practitioners in our nation's schools. Again, I challenge you to take a moment and review the educational leadership standards for aspiring and practicing school leaders and licensure requirements and structure (policies and procedures) in your particular state. After review, if you believe something needs to be changed for the better, might you make time to advocate for such change? If not you, who? If not now, when?

Reflection

Questions for Practicing and Aspiring School Leaders

1. What steps will you take to ensure you stay well-versed with regards to the educational leadership standards and licensure policies and procedures in your state?

2. Do you believe knowing the educational leadership standards and licensure policies and procedures in your state is important as an aspiring or practicing school leader? Why? Why not?

3. As a school district/building leader, how might educational leadership standards drive your leadership practices and the work you do in schools on a daily basis?

4. As a school district/building leader, how might you advocate for changes necessary to educational leadership standards (national and state) and licensure policies and procedures (state)?

5. As a school district/building leader, how might you get more involved with the many organizations mentioned in this chapter that are responsible for the development of the educational leadership standards in the United States?

Problem-based Scenario

The standards aren't up to standard

As a building (or district) school leader, you have been asked to serve on a committee at the state level. This committee has been charged with reviewing the current educational leadership standards for practicing school leaders in your state. That is, to be clear, the standards developed and adopted for practicing school leaders. As part of this committee, you are also charged with reviewing the evaluation processes for school leaders in your state. For all intents and purposes, note that the evaluation processes and accompanying rubrics are carefully and clearly aligned with the standards for practicing school leaders in your state. In preparing for the first committee meeting, you have been asked to review the standards and evaluation processes for practicing school leaders in your state. You are one of only a few practicing school leaders serving on the committee. The rest of the committee consists of policy makers, state education employees, community members, and the like, including individuals whose educational backgrounds ended when they graduated high school. Thus, you, along with a few other committee members, are "in the trenches," and conceivably have the practitioner experience and knowledge to make key suggestions to improve the current standards and evaluation processes for school leaders in your state. Upon reviewing the standards and evaluation processes in preparation for your first committee meeting, it becomes apparent that there are many discrepancies between the standards/evaluation processes and best practices - that is, school leadership practices that are best for students. It is evident to you as a practitioner that several of the standards and evaluation processes do not support and encourage these best practices, and likewise, only loosely align with the national standards (say, PSELs).

Discuss how you might exercise some political sensibility in presenting your suggested changes to the rest of the committee members at the first meeting (and possibly several future meetings). What might you need to be mindful of in advocating for such changes? How might you get your point across without losing the support of other committee members? What preliminary research might you need to conduct (and possibly present) in order to prepare for and support your suggestions? Where might you access such information and data? In generating your responses to these questions, remember that the majority of your audience are non-practitioners with little to no experience in the PreK-12 educational setting outside of their own experiences as a student in said setting.

Choose Your School Setting

Choose your role and then choose your school building/district setting before you respond to the scenario above. As you draft your response, please be cognizant of how your setting might affect how you respond to the scenario. Essentially, based on the characteristics listed, think about what we generally know about these characteristics, and, furthermore, how they impact schools/districts. How might they affect your decision-making with regards to the scenario, if at all? Be sure to clearly describe your school setting in your response.

Role: Superintendent, Principal, or Assistant Principal
Locale: Urban, Suburban, or Rural
Size: Small District, Medium District, or Large District
Diversity: No Diversity, Some Diversity, or Very Diverse
SES Status: 100% Free and Reduced Lunch (FRL), 50% FRL, or 0% FRL

Chapter 7

School Climate and School Culture

"The real role of leadership is climate control,
creating a climate of possibility."
~ *Sir Ken Robinson*

Y ou will never change the **school culture** until you change what you
do daily (**school climate**). The secret of your success in changing
the **school culture** will be found in your daily routine (**school climate**).
Both **school culture** and **school climate** are extremely important to a
school's success (or failure).

What's the Difference Anyway?

Before delving into this chapter, I believe we need to answer the following question: *What is the difference between school climate and school culture?* The answer to this question has often been debated. In fact, in my
experience, I have found that many individuals, especially in education,
often use the terms school climate and school culture interchangeably.
Furthermore, when I have had conversations with individuals throughout
the nation and around the globe, I have found that even as they attempt
to describe the difference between the two terms, they often appear
uncertain in their description. That is, they seem to lack confidence in
their explanation. Thus, my aim within this chapter is to dispel confusion
with regards to the two terms, and to describe the distinct differences
between the two. I once heard Todd Whitaker explain the difference
between climate and culture on a video he created with ASCD, using
a weather analogy. Now, I have tried explaining the differences several
times over to many folks, and I am here to tell you, the weather analogy

seems to do the trick. When I have used this method, not only do individuals clearly understand the difference, I have also begun to notice that, perhaps more importantly, they remember the difference. Thus, I like to use the weather analogy when explaining the difference between school climate and school culture.

First, let's break down the two by definition and I will include some weather analogy.

School Climate. The way a school feels when your stakeholders, including students, parents, staff, community members, and business owners, walk in the door. "Whereas some schools feel friendly, inviting, and supportive, others feel exclusionary, unwelcoming, and even unsafe" (Loukas, 2016, p. 1). It is the "weather today."

School Culture. The way in which a school does things. This includes values, traditions, perceptions, systematic items (e.g., do you have bells or no bells), etc. "Culture drives expectations and beliefs; expectations and beliefs drive behavior; behavior drives habits; and habits create the future. It all starts with culture" (Gordon, 2015, p. 2). It is the "weather over a long period of time."

Keeping with the weather theme, let's further describe this analogy. For example, it may be warmer in Alaska than California on a given day (school climate), however, we all know that overall it is colder in Alaska than in California over a given year (school culture).

To drive this point further home (i.e., the subtle differences between school climate and school culture), let's look at a few tweets from my friend Dr. Justin Tarte with regards to school climate and school culture:

> "*School climate* is how people act when the superintendent is in the room. *School culture* is how people act when nobody is around."

> "*School climate* is what is said in a staff faculty meeting. *School culture* is what is said in the parking lot after the meeting."

"*School climate* is how we speak to a child when their parent is present. *School culture* is how we speak to a child when nobody is around."

The Importance of Creating a Positive School Climate and Culture

"Culture is like a tree...it takes years to grow, yet it can be chopped down in minutes."

~ *Jon Gordon*

"You can tell a lot about a school's culture by the way the adults treat each other and students when no one is looking or listening."

~ *Dwight Carter*

"If you want to know about the culture of a school, see how the adults greet kids and you will learn a lot."

~ *Dr. Todd Whitaker*

"School environments vary greatly. Whereas some schools feel friendly, inviting, and supportive, others feel exclusionary, unwelcoming, and even unsafe" (Loukas, 2016, p. 1). The truth is, most of us can sense the climate/culture of a school as soon as we set foot in it. In fact, even school districts/buildings in close proximity to one another can be drastically different in terms of school climate and school culture. Perhaps even worse, most of the individuals in the negative school climate and school culture don't even notice it. They have become accustomed to it and no longer see how negative it is. When they hire a new individual, those individuals become just like the existing individuals in that school district's/building's culture. This concept is shared by my friend Dr. Todd Whitaker in an ASCD Short titled *Climate and Culture with Todd Whitaker*. He does an excellent job depicting this very concept.

See: https://www.youtube.com/watch?v=4IwZubnyr_c.

Perhaps the most important part of his presentation is at the very end, because it is here that he addresses how one might fix this problem when he states "Within an organization, we have to get a real handle on what is the culture, what is the driving force within the district, and then be able to alter that or improve it, either on a sub-culture basis or a school-wide basis or a district-wide basis" (Whitaker, 2016).

People ask me all the time what is the most important aspect in turning around a school. My answer is always the same: "You must focus on your school climate/school culture and your achievement data simultaneously." I know, easier said than done. I shared how you might tackle the achievement data in chapter four, so for this chapter we will focus on the importance of fostering a positive school climate/school culture. As you read through this chapter, I want you to think about your current school setting. Do you believe your school setting has a positive school climate and school culture? If not, how are you going to change that? You do not need to be in an administrative position to start leading the positive school climate/school culture initiative. It can start with anyone, from a custodian, teacher, assistant principal, principal, to the superintendent. I know, because I have witnessed it myself. So what is holding you back? You can start tomorrow.

"There are no neutral interactions in the building. You are either building culture or undermining it."

~ Jimmy Casas

In order to change your school's climate and culture, first you must know where you are in order to get where you want to go. I liken it to one of those marked areas on a map that say *You Are Here*. You know, the ones you see on Rest Area maps in the middle of nowhere, or shopping mall maps, theme park maps, etc. How could you possibly get where you want to go if you don't know where you are starting from? Thus, you may need to do some preliminary research on your school building/district. Depending on how in-depth you want to go, you could use anything from a Survey Monkey (10 questions) to one of Dr. Wayne K. Hoy's Organizational Climate Surveys.

See: https://www.surveymonkey.com/ to access Survey Monkey.

See: http://www.waynekhoy.com/ocdq-re.html for example of Hoy's Organizational Climate Surveys.

Nonetheless, you need to have a good pulse on the school climate/ culture as it is. Only then can you start planning how you are going to improve it, and, perhaps most importantly, sustain it. I strongly suggest surveying all of your stakeholders in order to gain as much information as possible with regard to your current setting. That being said, anonymous surveys are not for the faint of heart: if you are going to send them out as a school leader, you better have some thick skin. As I am sure you would suspect, oftentimes this gives stakeholders a passive-aggressive way to tee off on their school leaders. With that in mind, I offer this advice. Pay little attention to the highly positive remarks or highly negative remarks; oftentimes it is the remarks in between that offer the most accurate analysis and feedback. In my experience, the middle of the road remarks tend to be the most meaningful and useful feedback provided on any type of survey. That being said, go ahead and hit send!

As reported by Loukas (2007), most researchers agree that school climate and school culture are really a multidimensional construct. This multidimensional construct includes physical, social, and academic dimensions. I like to include discipline as the fourth construct, for two main reasons: (1) your discipline plan (whether it be black and white, have gray areas, or is a restorative justice model, etc.) can have an enormous effect on the school climate and school culture; and (2) many of you reading this may be aspiring school leaders, thus, your next step in the ladder may be serving as an assistant principal, and we all know assistant principals often get the joy of handling the bulk of the discipline. Using Loukas article (2007), let's further break down each of the dimensions in greater detail, and under each, discuss how we might positively affect each as a school leader.

Physical
This includes the appearance of the school building and classrooms, enrollment size and student to teacher ratio, the order and organization of the classrooms, availability of resources, and safety and comfort.

Appearance (Building & Classrooms). There is absolutely no excuse not to keep your school building(s) and classrooms meticulously clean and in tiptop condition. In middle/high school, I baled hay and straw for $5.00 an hour on area farms in order to save up $1,000.00 for my first car. It was a 1988 Isuzu I-Mark. Now, it was not brand new and it certainly wasn't the coolest first car by any means. But let me tell you, I kept it clean! What I am getting at here is this: you may not be in a brand-new school building with all the fancy bells and whistles, but you can still keep it cleaner than a brand-new school building. I have been in brand new school buildings that were dirty and old school buildings that were so clean you could eat off the floor. I bet you can guess which one had the positive school climate and school culture. As an administrator, keep your building and classrooms clean (you can ensure the classrooms are clean through feedback from walk-throughs and observations). Here are a few tips to help in this process: (1) treat your custodians with the utmost respect. I love the quote, "I treat/talk to the custodians the same way I treat/talk to the superintendent." Believe me, this will ease the process; and (2) any chance you get, pick up some trash. I used to love talking/walking with students, parents, and teachers in the hall of my school building and then stopping and picking up trash right in front of them. Don't be above it, it sets an example. I especially liked doing this in the crowded halls in between class changes. On that note, it may just become your legacy. I was touring the Ole Miss campus when I had first accepted a professor position there a few years ago. The man giving me the tour was going on and on about how wonderful Chancellor Robert Khayat was. I finally asked what was he most remembered for (as he never really got into specifics). He stopped, turned to me and said, "Chancellor Khayat is the reason Ole Miss was named *The Most Beautiful Campus in the United States.* When he became Chancellor, this place was not taken care of, but he changed that. In fact, he was known for walking around campus with a bunch of trash in his hands in between each trash can from picking it up himself." People remember those types of things, and so will your stakeholders. Months later I would run into/meet Khayat at the local gym. I was doing sit down rows and he came up, tapped me on the shoulder and said, "That's all you can lift? Put some weight on there." Coming from him (he also played in the NFL), he probably thought I was slacking. Nonetheless, I ended up introducing myself. He is certainly a great leader, and not just because he picked up trash on the campus of Ole Miss (To learn more about Khayat, be sure to read his book *The Education of a Lifetime*). Like Khayat, my high school baseball coach was never above it. Don Thorp is in every (and any) Hall of Fame that has to do with coaching high school baseball, and in some cases, football and basketball - as he coached those two sports for many years before focusing on baseball. He is legendary, to say the least, and I had the opportunity to play for him. But what I remember about him the most is this. As an eighth grader attending my first high school basketball game, I was in awe when I saw him sweeping the floor at halftime. I remember standing there looking through the double doors and watching him go up and down the gym floor with the broom. I thought, wow, there is Coach Thorp cleaning the floors ... ever since then, I have never been above it, and I never will be. As my mother used to say, "Every hand fits a broom." So, get to work and never be above it!

Enrollment Size and Student to Teacher Ratio. There are certainly some things that are harder to control than others, and enrollment size and student to teacher ratio are among them. However, here is my suggestion with regard to this particular area. First, be sure that your school building/district does an excellent job of ensuring that the students who attend your school actually belong at your school. That is, that they do reside within the district boundaries. If they do not, you need to have an efficient process in place to redirect such students to the district in which they are supposed to attend. In one district in which I served as a school administrator, we even employed an individual (with a six-figure salary) whose sole responsibility was to determine if students were supposed to be attending our school district. You are probably thinking to yourself, that seems like a high salary for such a position. But let me tell you, this individual had a lot of responsibility, and furthermore, this individual saved the district quite a bit of money. Secondly, as a school leader, one of your most tedious tasks will be developing the daily schedule as it pertains to your teachers and students. More specifically, you have to be innovative in how you schedule where your teachers and students will be (i.e., location) and what your teachers will teach (i.e., subject area). This takes time if you are going to get innovative about it. You will need to go through and analyze all of your teacher and staff files with regard to what subjects and grade levels they are licensed to teach. Furthermore, in order to do what is best for students, it may require teachers teaching subjects/grade levels they are certified to teach, but have not taught in years (or ever for that matter). This can lead to difficult conversations, but again, I always hung my hat on doing what is best for students. I personally have found it best to have teachers teaching multiple grade levels throughout the day, and in some cases, in more than one subject. Some of your teachers may be resistant at first, but for the most part, I have found that most enjoy the challenge and change. Another option is reaching out to local and regionally located educational service centers and proposing the need for additional staff. In some cases, they may fund the additional staff. That is, the additional staff will actually be employed by the educational service center but work in your school building/district. One other option is specifically for school district leaders (such as superintendents). District leaders might look at opportunities to pass a new levy or other funding options (local businesses) which would allow for the possibility of erecting a new school building and/or hiring more staff. I have personally witnessed how some superintendents become very innovative in how they fund such initiatives. Unfortunately, I have also seen how they will hit the community where it hurts if the community is not willing to support a new levy or the like. For example, when the threat of eliminating school transportation and or moving to pay-to-play for athletics is on the agenda if the given initiative does not pass, in many cases, voters will come out and support the initiative. However, I have seen communities who first tested the waters (i.e., voted no on a new levy and then experienced the repercussions of not having any school transportation and/or moving to pay-to-play athletics) only to quickly support the levy/new initiative next time it is on the ballot. Sadly, it can take years to recover from such damage and rarely have I seen a district go from pay-to-play athletics back to free athletics, even with the passage of a new levy. Nonetheless, school district leaders have to do what is best for students, even if that means making things difficult for the community in order to get a new levy passed or initiative supported. I don't necessarily agree with this process, but I am being transparent about it. I would bet it would be difficult to get any superintendent to admit to this tactic, but I promise you, it has been used, and it has worked. Unfortunately, the climate/culture will ultimately suffer and will need mending.

Order and Organization of the Classrooms. The order and organization of the classrooms is first and foremost the responsibility of the teacher in the classroom. One of the best compliments I ever received as a teacher was shared with me when I had recently accepted a new administrative position. One of the teachers in my new school was neighbors with my old principal from my day as a teacher. This teacher was naturally curious about his new school leader and asked him about me. My old principal went on to say I was one of the best teachers he ever hired. But as it applies to this particular concept, he also said "Denver never once sent a student to my office outside of a bloody fist fight in the six years he taught in my building. The students knew the buck stopped at his classroom door, not my office. Not only was he a great teacher, but he had the highest expectations for the students in his class, and when they were out of line, he handled it, he never sent them to me." When I heard that it brought a smile to my face. He was right, I never passed the buck, it started and ended with me in my classroom. As for the fist fights, well, I can only remember two in my six years in that particular district, and I will save you the details, but both times the students needed to be brought to the office. What I am getting at here is this, as a school leader, through walk-throughs and observations, you must support and encourage your teachers in having an orderly and organized classroom. However, I do want to note here that this does not mean a boring atmosphere that is organized and rigid. Rather, I envision an atmosphere more like Mr. Keating's (played by actor Robin Williams) class in the movie *Dead Poets Society*. See: https://www.youtube.com/watch?v=XtYRC00IoUs for an example. Now, I know we can't all be Mr. Keating, but we can all be enthusiastic about all that we do, and this especially applies to school leadership and teaching. Furthermore, Mr. Keating dresses the part. My best teachers always dressed the part, wore ties and jackets each day, etc. They took their job seriously, and the students took them seriously in all that they did from teaching to discipline. This may seem like a coincidence, but I strongly disagree. Organization is a tough one. I write this because I have worked with teachers whose classrooms appear unorganized. However, you might ask them for something and they will walk right over and pull it from some pile. That is, they know exactly where everything is in what we perceive to be a mess. Thus, I tread lightly in my approach to organization, with regards to this in particular. That being said, lesson plans, unit plans, aligned to the correct standards, and the like, do need to be organized. Again, this task can be supported and encouraged through regular walkthroughs and observations where there is an opportunity to review lesson plans and such. I have found that unorganized lesson plans usually lead to not-so-great teaching. Conversely, I have found that well thought out lesson/unit plans that are correctly aligned with the required standards lead to excellent teaching. Coincidence? I think not. Be brave, push your teachers to have an orderly and organized classroom while also being mindful that your teachers need a little anonymity. That is, teachers have different styles and personalities in all facets of teaching. Your job as a school leader is to tap into the myriad of styles and personalities and make them work for your students. Again, not everyone can be Mr. Keating, but everyone can be just as enthusiastic and passionately do their jobs.

> *"Classroom management is not about having the right rules ... it's about having the right relationships."*
> ~ *Danny Steele*

Availability of Resources. One complaint I hear from school leaders is that they have limited resources as it applies to this or that aspect of schooling. My response is always the same, "Have you looked for grants that might support that?" It amazes me how often school leaders overlook resources like grants. In my last two years of service in the

PreK-12 educational setting as a school leader, I served as a co-investigator[32] on 11 grants totaling close to $30,000. These grants allowed us to purchase classroom sets of iPads, Elmos (interactive document cameras), Chromebooks, headsets, charging docks/tubs, and equipment for our new robotics program. In addition, two separate grants supported the installation of an outdoor lecture area/community garden and supported our *We the People* team as they traveled to Washington, D.C. to compete in the National *We the People* competition. Basically, I got sick of my teachers complaining about what they did not have and what they needed, so I decided to do something about it. I challenged them to find grants to support what they wanted and needed. My pledge to them was that I would help in finding such grants and I would help write them and submit them. Most of my teachers accepted the challenge and we got to work. By the time I left that building, almost every need or want was met through a grant of some sort. In fact, most of the classrooms had a classroom set of iPads or Chromebooks with either a charging tub or charging dock, and the classrooms that did not could share with someone across the hall (we strategically placed the sets). Furthermore, some of my teachers used the grants to fund professional development opportunities. Below I have listed a few sites to get you started. Enjoy!

National Education Association: http://www.nea.org/grants/grantsawardsandmore.html
Grants for Teachers: https://teach.com/what/grants-for-teachers/
Edutopia: https://www.edutopia.org/grants-and-resources
TeachersCount: http://www.teacherscount.org/grants/

Safety and Comfort. Safety and comfort play a large role in all things school, especially as it applies to the climate and culture. Although safety and comfort are somewhat tied to discipline (e.g. where bullying, fighting, harassment, cyberbullying, etc. are involved), as previously reported,

---

32 Most PreK-12 educational grants are for teachers versus school administrators. Thus, as a school leader, you can help write them and even serve as a co-investigator on such grants, but oftentimes the teacher will be listed as the primary applicant/investigator.

I have made discipline a separate additional dimension, thus here we will focus on safety and comfort as it applies to school safety policies and procedures. It goes without saying that it is imperative that you address and have a plan in place for all possible emergencies. In the 21st Century, a lot has changed. Most school campuses are no-gun zones. When I was in high school, I remember when my friends (who were farmers and hunters) would have their hunting rifles hanging in the rear window of their trucks in the school parking lot. Oftentimes loaded and with the doors left unlocked. No one ever thought about shooting up a school. However, as we know, this is just not the case in today's world. We must plan and prepare our school buildings/districts for all potential emergencies. This includes active shooters, tornados, earthquakes, hurricanes, tsunamis, internal threat, external threat, lockdowns, fire drills, etc. Let me tell you from experience, the key to all of this is preparedness, and preparedness comes from practicing such drills over and over. This means more than the required number of times. Essentially, you want get your teachers and students to the point where they do not to think about what to do, they just do it. Remember, as a school building leader, you are in charge of the procedural aspects of such drills, while the superintendent/board of education implement the policies that you must adhere by. Thus, it is up to you to ensure the best procedures are in place in order to keep your students and teachers safe. Here are a few tips from my days as a school leader:

- Ensure you have long-range walkie-talkies that are regularly charged and work. Backup batteries are a must!
- Ensure everyone knows their role in all emergency situations no matter the time of day (see below).
- Practice drills throughout the school day, not just at the time of day that is convenient for you, your teachers and students. For example, try a drill during class transition when all the students are in the hallway, or when a grade level of students are at lunch. Switch it up so you can address any issues that may arise in order to be best prepared for the real thing.

- When there is a breakdown in any of your procedures, address it. I kept a clipboard and pad of paper to make notes during all of our drills.
- Constantly look for ways to be more efficient. For example, one year I discovered we had classrooms walking past each other to report to their designated tornado locations. This made no sense, but it had been that way for years. I went through and updated all the necessary tornado locations in order to allow for the best transition/flow to those areas, avoiding unnecessary congestion in the hallways. It took me a few hours, but they had been using those routes for years without someone deciding to fix it. Constantly look for ways to be more efficient in your procedures.
- Place visible numbers on the outside of each window of your school building. This will allow you to easily communicate with emergency response teams as to the location of a threat or crisis inside the school building.
- Implement some sort of camera and "buzz in" policy into the school building. No doors should be left unlocked or propped open throughout the school day.
- Ensure all contact information for emergency responders is saved in your cell phone and readily accessible for others in the building as well.
- Conduct a SWOT (stands for Strengths, Weaknesses, Opportunities, Threats) analysis to identify any and all internal strengths and weaknesses, as well as any external opportunities and threats. This should be completed at least once a year.
- There is no such thing as being over-prepared.

Below I have recommended a few books that apply to school crisis prevention, intervention, and preparedness. Also, if you ever need a great speaker on this particular topic for your school building and/or district, look up my colleague and friend, Dr. Gene Deisinger who is one of the best in speakers in this subject area.

Recommended Speaker on School Safety
Dr. Gene Deisinger

Visit: http://campusthreatassessment.org/index.php/faculty/bios/
gene_deisinger/

Recommended Books on School Safety
School Crisis Prevention and Intervention[33] by Mary Margaret Kerr

Proactive School Security and Emergency Preparedness Planning
by Kenneth S. Trump

Social
This includes the quality of interpersonal relationships between and among students, teachers, and staff, equitable and fair treatment of students by teachers and staff, degree of competition and social comparison between students, and degree to which students, teachers, and staff contribute to decision-making at the school. Remember, "what you permit, you promote" and "a culture can never rise above the worst behavior that is allowed" (Tarte, 2017). As it applies to the social dimension of school climate and culture, this is particularly important.

Quality of Interpersonal Relationships/Equitable and Fair Treatment of Students. It probably goes without saying that the quality of interpersonal relationships amongst students, staff, and administration play a key role in fostering and maintaining a positive school climate and school culture in a given school building/district. As a school leader, how will you ensure the relationships between students, staff, and administration are professional yet meaningful? I contend you start by treating them like human beings (or better yet, family) first, and staff/students second. It is like the quote, "people don't care how much you know, until they know how much you care" and/or "people do not remember what you said, but they do remember how you made them feel." It is the little things ... I used to study the yearbook year-to-year in order to learn every student's name coming into my school building (and not just know the names, but also pronounce them correctly). I used to enjoy surprising them in the

---

33 I especially like this book as it provides case studies that imitate/simulate real-life challenges and dilemmas.

hallway in between classes by saying "Hi Johnny, how is your day going?" Just to let them know I know their name. This rings true with staff as well; it goes a long way to learn a staff member's interests, hobbies, and their spouse and children's names. I used to look for opportunities to ask a staff member how their son Johnny played at their soccer game last night, ask how their spouse was doing, or check in on a sick family member. Likewise, as a school leader, you must ensure your teachers are fostering positive relationships with their students. As a former school leader, I often wondered why some students would sit up straight, listen, and work hard in some teachers' classrooms, and in others, do nothing but misbehave. Let me tell you, my friends, it all has to do with relationships (and a close second would be setting clear expectations). As Rita Pierson said, "Students don't learn from teachers they don't like!" She goes on to say, "You don't have to like all of your students, but the trick is, they can never know otherwise." She is right! It really is all about relationships. Once that is established, the possibilities are endless. Unfortunately, some adults (and in this case, teachers) just do not get this idea and refuse to buy into it. This is where I have had to have some of the most difficult conversations with teachers, who have "had it out" for one or more of our students, simply because they did not like them. As a school leader, I had no tolerance for this type of behavior, and neither should you. You have to ensure there is equitable and fair treatment of all students in your building/district. Remember, what you permit, you promote.

Degree of Competition and Social Comparison. I am a big believer in the mindset that some healthy competition breeds success. However, the keyword there is "healthy." For example, in my last role as a practitioner/school leader, I served in a school district that had three large middle schools that fed into one extremely large high school. At the time, I was an administrator at one of the middle schools. Each year, our particular middle school would have a large outdoor carnival for our students, their siblings, and parents - where we would have all kinds of games, and I would get in the dunk tank (the kids loved this particular aspect), etc. We had one of the best Parent Teacher Association's I have ever worked with. That being said, when we administrators got together, I used to say to the other middle school administrators things like, "How was your carnival this summer?...Oh, wait, that is right, we are the only middle school that does the carnival." This is just one example, but it was all in fun. In fact, the other middle schools in that district did other events for their students and parents, but we always tried to one-up them. This degree of competition and social comparison can be particularly important in the school house, and more specifically, in student-to-student, teacher-to-student, and teacher-to-teacher relationships. I was asked to serve on a committee in one particular school district that was struggling with this aspect both in the community and the school house. This community served a majority of students who were considered to come from extremely high SES backgrounds. Nonetheless, a string of suicides had rocked the community and the school. When serving on the committee, it was apparent that the degree of competition and social comparison had reached unhealthy levels. Two main themes were evident; (1) if you were not in AP courses, Gifted, or going to an Ivy League University after high school, you were seen as a failure by your peers (and in some cases, your parents); and (2) if you were not extremely rich, you were a nobody. The sad reality was, as it applies to the second theme, any student in that district would be considered high SES on a nationwide scale. For reference, some of the largest homes in that particular state were located in that community. Likewise, their per-student spending far exceeded that of any district in the area (the entire Central part of the state). To further highlight the fiscal resources available to this community, I will share a story once shared with me. The superintendent in said district at the time was approached by several football parents about installing a turf football field (replacing the grass). She declined, and furthermore said that it would not appear on the next levy that was set to be up for vote in the near future. The parents went around and asked for personal and private donations throughout the community. The next day, one of the parents showed up with a check to install the turf football field. To put that in perspective, turf football fields cost upwards of a million plus dollars to install. Nonetheless, with the help of all stakeholders, the district was able to work diligently to minimize the degree of competition and social comparison amongst students, and this degree of competition returned to healthy levels. This was accomplished through bringing in authors such as Rosalind Wiseman who spoke on her book *Queen Bees and Wannabes* (2002) [the movie *Mean Girls* was adapted from this book], implementing initiatives to improve the overall culture/climate, professional development for staff, and the like. I used this school district as an example because it is a district that is both high-performing and has a majority of students who would be described as high-SES. That is, I wanted to highlight that these tribulations are not just faced by school leaders serving in low-performing schools with a majority of students who would be described as low-SES. All schools have problems associated with them regardless of the demographics associated with the student population. Nevertheless, the degree of competition needs to be at healthy levels. Moreover, students should have self-worth regardless of what school they attend. This self-worth can be cultivated by school leaders who promote respect for themselves, their students, their parents, and their community members and business owners in all that they do. It goes without saying, but school leaders must believe that every student can learn and succeed. This goes a long way in building self-worth and confidence in your student population. Along these same lines, and perhaps worth noting here, as it applies to schools of high diversity, the cross-cultural competence of a school leader plays a vital role in building student self-worth as well. Although the school I used in the example is only somewhat diverse, school leaders serving schools with high diversity (and all school leaders for that matter) must value and embrace diversity, and celebrate the different cultures within their student population. For example, I served in a school that had recently experienced an influx of Somalian students who were recently relocated to the United States from refugee camps. Thus, I began to research Somalia, and learn more about their culture. Seems logical, right? However, I have conducted professional development in schools of high diversity and I am always amazed at the lack of knowledge school leaders have about their students (in general) and the different cultures from which they come. It goes a long way to make an exerted effort to learn more about your stakeholders. That is, more than you have to know. Furthermore, in order to truly lead for equity (see chapter 10), a school leader must know their students and their backgrounds. Although my example was mainly focused on the student-to-student aspect, it is all the same with the teacher-to-student, teacher-to-teacher, school leader-to-teacher, and even school leader-to-school leader aspects as well. That is, everything shared can be applied to all aspects with regards to the degree of competition and social comparison amongst these groups.

> *"The relationships among the adults (and students) within a school have a significant and far-reaching influence on the character and quality of the school."*
>
> ~ *Justin Tarte*

Shared Decision-Making. Though, I contend that some of the practices I share should go without saying, the more I visit and conduct professional development in schools, the more I am amazed that some of these practices simply do not exist. Thus, though it may seem an obvious statement, all decision-making must be collaborative. You can tell a lot about a school building/district by identifying the degree to which students, staff, parents, community members, and business owners contribute to the decision-making process. If you want true buy-in, you must proceed accordingly. In fact, the very definition of buy-in is "the fact of agreeing with and accepting something that someone suggests" (Cambridge Dictionary, 2017). The example sentence given is "if you want buy-in to go ahead with these plans, you'll need buy-in from the employees" (Cambridge Dictionary, 2017). Let me tell you from experience, if you want true buy-in from all stakeholders, you must include them in the decision-making process. If not, your initiative may fail, not because it was a bad idea, but because your stakeholders were not involved in the process of coming up with the plan. When it comes to all things school, be sure to include as many folks as possible in the decision-making process. Much like with my school turnaround story shared in chapter four, where I share how to create your world-class data team (i.e., Five C's), the first "C" stands for Collaboratively. Finally, by implementing shared decision-making, you will not only garner buy-in, but often I have found that in addition to the buy-in, these same folks are invested and want to help in ensuring that the initiative, whatever it may be, succeeds. That is, they want to help make it happen. So, remember, *team work makes the dream work!* and *many hands make light work!* Don't forget it! Besides, you have enough on your desk as a school leader, so don't be a micro-manager—share the load, empower others, and mentor future school leaders. But don't forget, *as a school leader you can delegate tasks, but you cannot delegate responsibility*. So, like Ronald Reagan said, "trust but verify." No need to micromanage, but it is okay to verify things are being done efficiently and correctly every once in while. After all, remember, it all stops at your desk. Proceed accordingly!

> *"The best school leaders don't force change...they facilitate change through collaboration and by empowering others."*
> ~ *Emily Sturchio*

Academic Dimensions
This includes quality of instruction, teacher expectations for student achievement, and the monitoring of student progress as well as promptly reporting results to students and parents.

Quality of Instruction. As reported in chapter one, this is the greatest difference I personally see between leading schools then and now. That is, the roles and responsibilities have changed. Part of those roles and responsibilities include being an instructional leader. A school leader must be able to evaluate teachers and provide meaningful and timely feedback in order to improve the quality of instruction in a given school building/district. This includes informal/formal walk-throughs, regular classroom visits (every classroom, every day), and informal/formal evaluations. In addition, a school leader must offer professional development that is meaningful to the staff, be it individualized professional development or whole group (see chapter three). The ability of a school leader to identify professional development specific to their school building/district is a vital skill and not an easy task. As we move to a more personalized and individual delivery of professional development, this task will get easier. However, as you read this book, I will assume most of you are still using and/or part of whole group professional development. I must be transparent in that there are times when whole group professional development is required (and the best option). However, many times, whole group professional development is made with the mindset of what the majority of your staff needs versus what each individual staff member needs. To truly improve the quality of instruction in a school building we must, of course, focus on improving each individual staff member. As previously reported in chapter four, utilizing student data to drive instructional practices throughout a school building/district is a skill set every school leader must have in the 21st Century. Again, school leaders must be instructional leaders and in layman's terms be able to explain to staff how to collect the data (e.g., formative assessments every day, every lesson), analyze the data (i.e., determine the cut score), and use it to guide instruction (e.g., interventions and enrichment).

Teacher Expectations for Student Achievement. As shared in an article I co-authored with Dr. Kelly Brown titled *Data-Driven Decisions: Using Equity Theory to Highlight Implications for Underserved Students* (Brown & Fowler, 2018), we aimed to identify how data is currently being used to solve the *what* and not the *why* as it relates to achievement gaps for marginalized students. As shared in the previous section, school leaders should (and are) utilizing quantitative data (i.e., assessment results) to drive instruction. However, as school leaders, we also need to be cognizant of the *why*. That is, in this particular article, essentially we argue that data does not tell the entire story, but only a portion of the story, as it relates to students (and their teachers). More specifically, in the article, we argue why these measures may not accurately reflect the knowledge level of underserved students, and we highlight the areas that may be needed to create a holistic picture of the social and academic needs of individual children. For example, as shared in chapter four with regards to my school turnaround story, we found that the trend data suggested that we were not growing African-American students in math from the time they hit our school building (middle school) to the time they left for high school. In order to attempt to identify the cause, in addition to the data, we discussed the possible *why* aspect. Basically, after discovering this outcome in the trend data (amongst others - this is just one example) we aimed to ensure that our teachers had the same expectations for all students/student achievement regardless of student demographics. This is just one example, nonetheless, school leaders must ensure teacher expectations for student achievement remain the same for all students, regardless of their demographics. That is, it would not be fair to expect less of underserved students. This is where I have found there is a need to support and implement culturally responsive teaching strategies, and an inclusive pedagogy that recognizes the diversity of all students, enabling them to access content, fully participate in learning activities, and demonstrate their knowledge and strengths on assessments. Maximum inclusion is the key here, and it must be maintained in all aspects of the school day.

Monitoring of Student Progress. In keeping with theme of 21st Century school leaders being instructional leaders, not just great managers, the monitoring of student progress and the prompt reporting of the results to both students and parents is vital. This can be supported by school leaders through feedback given in the evaluation process (e.g., walk-throughs and observations) and meaningful discussions with staff. In chapter one I shared some strategies on how to utilize technology to instantaneously share assessment data with both students and parents. Thus, it would go a long way for school leaders to be well-versed in the use of such technology in order to support teachers using it in their classrooms. Again, as I contended in chapter four, create a data team. This will allow you to ensure that your school building/district is data-driven. That is, to ensure you are constantly monitoring student progress.

Discipline

This includes building meaningful relationships with all stakeholders (students, staff, parents, community members, and business owners), fair and consistent handling of all discipline issues, open communication, taking absolutely nothing personally, revisiting your discipline plan, and taking advantage of the first interaction.

"When students can't read, we teach. If a student can't add, we teach. If a student doesn't behave, we NEED to teach...not just punish."

~ *Justin Tarte*

Building Meaningful Relationships. You quite simply have to be a servant driven leader if you want to build meaningful relationships with all stakeholders (and as it applies to discipline, this means your students and parents). In simplest terms, relationships take time: time to get to know people, time to care, time to listen, time to go the extra mile, time to be present and engaged in every interaction – with every student. Perhaps Northouse (2016) describes servant leadership best in his 10 characteristics of servant leadership:

1. Listening – Servant leaders listen first.
2. Empathy – Servant leaders see the world through the eyes of the other.
3. Heal – Servant leaders wish to make the injured healed.
4. Awareness – Servant leaders are aware of their physical, social and political environments.
5. Persuasion – Servant leaders persuade by the use of gentle nonjudgmental argument to create change.
6. Conceptualization – Servant leaders visualize the big future.
7. Foresight – Servant leaders use the past and present to plan for the future.
8. Stewardship – Servant leaders take responsibility.
9. Commitment to People – Servant leaders place a premium on the individual.
10. Building Community – Servant leaders seek to create union or synergy.

If you want to build meaningful relationships, start by implementing the characteristics above into your daily leadership routines. This will help eliminate and lessen disciplinary issues, and furthermore, will ease the process when you are dealing with them (i.e., communicating with the parent, student, etc.).

Fair and Consistent. It goes without saying that this should be how all discipline situations are handled, however, I have served in enough districts to know that not all school administrators are fair and consistent in handling discipline issues. In fact, in my experience, most are rarely fair and consistent. That being said, as a school leader, you can kill the climate/culture of a school district/building if you do not exercise and support equitable treatment of all students regardless of their demographics, who their parents are, and/or what athletics they participate in (e.g., the all-star football player, etc.). Here is my rule of thumb with regards to being fair and consistent in handling discipline. I always just pretended it was my son or daughter sitting across from my desk. Then, in my mind, I would always think about what I would want his/her assistant principal/principal/superintendent to say to him/her, and furthermore, how to handle the given incident fairly and consistently. When handling discipline, it is vital to be fair and consistent.

Open Communication. We used to invite each grade level (with their parents) over three days in the summer (usually in mid-late August) to kick off the school year. As the assistant principal, I would usually discuss and go over our discipline procedures/plan in our school handbook. It was during this segment of the presentation that I would always say "you can expect me to over-communicate with you. I will call, text, email, and mail all communication (for good and bad behavior) to you in a timely manner." Let me tell you, there is nothing better in aiding discipline than over-communicating with your stakeholders and, perhaps just as important, communicating good behavior as well as the bad. In one school district in which I served, we had a goal to communicate both the positive and the negative on a regular basis. At first it seemed time consuming and a daunting task in addition to our teaching responsibilities. However, it was not long before everyone began to buy in, as we started to both hear and witness the positivity it was spreading. In fact, the next school year the rest of the school buildings in the district started the same initiative. For example, if I had called a parent a few times to tell them how well their son/daughter was doing in school, when it was time to call them because their son/daughter was in a fist-fight, 100% of the time the call went better with that parent versus the parents I had yet to communicate with (we had close to 700 students in that particular school building). If you openly communicate, your parents will begin to trust you not only when you report the good, but also the bad. Open communication and over-communicating will only lead to good, in all things, not just discipline.

Nothing is Personal and First Interaction. I decided to combine these two, as they are somewhat interrelated. For a school leader, handling discipline must never be personal. Perhaps just as important, you must never hold any type of perception, preconceived notion, or judgments about a student. Furthermore, you must ensure your teachers do not have personal issues with their students. Now, as I write this, I bet you can think of a student that really got under your skin; you flat out did not like him/her for whatever reason. That is fine, you don't have to like all your students. You see, the trick is, it is perfectly fine if you don't like them all, however, they can never know it. In the late Rita Pierson's (2013) TEDxTalk titled *Every Kid Needs A Champion*, she does a great job sharing this exact concept (please see link). In the TEDxTalk, Pierson shares that one of her colleagues said, "They don't pay me to like the kids, they pay me to teach them." She then responded, "Kids don't learn from people they don't like." Furthermore, she said "While you won't like them all, the key is they can never, ever, know it." This was always my mindset, even before I ever saw Pierson's TEDxTalk. Thus, as a teacher, all of my students thought they were my favorite, and I would often hear them argue with one another about who was really my favorite. Later, when I was a school leader, all of my teachers thought they were my favorites and would often take pride in thinking so. Now, did I like all my students and teachers? The honest answer is no. However, they never knew otherwise. As for the first interaction after discipline, it always has to be a clean slate. If I suspended a student for fighting, say for five days, their first day back, I would actively seek them out, check on them, ask them how they are, and say, "Are we good?" (or the like) and give them a fist bump. I wanted them to know that we all make mistakes, but here and now, we are hitting the reset button, we are moving on. It is time to get back to learning and doing what we are supposed to do at school. Like adults, students want to be forgiven. I want that student to know there are no grudges from me, and I want that to be loud and clear. Now, word to the wise, be sincere about it, or it can be taken out of context (as sarcasm). A colleague of mine loved this concept when I shared it with him. However, to my surprise, he called me up and said it did not go as planned. Somewhat confused, I asked what he meant. Essentially, the student took it as mockery or sarcasm and the parent came in the next morning. So be sincere, or you may make things worse. It has to be natural.

Rita Pierson's TEDxTalk
Every Kid Needs A Champion
See: https://www.ted.com/talks/
rita_pierson_every_kid_needs_a_champion#t-391466

Discipline Plan. Depending on what type of discipline plan your school building/district implements, this could be more or less difficult. For example, if your district uses a black and white discipline plan, then this task of being fair and consistent can be relatively easy. That is, it is spelled out for you in black and white how to handle the given incident. However, if you are in a school building/district that has grey areas in their discipline plan and/or a restorative justice model, much more judgment is involved. Certainly, there are positives and negatives associated with all types of discipline plans. Thus, it is worth your time to research each and decide what is best for your school setting. There is a great TEDxTalk by Barry Schwartz (2010), titled *Using Our Practical Wisdom,* depicting the dangers of a black and white discipline plan where judgment is somewhat removed from the process (except the main example given is someone breaking the law and a courtroom judge). In a discipline plan that has grey areas, key judgments will need to be made that are fair and consistent with regards to discipline infractions. I highly recommend creating a discipline committee consisting of all stakeholders, and determine what type of plan best suits your stakeholders and school setting. Here's a hint, don't reinvent the wheel; identify 5-10 discipline plans in other school districts (preferably some black and white, grey, and restorative justice, etc.) and take all of the best discipline practices from them, and incorporate them into yours. One final thought: discipline should never be a double punishment. Do not allow your discipline plan to affect students academically. In addition, most of the effective school discipline plans I have created (or reviewed) have had a Positive Behavioral Intervention and Supports (PBIS) aspect incorporated within them. Although implementing PBIS is advantageous to many aspects of the school building/district, as it relates to the discipline plan, it encourages the continuous monitoring of student behavior. Thus, I would suggest incorporating it into your plan and/or building/district in one form or another. Now, let me forewarn you, after you watch Schwartz's TEDxTalk below, you might decide to go with a grey or restorative justice type of discipline model. Enjoy!

Barry Schwartz's TEDxTalk
Using Our Practical Wisdom
See: http://www.ted.com/talks/
barry_schwartz_using_our_practical_wisdom

To reiterate, do know that you will never change the **school culture** until you change what you do daily (**school climate**). The secret of your success in changing the **school culture** will be found in your daily routine (**school climate**). Again, both **school culture** and **school climate** are extremely important to a school's success (or failure).

Below I have shared some healthy culture killer phrases in education (particularly as it applies to teaching) that were shared with me recently on Twitter. As you can probably guess, healthy cultures do not use these phrases.

"We've always done it this way."
"I can't help bad parenting."
"He/she's too far behind to catch up."
"My students can't do that."
"I covered it in class and they didn't listen/learn."
"They don't pay me to like the students, they pay me to teach."

Fowler's Five

Finally, throughout my years of service as both a former school leader and a professor preparing aspiring school leaders, I have given much thought to creating a concise list of what I believe are fundamental aspects in being a successful school building/district leader. I have named them *Fowler's Five* (please see below). Enjoy!

1. Don't Sweat the Small Stuff

Don't sweat the small stuff. It is important to keep things in perspective. My grandpa Moran was a tank commander in World War II and fought in two major campaigns including the *Battle of the Bulge* and *Normandy*. My grandpa Fowler coal mined his entire life in the State of West Virginia before eventually dying from black lung disease. So remember, even on your most stressful day as a school leader, you are not on the beaches of Normandy and/or in the coal mines of West Virginia. I have always kept a model of a M4 Sherman Tank in my office along with an old oil Auto Lite head lamp (like those used in the coal mines when my grandpa mined) as a daily reminder that things aren't so bad, no matter how stressed out you may feel. You will need to determine what you need to place in your office as a reminder (or maybe it is not something you physically place in your office at all, a different approach is fine), but again, it is important to always keep things in perspective.

2. Always Do What is Best for Students

Always do what is best for students. I promise your school building, school district, state, our nation, and the rest of the world will be better for it. In every decision I made as a school leader, I always asked myself "what is the decision that is best for students?" This quite simply led me to the best possible (and sometimes, the most criticized) decision every time. However, I must share that in many cases, as with life in general, doing the right thing is often the hardest thing to do.

3. Do What You Can, With What You Have, From Where You Are

Do what you can, with what you have, from where you are. This is one of my favorite quotes by Theodore Roosevelt. quite simply, the truth is, as a school leader you may have a brand new school building or a dilapidated school building, a ton of technology or no technology, new books or outdated books, etc. However, at the end of the day, you have to do what you can, with what you have, from where you are. Do the best you can with what you have: at the end of the day, you can live with that.

4. Take Care of Yourself

Take care of yourself. While you are out there saving the world, don't forget to take care of yourself, your marriage, spouse, significant other, children, family, friends, health, faith, and hobbies. One of the biggest mistakes I see with school leaders is the lack in ability to maintain a good work-life balance (see chapter eight). In order for you to be the best you each and everyday, you need to take care of yourself. If you do not, the stakeholders you serve (especially your teachers and students) will not be getting the best you each and everyday. Be sure to prioritize your time and learn to say "no" if you cannot fit it in your schedule. I also discussed work-life balance in a podcast interview I did with *We Love Schools* (Episode 27, *Developing Leaders in Our Schools*).
See: http://www.weloveschoolspodcast.com/2016/06/developing-leaders-in-our-schools/

5. Be A Change Agent

Be a change agent. I once read you can always spot a change agent by the large number of arrows in their back. As they say, "No good deed goes unpunished." In some ways, this is true. However, I would rather be a change agent than go with the flow in order to keep the waters calm, especially if it ultimately means doing what is best for students. Do not maintain the status quo. Status quo in Latin means "the mess we're in." Be a change agent! After all, remember, the worst saying in any organization is "we have always done it this way." There will always be barriers...break through them! Sometimes you have to be the "lone nut" to initiate change or start a movement and create the all but necessary "buy-in." Although I do not agree with all of the statements made by Derek Sivers (2010) in conjunction with this video, it is a great depiction of a lone nut creating a movement. See: https://www.youtube.com/watch?v=fW8amMCVAJQ

Reflection

Questions for Practicing and Aspiring School Leaders

1. As reported by Loukas (2007), most researchers agree that school climate and school culture are really a multidimensional construct. This multidimensional construct includes physical, social, and academic dimensions ... and I added discipline. How will you maintain focus on all four dimensions as a school leader?
2. As a school district/building leader, what challenges do you foresee in attempting to maintain Fowler's Five?
3. As a school district/building leader, how might you help teachers in your building locate additional resources for their classrooms/your building/your district?
4. As a school district/building leader, how might you reward items such as excellent attendance, academics, and behavior in your school building/district?
5. Most discipline plans can be broken down into three categories: (1) black and white; (2) grey area; and (3) restorative justice – and many include a PBIS aspect. Which discipline plan do you foresee yourself using and/or supporting on your building/district? Why? Will you include PBIS as part of it? Why? Why not?

Problem-based Scenario

It All Starts with the Climate and Culture

As a building (or district) school leader, you have begun to notice that the climate/culture is a toxic one. Furthermore, you have begun to notice that it is now starting to affect you (much like the new fast-food employee in Todd Whitaker's ASCD Short shared at the beginning of the chapter).

However, you are determined to not allow the negative climate/culture to affect you, and furthermore, you are determined to lead the initiative in creating a positive school climate/culture throughout your district or in your school building. With that in mind, what steps might you first take in determining the current state of affairs as it applies to the climate/culture in your building/district? How will you ensure that through this process you are fostering, creating, and sustaining a positive school climate/culture in your building/district? Be specific in your tentative approach and plan in improving the climate/culture.

Choose Your School Setting

Choose your role and then choose your school building/district setting before you respond to the scenario above. As you draft your response, please be cognizant of how your setting might affect how you respond to the scenario. Essentially, based on the characteristics below, think about what we generally know about these characteristics listed below, and furthermore, how they generally impact schools/districts. How might they affect your decision-making with regards to the scenario, if at all? Be sure to clearly describe your school setting in your response.

Role: Superintendent, Principal, or Assistant Principal
Locale: Urban, Suburban, or Rural
Size: Small District, Medium District, or Large District
Diversity: No Diversity, Some Diversity, or Very Diverse
SES Status: 100% Free and Reduced Lunch (FRL), 50% FRL, or 0% FRL

Chapter 8

Work-Life Balance

"There's no such thing as work-life balance. There are work-life choices, and you make them, and they have consequences."
~ *Jack Welch*

"Show me an excellent school leader... you've got my attention. Show me an excellent school leader who is also an excellent spouse, parent, has a strong faith, has strong morals, is ethical, and takes care of their health...now you you've got my undivided attention. You think that stuff doesn't matter, you're dead wrong. We're molding the future minds of our society."
~ *Dr. Denver J. Fowler*

"Do not expect work to fill a void that non-work relationships should." ~ *Tim Ferris (Summarized by Reese Jones)*

Introduction

I strongly believe that, to a great extent, there is no such thing as work-life balance; rather, we make choices about what is most important to us and proceed accordingly. Nonetheless, for reasons of clarity, I will use the term work-life balance throughout this chapter (versus work-life choices). Now, aspiring school leaders might be asking themselves why I have devoted an entire chapter in a school leadership book to work-life balance. In contrast, practicing school leaders should know exactly why. The fact is, I theorize with great confidence that a majority of school leaders have a lousy work-life balance. Furthermore, I also theorize with great confidence that in some cases this lousy work-life balance has had negative consequences on the life of school leaders, both physically and emotionally. Thus, I included this chapter for two reasons: (1) I hope to make a case for and support the importance of maintaining a good work-life balance as a priority for aspiring school leaders; and (2) for practicing school leaders, I hope to emphasize the importance of maintaining a good work-life balance, and furthermore, that it is never too late to get back in balance. My efforts may have lasting implications on the very stakeholders you lead, as I would argue that in order to be the best you, each and every day, you must have a good work-life balance. There is no question that the stakeholders you lead need the best you, each and every day. There is no better time to start working on your work-life balance than now. So, let's get started!

Admittedly, as a school leader, I once had a lousy work-life balance. But as a great school leader, I was accurately self-reflective, and I was cognizant of all things at all times. That is, I was able to identify that my work-life balance was out of synch, and then take proactive steps to get that balance back in order. I want to share with you exactly how I accomplished this. Years ago I was asked to write an article on work-life balance for the American Association of School Administrators' *School Administrator* national magazine (Fowler, 2016). In this article, I shared my work-life balance story, and how I was able to balance things out. An abridged variation of the story below is in print and you can access this version via the reference I provided below. However, what follows is my full unabridged version of the story. Enjoy!

Journal
Fowler, D. (2016). Cats in the cradle: My work-life balance. *School Administrator* 73(3), 11-12.

Podcast
I also discussed work-life balance in a podcast interview I did with *We Love Schools* (Episode 27, *Developing Leaders in Our Schools*).
See: http://www.weloveschoolspodcast.com/2016/06/developing-leaders-in-our-schools/

Cats in the Cradle:
The Work-Life Balance of a School Administrator

Before beginning my story, I would like you to read the lyrics of the song titled *Cat's in the Cradle*, written by Harry Chapin (1974). As you will notice in my story, I make a play on the lyrics of the song for the title of each section, much as I did in the version that was published in *School Administrator*. You can also watch the video of Harry Chapin singing it at: https://www.youtube.com/watch?v=etundhqa724 for the full experience.

> My child arrived just the other day
> He came to the world in the usual way
> But there were planes to catch, and bills to pay
> He learned to walk while I was away
> And he was talking 'fore I knew it, and as he grew
> He'd say, "I'm gonna be like you, dad
> You know I'm gonna be like you."
>
> And the cat's in the cradle and the silver spoon
> Little boy blue and the man in the moon
> "When you coming home, dad?" "I don't know when
> But we'll get together then
> You know we'll have a good time then."
>
> My son turned ten just the other day
> He said, "Thanks for the ball, dad; come on, let's play
> Can you teach me to throw?"
> I said, "Not today, I got a lot to do."
> He said, "That's okay."
> And he walked away, but his smile never dimmed
> And said, "I'm gonna be like him, yeah
> You know I'm gonna be like him."
>
> And the cat's in the cradle and the silver spoon

Little boy blue and the man in the moon
"When you coming home, dad?" "I don't know when
But we'll get together then
You know we'll have a good time then."

Well, he came from college just the other day
So much like a man, I just had to say
"Son, I'm proud of you. Can you sit for a while?"
He shook his head, and he said with a smile
"What I'd really like, dad, is to borrow the car keys
See you later; can I have them please?"

And the cat's in the cradle and the silver spoon
Little boy blue and the man in the moon
"When you coming home, son?" "I don't know when
But we'll get together then, dad
You know we'll have a good time then."

I've long since retired, and my son's moved away
I called him up just the other day
I said, "I'd like to see you if you don't mind."
He said, "I'd love to, dad, if I could find the time
You see, my new job's a hassle, and the kid's got the flu
But it's sure nice talking to you, dad
It's been sure nice talking to you."
And as I hung up the phone, it occurred to me
He'd grown up just like me
My boy was just like me

And the cat's in the cradle and the silver spoon
Little boy blue and the man in the moon
"When you coming home, son?" "I don't know when
But we'll get together then, dad
We're gonna have a good time then."

I Don't Know When, But We'll Get Together Then

The very concept of work-life balance first occurred to me during my exit interview, while completing my superintendent internship (as part of my superintendent license program). I was very fortunate to work with a great group of superintendents during my internship, one of which had been a very successful superintendent for over 20 years in the same school district (and later became a very successful state superintendent). As we wrapped up my interview, he spoke to me about a recent trip he took with his son and how he was trying to play catch-up with his wife and children. Furthermore, as he choked up, he expressed that he felt he was the best superintendent anyone could ask for during his career, but that he had sacrificed significant time away from his family to be so. I got the feeling that he was sharing this information with me for a reason ... I felt as if he was saying "Don't let it happen to you." I did not know how to respond, there was a long pause, and I replied "yeah, kind of like the cats in the cradle song, huh?" with a sympathetic face and nodded in agreement. We parted ways, and to my surprise, shortly after this meeting he accepted a position to be a state superintendent. I thought perhaps he realized it was just too late to make up all of that lost time with his family.

Not Today, I Got A lot To Do

Several years into my tenure as a school administrator, I realized how difficult it is to maintain a work-life balance as a school leader. From the inside, the hustle and bustle and long hours seemed, and felt, normal, especially because everyone close to me professionally (such as the administrative team in my school district and colleagues in other districts) were on the same schedule (60-80 hours a week). But does that make it okay, just because everyone else is doing it? Isn't this in direct contrast to what we tell our own children, as well as our students? From the outside looking in, it is easy to see that your schedule is overwhelming. My wife used to tell me that I needed to slow down and be able to unplug completely when I was at home with her and our children (a task that I found very difficult to accomplish). I was running at 300 mph all day long and then I had to unplug and be a husband and father when I hit the door at home. Undoubtedly, I had started remembering my exit interview several years before. I was becoming the person that I had intentionally tried to avoid becoming; a school administrator with a lousy work-life balance and no time for my family. On top of that, I was no longer exercising regularly and my diet was horrible; I often skipped lunch during the school day.

Two things were becoming increasingly apparent: (1) I was an excellent school administrator and I was great at my job (in fact, at the time, I was named *Assistant Principal of the Year* in my state and was nominated for the *National Assistant Principal of the Year* in the United States); and (2) I began to see my personal life suffer (time away from family, friends, hobbies, etc.). Slowly and sadly, I was beginning to believe that the ideal school administrator is someone who is single with no children, or worse, someone who could stomach not seeing, or spending quality time with, their spouse and children, which I personally could not live with.

We're Gonna; Have A Good Time ~~Then~~ *Now*

After a while, I finally had enough. I decided to put my foot down and I got creative. I was not going to allow my job to interfere with me being a good husband and father. If I had to cover the football game Friday night, my wife and children met me there and we ate hot dogs and nachos with cheese and drank Coca Cola for dinner, together. I learned to completely unplug when I arrived home by mentally preparing for my arrival and by making adjustments to my drive home from work with the additions of good music, rolled down windows, taking the scenic route, and of course some good old prayer. I made time to work out during the hours that my family was fast asleep (early am or late pm). I made myself eat lunch, no matter how busy I was during the school day[34]. I learned to say no when asked to do things like serving on committees or volunteering for events on the weekends that interfered with "family time." I learned that even though I had a pile of things on my desk at the end of each day, it would still be there to work on in the morning. I learned to

---

34 I accomplished this by eating lunch with my students. Each day, I would place a table tent (with the words "Lunch with Dr. Fowler" written on it) on a lunch table in the cafeteria. Those students would come to the office conference room to eat lunch with me. This was a great way for me to get to know my students, hear their ideas and suggestions about how we do things at our school, and last but not least, ensure I ate lunch each day.

pace myself and realized that not everything had to be completed each and every day. I decided not to check my email after I left work or on the weekends. I fully engaged with my wife and children when I was at home by doing things like leaving my cell phone in the car when we were at the pumpkin patch, eating out, or attending a ball game.

Admittedly, these changes were hard to implement at first, but after a while they became routine. Furthermore, my colleagues respected and admired me for it. It wasn't until I implemented these changes that I began to realize just how out of sync my work-life balance had been. We were driving down the road the other day singing in the car, and I looked at my wife and kids with smiles on their faces and I realized all that I had been missing ... and that, my friends, that's the good stuff.

My thoughts on Faith, Family, Health and Purpose

"If you have failed in your faith, you have failed as a school leader. If you have failed as a spouse, you have failed as a school leader. If you have failed as a parent, you have failed as a school leader. If you have failed your health, you have failed as a school leader. If you have failed as a family member, you have failed as a school leader. If you have failed as a friend, you have failed as a school leader."

~ Dr. Denver J. Fowler

Building upon content previously mentioned in this book with regard to work-life balance (see chapter seven), I want to touch on what some may deem as personal topics as they may apply to your own work-life balance. I strongly believe work-life balance is one of the major issues in effective school leadership today (and with most jobs within most work-place settings). The times are changing, at least in the United States. It was not long ago that stores were closed on all holidays, Sundays, and the like. Nowadays, most stores stay open on Sundays and holidays, and many are open 24 hours a day, seven days a week.

There is no doubt that school leaders often experience high levels of daily stress, and struggle to balance the things that have to be done day-in and day-out. Often, something has to give, and unfortunately, it is usually our family members that suffer the most. They share us with so many others. I will never forget something that one of the best superintendents I ever worked for (Mr. Thomas Shade) said to my wife once. I had accepted my first administrative position as an Athletic Director and Assistant Principal at a middle school in the State of Ohio. My wife and I (along with our children) were attending the high school football game on this particular Friday night, as I was volunteering in the concession stand. We were standing by the fence watching the game and Mr. Shade walked up and greeted us. I introduced him to my wife and children and we spoke for a while. Before he left, he turned to my wife, and shook her hand, looked her in the eye and said, "Denver is doing a tremendous job here, and I want to personally thank you for sharing him with us." I will never forget that. It is so true. The significant others of school leaders, and their family members (namely children), truly share them with their respective school district. It can be hard on all involved. To further highlight this aspect of school leadership, I have often thought it would be an interesting photography experiment to take pictures of school leaders around the globe just before they accept their first full-time administrative position, then take one at the end of each school year thereafter, and put them side-by-side over a 10-year period. Unfortunately, I would hypothesize that we would see such individuals age and gain weight much faster than their peers. Furthermore, I believe these individuals' overall health would decline. Nonetheless, it would be an interesting experiment. Thus, be sure to make an exerted effort to maintain a healthy work-life balance. Will it be easy? Absolutely not. Can it be done? Absolutely. Remember, *action reveals commitment*, so make time to commit to the things that matter most: your faith, family, health, and purpose.

Faith

"Sunday morning I'm too tired to go to church. But I thank God for the work."　　　　　　　　　　~ Jason Isbell

Whatever your religion may be, make time for it. I will not use this section to project onto you my own religious beliefs. Nonetheless, I would argue that most religions are grounded in the idea of being a better human being. Thus, I feel confident in writing that you need to make time for your religion. Some of the most rewarding service I have been part of has been through my church. Make time to go to church each week and get involved; I promise you will be better for it. But remember, *standing in a church each Sunday no more makes you a Christian (or insert another religion) than standing in your garage makes you a car.* As my pastor would say, you have to put the words into action. I have been in some of the most challenging schools in the United States, where the demographics associated with my students (and parents) were truly heartbreaking. For example, while still an undergraduate student at The Ohio State University, during my student teaching observations in downtown Columbus, Ohio, I remember the elementary students coming to school with over/undersized flip-flops, t-shirts, and shorts in the middle of winter – with several feet of snow on the ground. Those students were in first grade. If school was canceled due to a snow day, those children did not eat. This experience had a lasting effect on me as an educator. It was then that I made the decision to serve in schools of high need. It is perhaps the hardest part of serving in the educational setting, that some of your students come to school without even their basic needs being met. They come from environments that are unsafe, where they are neglected, they are not fed, and they do not have things like heat in the winter months.

I have spent many restless nights lying awake thinking about how I could help better meet the basic needs of my students. When I was still a teacher, I would regularly donate my clothes and shoes to students who were in need, and loan them lunch money. As an administrator, I used to allow students to charge their lunches to my account, knowing it was unlikely they were going to pay me back (and I never asked them to). I did not care - I could not let my students not eat and go through the school day hungry. I also believe in the power of prayer. It is okay to pray for your students, and you should. I used to pray for my students, staff, and parents each and every day on the way to school. I ask that you have faith, my friend, if not in a religion, then in the fact that your school building/district may be the one and only place during your students' day (and in some cases, their life) that they actually feel safe, have heat in the winter months, and are fed a meal.

Family

"Time spent with family is worth every second." ~ *Unknown*

Do not neglect your family in the name of your workload/job. Being a school leader is not for the faint of heart. The hours, days, weeks, months, and years are long and oftentimes run together. However, you must make time for your family. Having raised one child to adulthood (she is now 21, and a future educator I might add), I know exactly what they mean when they say "don't blink." Oh, how the time flies. I remember sitting at her high school graduation thinking "where has the time gone?" The truth is, you will never be able to make up the time once it is lost. You had better learn to live in the now, and make the time now. If you don't, just like the retired superintendent I referenced earlier in this chapter, you will regret it. Although I am sad that my daughter is all grown up, I am at peace with it and myself because I know I was there for her every step along the way (and I still am). I have no regrets, because I made the time for her, regardless of how busy I was.

You must make time for your family. This applies not only to your children, but to your significant other as well. I will sum this section up like this. Have you ever been in an old school building where they have a picture of a former principal on the wall with their name and the years they served the particular school you are standing in? I have...and oftentimes, in my experience (because I like to find such pictures and plaques as a reminder to myself that I too will be forgotten) no one currently working there actually knew the principal, or could tell me anything about them. What I am getting at here is the fact that you too will be replaced, and, in some ways, forgotten. You are replaceable. Someday you will retire. Someday you will die. Someday you will be just vaguely remembered by former colleagues, and the like. As I write this, just one floor up from me in this building are paintings of all of the individuals who formerly served as the Dean of the School of Education here at The University of Mississippi. Of all those depicted in the hallway paintings, I personally only know three of them (and that is only because two of the former Deans still work here). As for the rest, maybe one or two people actively employed in the entire School of Education knew, knew of, or worked with them. This is not to say that you don't want to aim to have the largest and most positive impact possible on the school building/district and students in which you serve; it is to say that no one will remember that day you left a few hours early to catch your son/daughter's ballgame. However, your son/daughter will remember the day you did not attend their ballgame, and, sadly, they may think, like you, it is okay to miss their children's ball games. Lead by example! You truly only live once, and your children are only young once. Proceed accordingly.

Health

"The greatest wealth is health." ~ Unknown

As a former personal trainer, there is no doubt in my mind that health is truly a person's greatest wealth. After all, what do you have if you do not have your health? Nonetheless, I have struggled with this as well. That is, making time to exercise and eat healthy while maintaining a busy schedule. If a study were conducted, I bet there would be a statistically significant correlation between accepting an administrative position and losing one's health (i.e., mental health, stress, weight gain, bad eating habits, etc.). I know, I know...on top of finding time for your faith and family, I am now asking you to also make time for your health. It is a lot, but it is all worth it, I promise. As a former personal trainer and school administrator, I have found the *Body for Life* (2017) exercise routines and diet to be the most helpful for someone with a busy schedule; the exercise routine only requires a 20-minute run on the cardio days and at most 45 minutes in the weight room on upper body/lower body lift days. Even better, it is completely free. See: http://bodyforlife.com/ That will take care of the physical health, but I would contend that mental health is just as important. As I mentioned in chapter three, I conduct professional development each year in New York City at EDxEDNYC. I have never been one to show up to a conference (or the like) and just present and leave. I always stay for the entire conference. A few years ago, I was at EDxEDNYC and attended a presentation on mindfulness. The presenter was actively working with school building/district leaders in the New York City Department of Education (NYCDOE) to help these individuals better manage their stress levels. One particular aspect, was learning how to meditate once a day for 10-30 minutes. I must say, as he shared statements from some of the leaders in the NYCDOE, I became a believer in meditation. Although I could be more consistent, I do med-itate ever so often (mainly as part of Yoga classes I attend with my wife). For me personally, it has the same effect as a power nap. That is, I come out of it rejuvenated and feeling refreshed. All said, I believe you should give it a try and incorporate mediation into your daily routine. Mayer (2015) has listed the *10 Best Guided Meditations on YouTube* on her website. See: http://www.ilivethelifeilove.com/10-best-guided-medita-tions/ If you meditate once a day, even for only a short amount of time, I believe you will benefit from it. The presenter that day shared that school leaders who had experienced the most rewards from the process either meditate in the morning before the school day, directly after arriving home, or just before bed each night. Give it a shot, you may just find it will change your life.

Finally, as a former athlete and coach, I have found that helping coach and/or getting involved in adult recreation leagues has helped with both my mental and physical health. If you are able and interested, I strongly suggest getting involved in an adult basketball league, softball league, golf league, kickball league, etc. Not only is it a fun way to exercise (as the gym can be redundant), it is a great way to get involved with your stakeholders outside of the school day – further establishing those all-im-portant meaningful relationships with your stakeholders; parents, com-munity members, and business owners. Believe me, if you do this, you will start to see a different side of such individuals. It is a great reminder that, regardless of our title or position in the workplace, we are all human beings. I have found this experience to be extremely rewarding. For example, years ago when I was still a middle school teacher, I played in a soccer league with my principal and several other teachers. I must say, I half liked my principal going into the season, but after getting to know him outside of the school building, I realized he was a great person with a great sense of humor. This experience, coupled with getting to know him better, made me want to work even harder for him during the school day. At the end of the soccer season, we had a few beers together with our soccer team and vented to each other about all the things in the educational setting that needed to be improved, changed, and developed. During this conversation, I remember him saying, "I want to go back to the classroom. I miss teaching." Sure enough, a few years after, he did just that. Joining an adult recreation league where you have the opportunity to play alongside your staff, parents, community members, and business owners can be extremely beneficial to not only your health, but also the climate and culture in your school building/district. As a school leader, you need to stay healthy, both physically and mentally. By ensuring you are taking care of yourself (see chapter seven – *Fowler's Five*), your stakeholders get the best you, and at the end of the day, that is what is best for students.

Purpose

> *"Allow your passion to become your purpose, and it will one day become your profession."*   ~ Unknown

It would be doing you a disservice not to include this final section. Let me first ask you a few questions… "What is your purpose?" "Are you doing exactly what it is you want to do?" Wait, don't answer those questions just yet … hush … be still. Now, close your eyes … focus only on your breathing for the next 30 seconds. Then ask yourself "Am I doing exactly what it is I want to be doing?" The truth is, you only live once, so I ask that you dig down deep and first decide if you are doing what it is you truly want to do, and secondly, that you use the figure to help you in deciding your purpose (see Figure 4). I did not design or create this figure and I have had no luck referencing the original creator. Nonetheless, I felt it was worthy of sharing. I believe that to be the best at what it is we do, we truly have to be doing what it is we want to do. We need school leaders that have no other purpose than wanting to lead school buildings/districts. I am not saying that you cannot have a bunch of hobbies and side projects (or as the millennials call it "a side hustle"), but what I am saying is that in order to be an excellent school leader, you must have a passion for it - it must be your purpose. If it is not, not only will you suffer (being a school leader is hard work, perhaps especially if it is work you are not passionate about), but so will the stakeholders you serve. Find your purpose ... and if it is school leadership, great! If not, move on ... we cannot afford to have lackluster leaders in our schools. I am not trying to discourage anyone reading this book; rather, I ask that you rededicate yourself to the cause. If it is your purpose, proceed accordingly!

Figure 4: Purpose

Again, there is no such thing as work-life balance; rather we make choices about what is most important to us and proceed accordingly. It is imperative to be mindful of that as a school leader. Remember, every decision you make has consequences, both in your personal life and your professional life. Of the school leaders I have worked with over the years, the best of them always had one thing in common: they were sound decision makers. That is, they made decisions in a timely manner that were best for all stakeholders: students, staff, parents, community members and business owners. Conversely, of the school leaders I have worked with, the worst of them also had one thing in common: they were indecisive and lousy decision makers (when and if they finally made a decision). It makes me think of the quote, "Be decisive. Right or wrong, make a decision. The road of life is paved with flat squirrels that couldn't make a decision." So, remember, be mindful of your work-life balance, and make decisions on a daily basis that are conducive to maintaining a healthy work-balance. Start one day at a time, one decision at a time. Have you ever seen *What About Bob?* Baby steps...one step at a time. Eventually, like me, you might just realize how out of synch your work-life balance really was. This experience can certainly be eye-opening in and of itself.

Finally, I cannot finish this chapter without sharing, "don't let your work be all that you have." That is, quite frankly, I have met too many school leaders who truly only have their work and nothing else. My friends, this is unhealthy and you have to strive to have more. Remember those forgotten principals I wrote about earlier in the chapter that reside on the walls of old school buildings, or the paintings of all the former Deans? Sadly, it is true - you are replaceable, you too will be forgotten, and you too will someday die. In fact, it is very likely that you may not even get a picture on the old school building wall or a painting of yourself in the halls of a university. That being said, it is never too late to start living. In fact, you can start right now. My motto has always been "Work hard, play hard!" When I am working, I give 110% and anyone I have worked with will tell you so. But likewise, I give 110% in my personal life as well, and this is the key difference between myself and most individuals I know and have worked with over the years. That is, I know a lot of folks who give 110% at work, but unfortunately, a majority of them fall short when it comes to their effort outside of work. Don't let this be you, start today. Make a bucket list and start checking the items off one at a time. I can promise you this, you will be better at your job once you *take care of yourself* (see chapter seven – *Fowler's Five*).

Reflection

Questions for Practicing and Aspiring School Leaders

1. What steps will you take to be accurately self-reflective on a regular basis as an aspiring or practicing school leader?
2. Why do you believe having a good work-life balance is so important, not only for yourself and your family, but also for the stakeholders you lead and serve?
3. As a school district/building leader, what challenges do you foresee in attempting to maintain a good work-life balance?
4. As a school district/building leader, how might you advocate for and/or implement policy or procedures to help ensure your school staff/district-wide administrative team maintain a good work-life balance?
5. As a school district/building leader, how will you prioritize your time so that it is conducive to ensuring your faith, family, health, and purpose remain at the forefront of all that you do?

Problem-based Scenario

Little Boy Blue and the Man in the Moon

As a building (or district) school leader, you have begun to notice that your work-life balance is out of synch. However, you do not see an end in sight. In fact, in even thinking about spending more time at home or at the gym, you cannot fathom how you would be able to get all the things done you need to do on a daily basis as a school leader, while creating more time in your schedule for things like your family and your health. You feel defeated and, quite frankly, you don't know what to do. You love being a school leader, however you fear it is starting to take a major toll on your family and health. On a daily basis, you leave the house before your wife/husband and children are up, and you arrive home long after your wife/husband and children are asleep. After some deep reflection, you are determined to get your work-life balance in order. Please describe the possible ways you will ensure that you maintain a good work-life balance as a building (or district) school leader, specifically as it relates to your family and/or health. Furthermore, how do you plan to maintain a good work-life balance during the remainder of your career as a school leader? Please explain.

Choose Your School Setting

Choose your role and then choose your school building/district setting before you respond to the scenario above. As you draft your response, please be cognizant of how your setting might affect how you respond to the scenario. Essentially, based on the characteristics listed below, think about what we generally know about these characteristics, and furthermore, how they generally impact schools/districts. How might they affect your decision-making with regards to the scenario, if at all? Be sure to clearly describe your school setting in your response.

Role: Superintendent, Principal, or Assistant Principal
Locale: Urban, Suburban, or Rural
Size: Small District, Medium District, or Large District
Diversity: No Diversity, Some Diversity, or Very Diverse
SES Status: 100% Free and Reduced Lunch (FRL), 50% FRL, or 0% FRL

Chapter 9

Professional Learning Network

*"Circles they grow and they swallow people whole. Half their
lives they say goodnight to wives they'll never know..."*
~ *Eddie Vedder*

N ow why would I start the networking chapter with these lyrics by
Pearl Jam's own Eddie Vedder? Because you have to be careful -
professional networking should not mean neglect of other areas of one's
life. Unfortunately, I know too many people (many of whom are school
leaders) who confuse the two, and neglect their family; spouse, significant other, children, parents, etc., all in the name of networking. So, as
you read through this chapter, be cognizant of what I wrote in the previous chapter with regard to work-life balance and work-life choices. That
being said, within this chapter I aim to shine light on the importance of
building a professional learning network (PLN) and how it can help you
sharpen your school leadership skills, with the underlying mindset and
foundation that, "As iron sharpens iron, so one person sharpens another" (Proverbs 27:17). I contend that in building this PLN, the building
process needs to happen genuinely and authentically. That is, like any relationship, it needs to happen naturally and not be forced, and you need
to build your PLN without neglecting your family. In addition, there is
an African proverb which says, *"If you want to go fast, go alone. If you want
to go far, go with others."* I contend that in order to lead schools effectively in the 21st Century, you must regularly develop and collaborate with
your PLN. Professional Learning Networks can be made up of an array of
individuals, from stakeholders (i.e., students, staff, parents, community
members and business owners), to other aspiring and practicing school/

district leaders (locally, nationally, and globally), to classmates (e.g., a cohort you are part of as you complete your degree/licensure program), to a spouse/significant other, close friends and family members. All of these individuals can (and should) be part of your PLN. This chapter will aim to highlight some strategies and resources you can use to build your PLN and collaborate with your PLN to assist your own personal and professional growth.

Know Your Tribe

Before we dig further into this chapter and the necessity of networking and building a PLN, I need to ensure you are choosing individuals to be part of your network that are going to help you in your own personal and professional growth, in order to receive the full benefits of your network. An easy way to put this is that we all need someone that is part of our network who is willing to be honest with us at all times, who pushes us to dream big, expands us, believes in us, forces us to be great, and in essence, challenges us in all we think, say, and do. I once read a quote that my old college buddy, former NFL player and current actor, Drew Carter, posted on Instagram that read:

> Be around the light bringers, the magic makers, the world shifters, the game shakers. They challenge you, break you open, uplift and expand you. They don't let you play small with your life. These heartbeats are your people. These people are your tribe.

Does this quote not make you want to be around such people? These are the type of people I want to associate with, and likewise, these are the type of people I want in my PLN (i.e., tribe)! Don't you? Now, how do you find your tribe? Here is what Jennifer Pastiloff (2017) writes:

> Find your tribe. You know, the ones that make you feel the most you. The ones that lift you up and help you remember who you really are. The ones that remind you that a blip in the road is just that, a blip. They are the ones that when you walk out of a room, they make you feel like a better person than when you walked in. They are the ones that even if you

don't see them face-to-face as often as you'd like, you see them heart-to-heart. You know, that kind of tribe. Who's your tribe?

Sounds easy enough, right? Just choose to interact with and be around such people in your life. I would not make time for anyone else. However, some of you will be better at, and more natural at, networking than others, and we will cover this particular aspect later within this chapter. Moving forward, here are a few more quotes to drive it home: "you can't do epic things without epic people," "your vibe attracts your tribe," and perhaps my favorite by Seth Godin (2017):

> A tribe is a group of people connected to one another, connected to a leader, and connected to an idea. For millions of years, human beings have been part of one tribe or another. A group needs only two things to be a tribe; a shared interest and a way to communicate.

You can take these quotes to heart as much and/or as deeply as you would like. That said, might your shared interest be *best practices for school leaders* and your way to communicate be both *virtually and face-to-face*? After all, it is the 21st Century and there are multiple (and effective) ways to communicate with individuals from around the globe (e.g., Twitter).

We must also be protective of who is in (and remains in) our tribe. This aspect of networking reminds me of something my old high school baseball coach and athletic director Coach Don Thorp said to me once in high school: "If you hang around the dumpster long enough, you begin to look and smell like trash." He said this to me because he thought I was starting to run around with the wrong crowd. Looking back at that time in my life, he was right. What I am trying to convey here is that you should be mindful of who is in your network, that is, your tribe. Another quote I like is "show me your friends and I will show you your future" (a quote associated with Solomon – see Proverbs). The people you surround yourself with, and with whom you spend most of your time, influence you, whether you like it or not, both positively and negatively. Likewise, folks outside your network will associate you with the members of your network (like the dumpster quote). Therefore, choose wisely!

Remember, you can always carefully, politely, and politically slide someone out of your network without the need to burn any bridges. After all, it is your network. Do not ever feel that you need to keep in your network someone that is toxic, negative, and does not contribute to your own personal and professional growth. As Kimberly "Sweet Brown" Wilkins (2012) once said "Ain't nobody got time for that." Furthermore, as Lou Holtz (2017) once said in a commencement speech (https://www.youtube.com/watch?v=TSae0t8xtiY), as an individual "you're either growing or dying." If someone in your network is not contributing to your growth, I would think twice about keeping them in the network. However, I am also fully aware that you may work closely with someone in your school building/district that you would never have in your tribe. This is where servant leadership comes in with regards to your tribe. As leaders, we often have to learn to work with the broken. That is, the individuals I am talking about kicking out of your tribe are the same individuals I would challenge you to mentor[35], especially if you work closely with such individuals on a daily basis. It is that "treat people the way they should act, and often, they will begin to act that way," analogy. This could mean showing someone respect even when they show you none, going the extra mile for someone even when you are too tired to do so or they do not deserve it, and it means leading by example in all that you do and say. I love the quote, "How we walk with the broken speaks louder than how we sit with the great." This is servant leadership at its best, and I would argue all school building/district leaders need to be servant leaders. As Jon Gordon (2017) says, servant leadership is described with words such as "selfless acts of love" and "serving others by doing the little things." As a school building/district leader, there are endless opportunities to serve others, so be strategic in where and who you serve, and always serve your tribe (even those on the fringes). I felt compelled to include this, as I believe the individuals who may not be fully in your tribe yet, might someday be. I have personally experienced this. That

---

35 The word "Mentor" meaning someone who teaches or gives help and advice to a less experienced and often younger person comes from the ancient Greek language. The name is derived from a character found in Homer's Odyssey named Mentor (in Greek MENTΩP). Mentor was the trusted friend of Odysseus.

is, someone who was barely on the fringes of my tribe, later becoming a full-fledged member. This can only be accomplished through servant leadership, a lot of patience, constructive criticism, and encouragement. This type of transition will in large part depend on how you lead and mentor the "broken," and the "selfless acts of love" you will be willing to offer those individuals who need some help. After all, our purpose as leaders is to create other leaders, and as Jack Welch (2017) said, "Before you are a leader, success is all about growing yourself. When you become a leader, success is all about growing others." Now that we have all of that covered, let's delve into the importance of your network, how you might grow your network, and how your network can contribute to your own personal and professional growth as a school leader.

The Importance of Building Your Professional Learning Network (PLN)

"Networking is not about collecting contacts, networking is about planting relationships."
                                                                 ~ *Unknown*

The power and influence of your PLN is immeasurable. In chapter three, I discussed using Twitter chats for free professional development. Along these same lines, Twitter and other social media are great ways to build your PLN. I cannot count how many times I have been at a conference and randomly met someone in a crowd that I have only previously interacted with on Twitter or other forms of social media (e.g., LinkedIn, Instagram, WordPress, Facebook, etc.). It is almost like you already know them (think back to what I shared from the social media strategist Leishman, from MIT, with regard to the four main benefits deriving from social media presence – *learning, network, visibility,* and *reputation*), and essentially, they become part of your PLN – someone you learn from and someone that at times may learn from you. Members of your PLN are not only folks you can learn from, they are individuals you can often consult about the issues you are facing in your own school building/district on a daily basis. In many cases, these individuals have experienced, or are experiencing, those same issues. For example, this might be the case when federal and state policy affects all school districts in a given state or across the nation, and school leaders are all dealing with similar problems and issues stemming from a newly adopted policy. You and the members of your PLN can work together to determine the best solution for such problems. Those of you reading this book who have been part of a cohort-based program as part of your formal education experiences know exactly what I am trying to convey here, albeit, perhaps on a smaller scale. In the cohort model, all students are going through the same coursework together at the same time. Thus, the commonality they share is the courses (i.e., school building/district) and the course requirements (i.e., federal and state policies). As a professor who has taught in cohort-based educational leadership programs for many years, and as someone who completed their Master's and Doctoral programs in cohort-based educational leadership programs, I can share this ... the best and most productive cohorts I have taught or been part of have exhibited behaviors that I also consider to be conducive to building and interacting with your PLN. These behaviors include things such as taking a genuine interest in each cohort member as a human being first and foremost, and as an aspiring school leader/classmate second; building trust, effective communication, and being a team player truly invested in the success of each and every member of the cohort. Essentially, you do what you can to help the members of your PLN and members of your PLN do what they can to help you. Like all relationships, you truly *get* what you *give* when it comes to your PLN. In addition to Twitter, there are several Facebook pages you can "like", LinkedIn groups you can "join", Instagram feeds you can "follow", blogs you can "follow" and the like that you can get involved with and likewise, aid in the effective building of your PLN. You can start right now! Get on it! Start networking!

So, where might you start? First, it is important to realize that not everyone is a natural networker. That is okay, "fake it until you become it" (Cuddy, 2012). Anyone I know would tell you that I am a huge networker. But personally, I have found that my networking capabilities are very much mood and context dependent, and that is not necessarily a good thing (although some argue that everything is context related, but we won't go there – at least not in this book). There are times (probably the majority of the time) where I have the approach of the lyrics of a song titled *Misfit* by Elefant, "Tell me your name, tell me your story, cause I'm into it..." However, there are other times where I like and value my alone time and want to be left undisturbed. An example would be when I am with my family at a ball game or the like – only because I strongly believe they deserve my time and attention in those moments and I refuse to chat it up with the person next to me and neglect my family. Nonetheless, most of the time I am up for some good old networking, whether it be face-to-face or virtually, through social media and the like. In fact, I usually leave conferences with a stack of business cards. Upon arriving home, within a few days of the conference, I always sit down and drop a line or two to every single person who gave me a card. I have personally found this to be a good practice and a way to stay connected with such individuals, who often end up being part of my PLN. Nevertheless, not everyone is naturally great at networking. In fact, it may take some significant effort and practice on your part. You might have to step out of your comfort zone and go for it! Remember, most personal growth happens right outside the boundaries of comfort. If you are an individual that is apprehensive about networking or it is out of your comfort zone to do so, I highly suggest watching Cuddy's TEDxTalk titled *Your Body Language Shapes Who You Are* (2012). Although a majority of the TEDxTalk is focused on Cuddy's research on body language, I would contend the best and most influential part of the speech is when she gets to the "fake it until you become it" part. You can access it here: https://www.ted.com/talks/amy_cuddy_your_body_language_shapes_who_you_are/up-next.

Secondly, I highly recommend starting with social media. A great place to begin is with Twitter/Twitter chats. Again, as I mentioned in chapter three, start with searching some hashtags of particular interest to you (or issues you may be experiencing) and see who else out there is talking about those same interests and issues. You would be surprised at how many aspiring or practicing school leaders are discussing in depth the same issues or interests you have. With regards to the Twitter chats, you can easily search topics and areas of interest by accessing this chat calendar that is focused on education chats only. See: https://sites. google.com/site/twittereducationchats/education-chat-calendar

Thirdly, I suggest joining and actively being involved in professional organizations. If you are an aspiring or practicing superintendent, perhaps you would join the American Association of School Administrators (AASA) or the National Association of School Superintendents (NASS). In addition, there are similar state organizations you can join. For example, in the State of Ohio, there is the Buckeye Association of School Administrators (BASA) and Ohio School Boards Association (OSBA), both organizations you would want to join if you were an aspiring or practicing superintendent in that respective state. Although I will not present each state superintendent organization within this book, most (if not all) states have similar organizations, which are relatively easy to locate via the Internet with a quick search. Many of the state organizations are state affiliates of the national organizations. Thus, they work hand-in-hand and often offer membership discounts to members of both organizations. In addition, if you are an aspiring principal or practicing principal, perhaps you would join the National Association of Secondary School Principals (NASSP) (for middle to high school principals) or National Association of Elementary School Principals (NAESP) (for elementary to middle school principals), both excellent organizations. Just as with the superintendent organizations, there are state organizations for aspiring principals and practicing principals as well. Still using the State of Ohio as an example, there is the Ohio Association of Secondary School Administrators (OASSA) (for middle to high school principals) and the Ohio Association of Elementary School Administrators (OAESA) (for elementary to middle school principals). Again, such state organizations can be found with a simple Internet search. In addition to the advantage of building your PLN, there are many other benefits from joining these organizations as well. This includes things such as legal assistance, access to vacancy announcements, legislative updates, advocacy and a collective voice with regards to all things policy (this particular aspect will be discussed in chapter 11), professional development opportunities (think licensure renewal), committee service opportunities, monthly publications, and more. In fact, my two favorite monthly publications to read with regards to the practitioner world are *School Administrator* released by AASA, and *Principal Leadership* released by NASSP. Most state organizations release monthly or quarterly publications as well. For example, OASSA releases the OASSA e-update and legal update monthly. For examples, see: http://www.oassa.org/images/uploads/920a89732789b0d4c0ecbe21e90b762c.pdf and http://www.oassa.org/images/uploads/8676c58b9e08e9dbc4da90522450f9fa.pdf. In addition to joining these organizations, it is important to attend the annual conferences. This is a great place to build your PLN face-to-face and learn about the latest and best practices for school leaders at both the district and building levels. At the end of this chapter I have provided information relating to the conferences of professional organizations mentioned within this chapter. Finally, I see it as advantageous to help further bridge the gap between the PreK-12 educational setting and the higher education setting for both aspiring and practicing school leaders to be members of, and actively involved with, professional organizations for professors of educational leadership. Likewise, professors of educational leadership should be involved with, and active members of the organizations for practicing school leaders. Just as with the aforementioned organizations, there are international, national, and state organizations for professors of educational leadership. At the international level, there is the International Council of Professors of Educational Leadership (ICPEL). At the national level, there is the American Educational Research Association (AERA – Division A) and University Council for Educational Administration (UCEA). At the state level, for example, in the State of California, there is the California Association of Professors of Educational Administration (CAPEA). As with the monthly publications associated with AASA and NASSP, many of the organizations for professors of educational leadership have several print outlets, mostly in the form of peer-reviewed journals. For example, CAPEA publishes a yearly journal titled *Educational Leadership and Administration: Teaching and Program Development*. ICPEL publishes several peer-reviewed journals (see: http://www.icpel.org/journals.html) as well as books (see: http://www.ncpeapublications.org/index.php/ncpea-press-books). UCEA publishes several peer-reviewed journals as well (see: https://members.ucea.org/member_journals) and books, mono-graphs, and reports (see: http://www.ucea.org/resource_category/books-monographs-reports/). AERA publishes several peer-reviewed journals (see: http://www.aera.net/Publications/Journals) and books (see: http://www.aera.net/Publications/Books).

Again, in addition to all the publications you will have access to as a member, all of these organizations have annual conferences that I would highly suggest you attend if possible. When I was still a practitioner, I always prioritized the "practitioner" conferences over the "professor" conferences. However, in my current role of preparing future school lead-ers, it goes without saying that both remain a high priority, and I am still actively involved with several of the practitioner organizations as much as I am involved with the professor organizations. Nonetheless, if I were you, I would join and attend as many as possible. That being said, my colleagues in the PreK-12 educational setting would always ask why I was attending and/or joining the "professor" organizations/conferences when I was still a practitioner. My answer was always the same, "if we want to bridge the gap between the PreK-12 educational setting and the higher education setting, it starts with me/us." I am fully aware that you cannot be out of the school building/district office all the time, and to do so might open you up to much criticism from all the stakeholders in which you serve (including your school board members). Thus, do the best you can and attend as many conferences as possible. I can promise you two things will most certainly come from it: (1) you will build a vast PLN; and (2) you will become better at what you do by learning from other school leaders throughout the nation and around the globe. The members of these organizations, the monthly publications they produce, and the annual conferences (specifically the keynotes and presentations you attend) will challenge you to think differently about issues you may be facing in your school building/district, and how you might address such issues. In summation, by joining such organizations and attending such conferences, you will experience personal and professional growth, and it most certainly will make you a more effective school leader.

Lastly, I want to share an exercise I like to do with my graduate students, who are all aspiring or practicing school leaders. The activity is focused on allowing them to identify and think more deeply about their current PLN, early in their careers/the program. In keeping with the theme of the course text I require and utilize with said course, titled *Leadership for Increasingly Diverse Schools* (Theoharis & Scanlan, 2015), the in-class assignment is called *Creating a Community of Practice (COP) Sociogram*. During this activity, I usually require my students to create this sociogram centered on or around a particular topic such as *leading for social justice in schools*. For this chapter, I would like you to complete this activity focused solely on your current network, your tribe or extant PLN. I would argue that most of us, to some level or varying degree, have a PLN, though, you may have never thought of it as this and/or you will need to dig deep and think more in-depth about it. That is exactly what this sociogram exercise will allow you to do; think more deeply about the individuals in your life that you turn to for help, advice, direction, or feedback. To begin, get out a blank piece of paper and a pencil, and then follow the directions below. If you are reading this book as part of a book study or course, it will certainly be beneficial to discuss and answer the questions included in the last step (Step 5) with other individuals completing this exercise. The sociogram directions below have been altered, but are derived from Theoharis and Scanlan (2015, p. 7):

Step 1. Write your name in the center of the paper with a rectangle around it.

Step 2. Begin with the question: In my role as an aspiring or practicing school leader, to whom do I turn for help, advice, direction, or feedback when I am wrestling with various questions and issues? Generate a list of names randomly around your piece of paper (all around your name).

Step 3. After you have created an initial list, go back to each name and add two details:

    (1) Put a shape around each name to correspond with various roles.
        Circle = Teacher
        Square = Administrator
        Triangle = State/County/District/Central Office
        Diamond = Other

(2) Inside each shape, add a number 1-4

    1 = weak (reliable but don't talk to very often)

    4 = strong (reliable and talk to often);

    2 or 3 for those individuals that fall somewhere in the middle of those two poles – use your best judgment

Step 4. Draw two lines (=) to your 4's, draw a solid line to your 3's (-), draw a dashed line (- - -) to your 2's, and a faint dotted line (....) to your 1's.

Step 5. Look at your initial sociogram and consider the reflection prompts below, and, if possible, discuss them with someone else who has completed this exercise.

> *What do you notice about the individuals you have identified, the variations of roles they represent, and the relative strength of these relationships?*

> *Who could be added to this sociogram if you took some of the individuals on it and asked them to create a sociogram?*

> *What dimensions of diversity are hidden on this sociogram? Think ... How diverse is my network by race and ethnicity? By gender? By religion? By geographical region (globally and nationally)? By roles and responsibilities?*

> *Think back as far as you would like ... How has the composition of this sociogram changed over time? How would you like it to change in the future?*

This exercise is meant to get you thinking about your current network/PLN, and how you might work to expand it in both the short-term and long-term based on the sociogram you created. Again, if you completed this exercise alone, that is fine, but I would highly suggest having someone you know (perhaps someone on your sociogram) complete the same exercise and then discuss the results with them (see Step 5 reflection prompts to consider and discuss). This is a great way to gather feedback. Remember, with sociograms (and PLN's), it is all about quality, not quantity. That is, more names does not necessarily mean you have a "better" sociogram, and likewise, fewer names does not necessarily mean you have a "lower quality" sociogram. Proceed accordingly...

Finally, I would contend that much of my own PLN stems from two areas: (1) my service to many of the organizations to which I belong; and (2) my relationships with the individuals I am connected to through such organizations. I have been volunteering and serving as much as my time allows (in any capacity possible) while being mindful of my work-life balance. This includes committee service, editorial service (serving as a journal and conference proposal reviewer), writing for/publishing in monthly publications and peer-reviewed journals, presenting at conferences, chairing sessions at conferences, conducting book reviews, participating in organization-sponsored Twitter chats, and the list goes on. In addition, I aim to build strong and lasting relationships with the individuals I am connected with through the organizations I am actively involved with. After all, these people are part of my tribe, we do much of the same work, and we are passionate about a lot of the same things, namely preparing effective school leaders to lead our nation's schools. So, remember, your PLN should start with service and relationships, and then grow from there!

Suggested Twitter Chats/Twitter Resources

Below I have shared the hashtag of several Twitter chats and Twitter resources for aspiring and practicing school leaders alike. These days/times were accurate at the time this book was written, but be aware that the days/times of Twitter chats can change from time-to-time. This should get you started. Enjoy!

Twitter Chats:

#LeadUpChat – Saturdays, 9:30 a.m. EST
#SATChat – Saturdays, 7:30 a.m. EST
#SuptChat – First Wednesday of every month, 8:00 p.m. EST
#EdChat – Twice weekly, Tuesdays, 12:00 p.m. and 7:00 p.m. EST
#Admin2B – First Monday of every month, 8:00 p.m. EST
#PrincipalLife – Wednesdays, 9:00 p.m. EST
#PSChat – Mondays, 8:30 p.m. EST

The Twitter resources shared below are hashtags used daily to share motivational quotes, handouts, PDFs, and rubrics supporting educational leadership. Essentially, they are active 24/7, you just search the hashtags (for example, if using the Twitter app on your smart phone, search the hashtags listed below in the "Search Twitter" section of the app [see the little magnifying glass icon right next to the home icon] – then you can choose "Top," "Latest," "People," "Photos," "Videos," "News," and "Periscopes" – all connected to the hashtag you are searching for).

Twitter Resources:
  #EdLeadership
  #EdAdmin
  #EdLeader21
  #Leadership
  #LeadwithGiants
  #LeadFromWithin
  #MondayMotivation
  #PrincipalsInAction

Organizations to Join (with current links)

Below I have shared several of the international and national organizations mentioned previously in this chapter. I have deliberately excluded state organizations, and trust you can seek these out on your own in your respective State.

Aspiring/Practicing Superintendents:
  AASA – www.aasa.org
  NASS – www.nass.us

Aspiring/Practicing Principals:
  NASSP – www.nassp.org
  NAESP – www.naesp.org

Aspiring/Practicing Professors of Educational Leadership:
    ICPEL – www.icpel.org
    AERA – www.aera.net
    UCEA – www.ucea.org

Conferences to Attend (with current links)

Aspiring/Practicing Superintendents:
    AASA's Annual National Conference on Education – http://nce.aasa.org
    NASS's Annual National Conference – http://nass.us/pages/professional-learning

Aspiring/Practicing Principals:
    *NASSP's Annual National Secondary Principals Conference – https://nassp.org/professional-learning/conferences
    *NAESP's Annual National Elementary School Principals Conference – http://www.naespconference.org
    *Note: Last year they held their conferences together for the first time. Thus, be cognizant that this process may continue.

Aspiring/Practicing Professors of Educational Leadership:
    ICPEL's Annual Conference – http://www.icpel.org/events.html
    AERA's Annual Meeting – http://www.aera.net/Events-Meetings
    UCEA's Annual Convention – http://www.ucea.org/events/

Other national organizations/conferences worth mentioning:
    ASCD – http://www.ascd.org/Default.aspx
    AMLE – http://www.amle.org/home/tabid/401/default.aspx

Reflection

Questions for Practicing and Aspiring School Leaders

1. What steps will/might you take in order to build and maintain your PLN?
2. Do you believe maintaining a healthy PLN is important to your personal and professional growth as an aspiring/practicing school/district leader? Why? Why not?
3. As a school district/building leader, how might you mentor others with the goal of having such individuals join your PLN someday?
4. As a school district/building leader, how will you balance your networking with your work-life balance and work-life choices?
5. As a school district/building leader, how might you join and get more actively involved with the many organizations (and conferences) shared within this chapter?

Problem-based Scenario

Networking, Service and Relationships

As a building (or district) school leader, you are now fully aware it is vital to create, grow, and maintain a healthy PLN for your own personal and professional growth. However, upon completing the sociogram exercise within this chapter (if you have not yet done so, do so now), you have come to realize that your PLN is almost non-existent, and furthermore, the individuals in your PLN are not people you consider to be highly reliable and/or you do not regularly talk to/interact with. In addition, as you reflected on your sociogram, you began to think of individuals you would like in your PLN who did not appear on your sociogram. Additionally, there are several individuals that did appear (maybe on the fringes) or did not appear at all, on your sociogram (you might work directly or indirectly with many of these individuals). These are individuals that fall under one of two categories: (1) they need to go, that is, they are toxic and negatively contributing to your personal and professional growth (think the dumpster quote shared at the beginning of this chapter); and/or (2) they need some mentoring before they can become full-fledged members of your PLN or continue to be part of your PLN. Nonetheless, with regards to such individuals, as a servant leader (all effective leaders are), you know the right thing to do is mentor these individuals in hopes that someday they may join your PLN. Briefly outline (in 'to-do list' form with tentative due dates) the steps you plan to take in order to create your PLN, grow your PLN, maintain your PLN, and help mentor those individuals who are not yet a part of your PLN (or are on the fringes) over the next year. With reference to the thoughts shared within this chapter, think about what type of people you want in your PLN (your tribe, your network), and what type of people you want to be associated with, as you draft your outline.

Choose Your School Setting

Choose your role and then choose your school building/district setting before you respond to the scenario above. As you draft your response, please be cognizant of how your setting might affect how you respond to the scenario. Essentially, based on the characteristics listed below, think about what we generally know about these characteristics, and furthermore, how they generally impact schools/districts. How might they affect your decision-making with regards to the scenario, if at all? Be sure to clearly describe your school setting in your response.

Role: Superintendent, Principal, or Assistant Principal
Locale: Urban, Suburban, or Rural
Size: Small District, Medium District, or Large District
Diversity: No Diversity, Some Diversity, or Very Diverse
SES Status: 100% Free and Reduced Lunch (FRL), 50% FRL, or 0% FRL

Chapter 10

Leading for Inclusiveness

"Excellence in education requires equity, not elitism."
                                                    ~ *Pasi Sahlberg*

"If a child can't learn the way we teach (or lead), maybe we should teach (or lead) the way they learn."
                                                    ~ *Ignacio Estrada*

Leading for Equity, Equality, Social Justice, Inclusion, and Multiculturalism in Schools

As school leaders, we must lead and pave the way when it comes to equity, equality, social justice, inclusion, and multiculturalism in schools. In order to do so, school leaders must be well-versed not only in the terminology, but also fully understand the implications of implementing particular policies and procedures and how they affect the school setting, and specifically the students. As one might suspect, "schools in the United States have historically responded to dimensions of diversity by privileging some and marginalizing others" (Theoharis & Scanlan, 2015, p. 1). Nonetheless, although historically this has been the norm, school leaders must advocate for policies at the federal, state, district, and local levels in order to ensure all students have equitable educational opportunities within the PreK-12 educational setting and beyond, regardless of their dimensions of diversity (see chapter 11). However, still today, certain students enjoy privileges that others do not. Theoharis and Scanlan (2015, p.1) wrote:

> Dimensions of diversity that have enjoyed privilege include being white, of European heritage, of moderate to high socioeconomic status, Christian, heterosexual, native English speaking, and without disability. By contrast, dimensions of diversity that have been marginalized

include being of color; of non-European heritage; of low socioeconomic status; non-Christian; LGBTQ; of limited proficiency in English; or with a special need or disability. Schools consistently fail to provide equitable educational opportunities to students across these dimensions of diversity.

This trend must change and it starts with school leaders (and school teachers) reaching out to their policy makers with a collective voice in an effort to address such inequities. After all, who knows what is going on in the trenches better than the folks who are in those trenches (i.e., the practitioners). Thus, we must shed light on these inequities and how they are affecting our students. It reminds me of the quote, "If not us, who? If not now, when?" It starts with you, and it starts now.

Key Terms

In writing this chapter, I felt obligated to provide some general definitions of several key terms. This decision stems from my own experiences in discussing equity with researchers and scholars around the globe, not only as it applies to the educational setting, but in general. During such conversations, I have found there to be a common theme occurring that is somewhat troubling to say the least. That is, certain terms are used interchangeably and/or inaccurately. Thus, I felt compelled to provide some shared definitions (and notes to help you further process the definitions) of several key terms as it applies to this particular chapter, not only as it applies to equity, but as it applies to other terms that often become a source of conversation when discussing equity. I believe this will be helpful to you, not only as you read this chapter, but also as you join the fight in leading for equity, equality, social justice, inclusion, and multiculturalism in education. As you read through each term, begin to think about how they might be applicable to the educational setting.

Key Terms:
> Implicit Bias: "Also known as implicit social cognition, implicit bias refers to the attitudes or stereotypes that affect

our understanding, actions, and decisions in an unconscious manner" (Kirwan Institute for the Study of Race & Ethnicity, The Ohio State University, 2017).

Explicit Bias: Explicit bias refers to the attitudes and beliefs we have about a person or group on a conscious level (Perception Institute: Research, Representation, Reality, 2017).

> Note: "Explicit bias is <u>conscious</u> bias; implicit bias is <u>subconscious</u> bias. Everyone has natural implicit and explicit "cognitive" bias. It's part of being human and what shapes our actions and attitudes" (DeMichele, 2016).

Multiculturalism: The preservation of different cultures or cultural identities within a unified society, as a state or nation.

Social Justice: Justice in terms of the distribution of wealth, opportunities, and privileges within a society.

Pluralism: Pluralism can be defined as a society in which members of diverse ethnic, racial, religious, and social groups maintain participation in and development of their traditions and special interests while cooperatively working toward the interdependence needed for a nation's unity. Pluralism is being practiced, taught, and expanded in community, preschool, elementary, high school, and college campus programs (England, 1992 [Abstract]).

> Note: Pluralistic approaches are educational concepts which acknowledge the value of linguistic and cultural diversity. According to these approaches, the learning of all languages and cultures should be fostered in the education setting.

Inclusion: "Inclusion requires the recognition of all children as full members of society and the respect of all their rights, regardless of age, gender, ethnicity, language, poverty or impairment. Inclusion involves the removal of barriers that might prevent the enjoyment of these rights, and requires creation of appropriate supportive and protective environments" (UNICEF, 2007, p. 1).

LGBTQ: Lesbian, gay, bisexual, transgender, or questioning.

Equality: A state of being equal, especially in status, rights, and opportunities.

Equity: The quality of being fair or impartial ... it is giving everyone what they need to be successful.

Note: Equity and equality are two strategies we can use in an effort to produce fairness. Equity is giving everyone what they need to be successful. Equality is treating everyone the same. Equality aims to promote fairness, but it can only work if everyone starts from the same place and needs the same help.

Equity Versus Equality

Before we delve into leading for equity in schools, I believe it is advantageous of me to discuss the long debated topic of equity versus equality, namely as it applies to the school setting. Likewise, I will share my thoughts as it applies to each. To fully understand the difference between equity and equality, I have provided a visual below (see Figure 5).

Figure 5: Equality versus Equity

What do you see when you look at the figure? What differences do you see between the image on the left representing *equality* and the image on the right depicting *equity*? As you can see in the image, equality is equal. That is, in this particular case, providing a crate for all. However, as you can see, equal is not always fair (not everyone can see the game). Equity is providing what each of the individuals need. That is, in this particular case, providing as many crates as each individual needs in order to see the game. Essentially, I would argue that we need to lead for equity in schools (although, worth noting, equality is a good thing as well, especially when it comes to things like equal rights – think the right to vote, etc.). This type of leadership (and teaching) provides the resources (including instruction) that each student needs to be successful and reach their full potential. Enrichment, intervention, and the like come to mind. Makes sense right? However, as educators, we struggle to implement such processes, namely because it is time consuming. Much like the argument that each student should be on an Individualized Education Plan (IEP). We all know that this makes perfect sense, that is, an individualized education plan for each student, and would be best practices, however, it is time consuming. Sticking with instruction, let's think about a relatively new term (in the grand scheme of things) in education: enrichment.

I visit schools often, and I find that most teachers and administrators struggle with what to do with their high achieving and gifted students. That is, the students that "already get it." As school leaders, we must provide such students with the resources to grow them well beyond proficiency – the content they "already get." This tends to be a difficult task, as for decades, we have almost solely focused on proficiency, that is, ensuring all students are proficient with respect to each grade level (i.e., what they should know by/in a particular grade) versus growing all students. This is where the other big debate in education lies – proficiency versus growth. Is it better to focus on the growth of each student from the beginning of each school year to the end? Or is it better to focus on each student being proficient in each grade level? Historically, the focus has been on proficiency. When the focus is on proficiency, we see a model where teachers and school leaders focus on the students who are "not getting it" (often the middle to low students) while the students who "already get it" (high students) are often left to the wayside. Worth noting here, astoundingly, I have even heard presenters say to "focus on the bubble students (i.e., middle students) only" with regards to state assessments. Essentially, their argument is this, to "not focus on the students who you know will perform well on the state assessment, and don't focus on the low students who will never do well on the state assessment no matter what you do, rather, focus on the bubble students because they are the students who will help your state report card." I remember attending a professional development many years ago when the presenter said this ... I literally about fell out of my chair. Nevertheless, in the growth model, teachers and school leaders focus on growing each student from the beginning of each school year to the end, this includes your low, middle, and high students. That all being said, I would argue that the best model is to focus on both proficiency and growth, versus one or the other. It is not enough to ensure students are proficient, and in many cases, it is not enough to focus on just growth, as some students start far below what is considered to be proficient in a given grade level. Thus, I would argue that we need to be cognizant of both the proficiency and growth of each student in our schools. In an era of socially promoting students[36], it is certainly important to ensure students are proficient at their given grade level, and if they are not, we need to find a way to fill in the gaps (e.g. after school and summer programming), however, growth should be a constant focus as well. Again, let me reiterate that I do not believe it needs to be one or the other, rather we should focus on both. The real issue is, how do we accurately judge growth and proficiency (see Figure 6). Without an excellent way to measure both growth and proficiency in such a way that allows each student, regardless of their demographics to show their

---

36 Socially promoting students refers to the process of allowing a student to move on to the next grade level regardless if they are academically ready to or not. Such a decision is usually made based on the student's age. For example, to avoid a 16-year-old from attending middle school with say, 11-year-olds, school systems will socially promote the student to high school even if they continually fail the highest grade in middle school (usually 8th grade). This process has an effect on the national graduation rate as many of these students never graduate high school as they are continually socially promoted without ever catching up with their peers academically.

knowledge and abilities (e.g., state assessments, standardized tests, etc.), it doesn't matter what you focus on, be it growth or proficiency, as no true measure exists. This can be detrimental to a student, especially those students who have been historically marginalized. Much like the fish depicted below and within Einstein's quote, biased assessments might have such students believing they are stupid their whole life. There are no easy answers, but we have to do better.

Figure 6: Assessing Growth and Proficiency

"*Everybody is a genius. But if you judge a fish by its ability to climb a tree, it will live its whole life believing that it is stupid.*"

Albert Einstein

"*Only by eliminating opportunity gaps can we eliminate achievement gaps.*" ~ *Diane Ravitch*

Now, as we think of social justice, especially as it applies to education and "justice in terms of distribution of wealth, opportunities, and privileges in society", we tend to think about things like school funding and biased state assessments, to name a few. Only here are we beginning to address the real elephant in the room—the systemic issues—such as the fact that schools are not equally funded (including per pupil/student spending) and that state assessments tend to favor certain students while disadvantaging others. As we begin to think of systems of oppression, let's take a look at another image developed by Paul Kuttner (2015) depicting equality versus equity (see Figure 7).

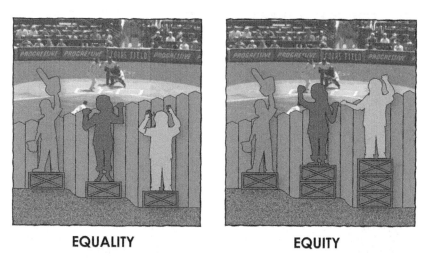

EQUALITY   **EQUITY**

Figure 7: Equality versus Equity 2.0 (Kuttner, 2015)

What do you see when you look at the figure? What differences do you see between the image on the left representing *equality* and the image on the right depicting *equity*? In this figure, we have a lot more going on. We might conceive that the lower ground represents historical oppression. Whereas the higher fence represents systems of oppression (like school funding, state assessments, etc.). Finally, we might conceive that the hole in the fence to be persistence. That is, the most resilient and persistent individuals often find "ways around" such historical and systemic oppression. Now, the million-dollar question is, as a school leader, what can you do about these issues? First, we can advocate for policy that supports systemic changes at the local, state, and federal levels. We can help adopt school policy (and in some cases, procedures) along with our school boards and administrative teams to ensure we are leading for "ways around" such systematic oppression in order to ensure each and every student in our building/district reaches their highest potential. By first being aware of such systematic oppression, we can begin to identify "ways around" such a system, and lead all stakeholders in the direction of removing the real problem, the fence itself. Removing the fence, well, that is social justice. However, we still have a long way to go in removing this fence, and the height of the fence seems to change depending on where the baseball field (i.e., school district) is located (i.e., zip code).

> *"If I can look at your zip code and I can tell whether you're going to get a good education, we've got a real problem."*
> ~ *Condoleezza Rice*

More often than not, a child's zip code determines the type of education they receive, and in many cases, their future. When it comes to school funding, the equality versus equity debate can become even more heated. Likewise, I often find myself on both sides of the debate. On one hand, I could argue that equal distribution of financial resources to all schools across the United States would be, well, equal. However, as discussed earlier, equal is not always fair. For example, if we look at some of the nation's largest school districts such as New York City Public Schools, Puerto Rico Public Schools, Los Angeles Unified School District, Chicago Public Schools, (United States Department of Education, 2009), would it be equitable to provide them with the same financial resources as, say, the smaller school districts across the nation? Obviously, the answer is "no". However, on a much smaller scale, take the State of Ohio, where schools are almost solely funded by property taxes—it might make more sense to fund schools equally. In the Ohio model, again, because schools are funded by property taxes, we truly see how a child's zip code determines the quality of education they receive, and often, dictates their future. For example, one could argue that the zip code determines things like the quality of facilities, teacher and administrator salary rates, resources for students and teachers such as the newest textbooks, technology (e.g., 1:1, SmartBoards, etc.), and more. Thus, one would most likely argue for equal funding. In contrast, the stake-holders of Cleveland Metropolitan School District, Cincinnati Public Schools, and Columbus City Schools, might argue that equal funding in the State of Ohio is not fair, as they are the larger school districts in the state and require more financial resources. As you can see, although equality as it applies to financial resources sounds good in theory, in fact it may not be enough. However, here in lies the problem. Let's stick with Ohio for practical purposes, and let's look at what the spending per student looks like in the State of Ohio. To magnify this problem, let's just look at Franklin County (i.e., Central Ohio). Furthermore, let's look at two school districts in Franklin County that share school district boundary lines. In an article by O'Donnell (2016), it was reported that Grandview Heights Schools (GHS) spends $16,227.00 per student each academic school year. In the next district over, as reported by the Ohio Department of Education (2017), Columbus City Schools spends only $9,845.00 per student each academic school year, almost half the amount GHS spends on their students (and worth noting, this article was published a year after the article reporting GHS's per pupil spending, so I might argue a larger discrepancy may actually exist). This certainly is not fair either. Therefore equity, even as it applies to financial resources, may be the answer. That is, for example and quite simply, putting all funds generated from property taxes in the State of Ohio into one large pot, and then by using a formula that incorporates all student demographics and school district characteristics (including enrollment size) equitably distributing the funds across the state (i.e., giving each school district and student what they need as it applies to financial resources). Only then can we begin to lead for equity as it applies to school/per pupil/student funding. That is, each school district would be starting at the same place, at least with regards to the financial resources they receive. That is applicable to other school districts because of how it would be allocated (i.e., based on enrollment size, students on free and reduced lunch, etc.). Thus, school leaders could begin to lead for equity using such monies to provide for each student and teacher what they need in order to reach their full potential (i.e., however many crates necessary for each student to see the game). Now, I am not naïve in that such a formula is both difficult to come up with, and furthermore, will most likely <u>not</u> keep all stakeholders and policy makers happy. As I have been part of many committees who have discussed this very idea of an equitable way to fund schools, I will refrain from reporting in my book the often sad and ridiculous reasons stakeholders in the "nice" zip codes give in defense of our current school funding system. Worth adding here, who do you think is more well-connected to the individuals responsible for creating policy, the parents in the "nice" zip codes, or the parents in the "not so nice" zip codes. I will leave it at that. Someone's voice is heard, and the other's is not. This has got to change. Regardless, as school leaders we have to start somewhere. With no immediate change in sight with regards to equitable funding for our nation's schools, school leaders must become innovative in how they obtain additional resources in order to ensure all students and teachers have the resources they need to reach their full potential. I see leading for equity in schools as school leaders doing what they can and need to do in order to provide the resources necessary for both their teachers and students to thrive and succeed. Thus, I have included several links to grants/grant websites at the end of this chapter (also shared in chapter seven). Again, as we know, and as I have previously mentioned in this chapter (and I have personally experienced this myself - first as a student in the PreK-12 educational setting, later as a teacher, and even later as a school leader), a zip code often determines the type of education a child receives, the funding a school receives, and the per student spending in a given school building/district. Thus, until we have a systemic reform with regards to equity as it applies to school funding and per student spending, school leaders must seek out and utilize innovative strategies to obtain additional resources for their students and teachers. One way to do this is to obtain grant money.

Worth noting, most grants are for educators, that is, school administrators cannot directly apply for them. However, as I reported in chapter seven, my last two years as a school administrator I applied for and obtained several grants for our school building totaling just under $30,000.00 (see p.146).

That being said, grants are not the only answer as I have both seen and heard of some pretty innovative strategies from school leaders around the globe with regards to leading for equity in their schools/ districts. Perhaps one of the most innovative strategies I have heard of was quite intriguing indeed. I was at the American Educational Research Association (AERA) annual conference in Washington, D.C. and attended a presentation on school leadership. During the presentation, the presenter (a practicing principal) said they were able to obtain funds to become a 1:1 school,[37] but had soon quickly realized that a majority of their students had no way to connect the provided devices to the Internet at home; many of their students were considered low socioeconomic...parents could not afford Internet service. To make things worse, this was problematic since many of the teachers in the school building had anticipated the 1:1 initiative and attempted to flip their classrooms since becoming 1:1, which required access to a Learning Management System (think Blackboard, Canvas, or the like) via the Internet. What the principal shared next was truly thinking outside of the box. To address this issue, the district installed Internet ports on all of their school buses. Then they worked with local business owners and the like to strategically park their buses around the district after the end of each school day/bus route. Thus, the students would access Internet via the ports on the strategically parked school buses throughout the district (which were connecting to the school WiFi). The presenter reported that 100% of their students now had access to the Internet after school hours. Amazing, huh? When I hear about stories like this, I think of that hole in the fence in the picture shared earlier in this chapter ... that hole represented persistence. When I heard this story at AERA, I was truly amazed, not only by the innovative idea itself, but by the sheer persistence of the school leaders in that building/district to ensure their students had the resources they needed to be successful and thrive. That is an example of a school leader leading for equity! It reminds me of a TEDxTalk I watched years

37 The term one-to-one (or 1:1) refers to programs in schools that provide all students with a device such as a laptop, netbook, tablet computer, or other mobile-computing device. Essentially, 1:1 refers to one computer for every student (EdGlossary, 2017).

ago. In the presentation, the principal shared her slogan "So what! Now what?" Ever since I watched this TEDxTalk, whenever someone goes on and on about how bad things are in education, or a problem that exists in their school, I always respond with a "So what! Now what?" mentality. That is, my thought is always ... thanks for highlighting everything wrong with education, your school, etc., now what are you going to do about it? Likewise, I used to tell my teachers, "Complaining about a problem without proposing a solution is called whining." You can watch the TEDxTalk here titled *How to Fix a Broken School: Lead Fearlessly and Love Hard*: https://www.ted.com/talks/linda_cliatt_wayman_how_ to_fix_a_broken_school_lead_fearlessly_love_hard#t-591015. Enjoy!

Where Do We Start? Conducting an Equity Audit Data Collection and Analysis, and Creating an Equity Audit Implementation Plan

When conducting professional development and/or presenting on the topics of school leadership and equity, equality, social justice, inclusion, and multiculturalism, I am often asked the same question in some way shape, or form, "Where do we start?" or "How do I know where my district/school stands regarding equity?" I always answer by suggesting the following: (1) conduct an *equity audit data collection and analysis*; and (2) based on those results, create an *equity audit implementation plan* with measurable goals. For example, I am currently responsible for teaching a course in our graduate program titled *Equity and Diversity in Educational Leadership*, and one of the assignments requires students to do just this. The assignment stems from the course textbook we use titled *Leadership for Increasingly Diverse Schools* by Theoharis and Scanlan (2015) - see the list of recommended books on equity at the end of this chapter. I have found that my students enjoy this assignment, and it allows them to have a true pulse on all things equity within their respective school buildings/districts. Furthermore, and perhaps most importantly, they analyze the data collected, and create an equity audit implementation plan that includes seven main elements for each goal they decide to create. The seven main elements for each goal include: (1)

Action Step; (2) People Involved; (3) Purpose; (4) How It Will Happen; (5) When It Will Happen; (6) Support in Place; and (7) Evidence of Progress. The goals in the implementation plan should stem directly from the data collected and analyzed in the first step in the process, the equity audit. I believe this is an excellent place to start in attempting to identify objectives and goals to put in place to ensure you are leading for equity in your school/district. Likewise, you may be surprised by how much work needs to be done with regards to ensuring your school is an equitable environment for all stakeholders. You can locate and use the equity audit and data collection form here: http://s3-euw1-ap-pe-ws4-cws-documents.ri-prod.s3.amazonaws.com/9781138785939/Equity-Audit-Data-Collection-and-Analysis.pdf .

In the table below (see Table 7), I have provided a simple example of how Theoharis and Scanlan (2015) suggest setting up your equity audit implementation plan. If you are a practicing school leader, I highly suggest creating a committee or team to assist in this equity audit process. This will allow for additional input from all stakeholders including students, teachers, parents, community members, and business owners.

Table 7: Equity Audit Implementation Plan

Goal	Action Step	People Involved	Purpose	How it will happen?	When it will happen?	Support in Place	Evidence of Progress

In addition and worth mentioning here, as leading for inclusion is just as important, for this same course (using the same course textbook), my students conduct several observations focused on and around *inclusive leadership and disability*. The authors (Theoharis & Scanlan, 2015) have created four forms to be completed during an observation focused on: (1) belonging; (2) classroom environment; (3) supporting behavior; and (4) co-teaching. This is a great way for both aspiring and practicing school leaders to ensure an inclusive pedagogy is being implemented in all classrooms in a given school/district. I highly suggest using the observation forms for informal evaluations (also sometimes referred to as walk-throughs). An example form (co-teaching) can be found here: http://s3-euw1-ap-pe-ws4-cws-documents.ri-prod.s3.amazonaws.com/9781138785939/Co-Teaching-Feedback-Form.pdf. All four forms can be found here with the Chapter 2 additional resources: http://routledgetextbooks.com/textbooks/9781138785939/.

Remember, as school leaders, we are the voice for our students, teachers, and all stakeholders. We must do our part in ensuring we are creating an educational environment in which all students, regardless of their dimensions of diversity, have the opportunity to thrive and succeed. We can accomplish this through a number of avenues such as influencing systemic (including instructional practices and resources) reform (federal and state) as well as reform at the local levels (county and district). To do so, school leaders must stay abreast of current educational policies (and in some cases, procedures) affecting their students and teachers both on a national level, and within their respective school building. Only then can we begin to advocate for educational reform efforts that will someday allow all students to have a just, equitable, and inclusive education. As I write this, I must say that it is truly disheartening and hard to believe that in the 21st Century, here in the United States of America, some students enjoy privileges that others do not. This must change and it starts with you. In chapter 11, I have highlighted the importance of educational policy, as well as how school leaders can successfully advocate for all stakeholders, including students, staff, parents, community members and business owners. In addition, I have provided several advocacy groups you can join in an effort to both stay abreast of current educational policies as well as help advocate for (and in some cases, against) new or changes proposed to current policies.

Recommended Books on Equity

Griffiths, D. (2013). Principals of Inclusion: Practical Strategies to Grow Inclusion in Urban Schools. Ontario, Canada: Word & Deed Publishing.

Griffiths, D., & Lowrey, S. (2017). The Principal Reader: Narratives of Experience. Ontario, Canada: Word & Deed Publishing.

Nieto, S., & Bode, P. (2012). Affirming Diversity: The Sociopolitical Context of Multicultural Education (6th ed.). Boston, MA: Pearson.

Redman, G. (2003). A Casebook for Exploring Diversity (2nd ed.). Upper Saddle River: NJ: Pearson Education.

Spring, J. (2001). Deculturalization and the Struggle for Equality: A Brief History of the Education of Dominated Cultures in the United States (3rd ed.). New York, NY: McGraw-Hill.

Theoharis, G., & Scanlan, M. (2015). Leadership for Increasingly Diverse Schools. New York, NY: Routledge.

Online resources for our course textbook can be found here: http://routledgetextbooks.com/textbooks/9781138785939/

Recommended Grants

National Education Association: http://www.nea.org/grants/grantsawardsandmore.html

Grants for Teachers: https://teach.com/what/grants-for-teachers/

Edutopia: https://www.edutopia.org/grants-and-resources

TeachersCount: http://www.teacherscount.org/grants/

Reflection

Questions for Practicing and Aspiring School Leaders

1. What steps will you take to ensure you are leading for equity, equality, social justice, inclusion, and multiculturalism in your school?

2. How will you stay abreast of current educational policies (and in some cases, procedures) at the federal, state, and local levels? Please explain.

3. As a school district/building leader, how will you advocate for your stakeholders at the federal, state, and local levels? Please explain.
4. As a school district/building leader, how might you ensure your teachers understand the terminology and importance of equity, equality, social justice, inclusion, and multiculturalism in your school?
5. As a school district/building leader, how might you know *where to start* in identifying inequities that may exist in your school/district?

Problem-based Scenario

So what! Now what? - Inclusive Leadership and Disability

As a building (or district) school leader, you have conducted several informal walk-throughs at the beginning of the academic school year in your school building/district. In doing so, you have noticed that many of the classroom practices by teachers are not conducive to an inclusive pedagogy. That is, in particular, in classrooms where co-teaching is taking place (i.e., a classroom teacher and inclusion teacher) you notice a clear distinction between the co-teachers with regards to numerous items in the classrooms such as leadership in the class, accommodations and modifications, behavior management, access to all students, grouping, and active learning structures and learning styles, to name a few. Using the form found here: http://s3-euw1-ap-pe-ws4-cws-documents.ri-prod.s3.amazonaws.com/9781138785939/Co-Teaching-Feedback-Form.pdf, how might you begin to use observations (and the provided form) and timely/meaningful feedback to support teachers (if you are choosing to be a principal/assistant principal for this scenario) or principals/assistant principals (if you are choosing to be a superintendent for this scenario) in an effort to lead for inclusion?

Choose Your School Setting

Choose your role and then choose your school building/district setting before you respond to the scenario above. As you draft your response, please be cognizant of how your setting might affect how you respond to the scenario. Essentially, based on the characteristics listed below, think about what we generally know about these characteristics, and furthermore, how they generally impact schools/districts. How might they affect your decision-making with regards to the scenario, if at all. Be sure to clearly describe your school setting in your response.

Role: Superintendent, Principal, or Assistant Principal
Locale: Urban, Suburban, or Rural
Size: Small District, Medium District, or Large District
Diversity: No Diversity, Some Diversity, or Very Diverse
SES Status: 100% Free and Reduced Lunch (FRL), 50% FRL, or 0% FRL

Chapter 11

Educational Policy

"Note to politicians: Going to school doesn't make you an education expert any more than getting a driver's license makes you a NASCAR driver." ~ *Unknown*

Introduction

I have used the phrase "in the trenches" before in this book, and I find the analogy of soldiers fighting a war while officers send orders from afar quite apt to our battle as school leaders and teachers dealing with policymakers. quite apt, and extremely troubling indeed. Admittedly, before 2015, I was not actively involved or well-informed when it came to educational policy at the federal and state levels. However, after being named the *Assistant Principal of the Year* (APOY) in the State of Ohio, I was exposed firsthand to the importance of advocacy and staying abreast of educational policy, through my experiences with the National Association of Secondary School Principals (NASSP). Due to the fact that I was named the APOY in the State of Ohio and nominated for the APOY in the United States, I had the opportunity to visit Washington, D.C. and spend time on Capitol Hill, advocating for our nation's educators and school leaders. This afforded me the opportunity both to speak on Capitol Hill and to spend considerable time discussing key issues affecting the PreK-12 educational setting with Congressmen, Congresswomen, State Senators (representing several states), and their Educational Policy advisors/teams. This experience was eye-opening, to say the least. Although previously I had paid only slight attention to the political landscape and educational policy as it applied to the PreK-12 educational setting, after this experience I became much more involved, and regularly advocated on behalf of my stakeholders: students, staff, parents, community members and business owners.

Quite simply, after this experience with NASSP, I realized how easily you can access such individuals (i.e., Congressmen, Congresswomen, Senators, and their Educational Policy advisors/committees) and furthermore, just how important it is for practitioners to inform these elected officials of how the policies that they vote on affect the work we do on a daily basis "in the trenches." I also found that, unfortunately, many of the educational policy advisors are typically fresh out of law school with no practitioner experience in <u>any</u> workplace setting, let alone experience in the educational setting. This was troublesome to say the least. Thus, I found that in addition to advocating, I was doing a lot of teaching on Capitol Hill. I found the best approach was to not assume that anyone I was meeting with knew anything about the Bills[38] I was meeting with them to discuss. With this approach in mind, I would first carefully and clearly outline many of the Bills I was advocating for (or against), before I shared how the Bill directly affected our stakeholders, namely students. What I am getting at here is that one should not assume that folks on Capitol Hill are necessarily well-versed in the Bills they are voting on and how such Bills affect the PreK-12 educational setting across the United States. The same is true at the state and local levels. That is in large part why I have included this chapter.

I contend that it is our duty as school building/district leaders to understand the importance of staying abreast of the educational policies (and proposed Bills) as well as the importance of advocacy (for or against) such Bills, based on how they will ultimately affect our stakeholders. To do otherwise is negligent (at the very least) on our part as school leaders. After all, we, along with our students and staff, are "in the trenches" on a daily basis. So, who better to explain how educational policy affects the PreK-12 educational setting than us (you). I know, I know...you are thinking *how will you carve out the time to do this?* How can you get involved with advocacy in a way that works with your daily schedule? In this chapter I have provided several resources that enable

---

38 A Bill starts either in the House of Representatives (U.S. Congresswomen and Congressmen) or in the Senate (U.S. State Senators). Bills are essentially legislative proposals that, if enacted, carry the force of law (GovTrack, 2017). This is similar to how Bills are passed at the state level as well.

school/district leaders to stay involved with advocacy efforts without a huge time commitment. In order not to overwhelm the reader, I have decided to focus on two organizations I believe are doing an excellent job when it comes to readily informing school building/district leaders with regards to educational policy. The organizations shared within this chapter, including the American Association of School Administrators (AASA) and NASSP, have made information relating to advocacy and educational policy readily and easily accessible. It is my hope that you will use these resources to your advantage and join the advocacy groups mentioned. Our policy makers at the federal, state, and local levels need to hear from you with regards to key issues shaping the Pre-K educational setting. You owe it to your stakeholders to get involved and ensure that the only Bills that are passed and signed into law are those that truly mandate "what is best for students."

Advocacy (and Lobbying)

Now, perhaps more than at any other time in history, it makes sense for school/district leaders to advocate on behalf of their stakeholders: students, staff, parents, community members and business owners. As previously mentioned, school building/district leaders and educators alike are serving in the trenches on a daily basis. Thus, with much urgency, I both challenge and encourage aspiring and practicing school leaders to regularly inform policymakers, with the goal that the said policymakers will make informed decisions when it comes to creating and voting on education policy. I might contend that the best way to do this is to get involved with advocacy efforts with other school building/district leaders (i.e., a collective voice) in relation to the organizations and associations to which you belong (or should belong). In addition, by contacting, and building relationships with, elected officials (i.e., policymakers), one can use such relationships to leverage and influence public policy decisions affecting the educational setting in the United States. In my experience, this should and can happen at the local, state and federal levels. In keeping theme with other chapters in this book, I have provided resources for the federal level with the thought in mind that you will seek out similar information in your respective state (including your locally elected representatives) – to help with this search, please refer to the *State Policy Trends* reported later in this chapter. Now, before we go any further, I believe we must cover the basics of advocating by answering some key questions. *What is advocacy?* and *How does one advocate?* Here is what appears on the NASSP website with regards to *Learning the basics of advocating on behalf of schools and principals* (NASSP, 2017) - some excellent, accurate and very informative content:

> *What is advocacy?*
> Advocacy is organized activism in support of an idea or cause. As an advocate for middle level and high school principals, assistant principals, and aspiring school leaders, you can help focus policy makers' attention on secondary school reform in order to ensure all students graduate from high school, college and career ready.
>
> Advocacy consists of constituents contacting their elected officials about issues that are important to them, and establishing relationships with these legislators. These relationships are then leveraged to influence public policy decisions. By establishing relationships and champions, you encourage public officials to make a commitment to you and all the members of NASSP.
>
> People often ask how advocacy is different from lobbying. Lobbying is an effort to influence the thinking of legislators or other public officials for or against a specific cause or a specific piece of proposed legislation. Advocacy is the promotion of a cause, idea, or policy. In other words, your active support of improved school leadership and of secondary schools is considered advocacy.
>
> *How do I advocate?*
> There are many ways to make your voice heard.
>
> ■ Communicate with your members of Congress
> ■ Establish relationships with lawmakers and congressional staff

Makes sense, right? For clarity, I contend that in every meeting (or interaction) with policy makers, one can advocate and lobby at the same time. That is, though advocacy and lobbying are certainly two different things, in my experience much of my time spent on Capitol Hill would be defined as both advocacy and lobbying, by definition. In essence, in most if not all meetings (and in some cases, phone calls, letters, and emails), I was both attempting to "influence the thinking of legislators" by informing them of the potential effects of a particular Bill, while also promoting policy (some of which was yet to be on the floor – that is, it still needed to be written into a proposed Bill). The section of the NASSP website referenced above provides examples of how you can establish relationships with lawmakers as well as how you can effectively communicate with them. The latter, I believe, is the biggest barrier to principals/superintendents advocating; they often find it difficult to easily access and locate members of Congress. The good news is that NASSP has provided links for both the House and the Senate on their website. They are:

> The United States House of Representatives
> https://www.house.gov

> The United States Senate
> https://www.senate.gov

If you prefer a phone call versus an email/letter, you can also call the U.S. Capitol switchboard at: (202) 224-3121 and simply ask for your Representative or Senator. Easy enough, right?

Finally, with regard to where and how to start advocating, NASSP has clearly broken down best practices for *emailing, phone calls,* and *social media* as it applies to interacting with members of Congress. To this end, I believe this aspect of the NASSP website will be the most helpful to individuals who are new to advocating. For those of you not familiar with the "ins and outs" of Capitol Hill, NASSP has included an overview of *Capitol Hill Basics* such as *How a Bill Becomes a Law, How Committees Work, The Budget and Appropriations Process,* and *Congressional Calendar* (for both the House of Representatives and Senate). You can find this information here: https://nassp.org/advocacy/federal-grassroots-network/advocacy-materials?SSO=true

Other resources include:

Committees of Interest to NASSP: https://nassp.org/advocacy/federal-grassroots-network/advocacy-materials/committees-of-interest-to-nassp

Capitol Hill Glossary: https://nassp.org/advocacy/federal-grassroots-network/advocacy-materials/capitol-hill-glossary

Web Resources: https://nassp.org/advocacy/federal-grassroots-network/advocacy-materials/web-resources

You can visit this portion of the NASSP website in its entirety here: https://nassp.org/advocacy/federal-grassroots-network/advocacy-materials

In addition to NASSP, the American Association of School Administrators (AASA) – The School Superintendents Association, is also actively involved in advocacy efforts. The main difference between the two organizations is that most of the resources shared here from the NASSP are free, regardless of whether or not you are a member, whereas many of the resources from the AASA do require from the AASA do require you to be a member. That being said, I would recommend joining the AASA if you are an aspiring or practicing superintendent/district school leader. To be clear, in layman's terms, NASSP is the middle school/high school assistant principal/principal association and AASA is the school superintendent association. All that being said, much like the NASSP website, AASA has numerous resources for school building/district leaders. As reported on the AASA (2017) website as it relates to *Policy and Advocacy*:

> AASA represents the dreams, educational expertise and concerns of nearly 10,000 local school system leaders to the three branches of the federal government.

> AASA enables the advocacy of its membership by sharing timely information that creates meaning out of the complex issues

surrounding any education policy. AASA members consistently rate AASA's advocacy for the profession of school administration as a top member benefit. Nobody else represents the voices of school superintendents on Capitol Hill. Advocacy is where AASA's voice on education policy comes to life. Every day, whether it is fighting for funding, a better relationship between federal, state and local governments, or for programs that make a difference for children, AASA is standing up for public education in Washington, D.C.

The AASA website breaks down their advocacy section into several subcategories including: (1) Policy and Advocacy Blogs; (2) About Policy and Advocacy; (3) Public Policy Resources; and (4) National Rural Education Advocacy Coalition (NREAC). Two of the blogs in particular are worth highlighting - you can access them here:

The Leading Edge Blog: http://aasa.org/policy-blogs. aspx?blogid=84002#

The New IDEA Blog: http://aasa.org/idea-blog. aspx?blogid=84005

Please note, *The New IDEA Blog* is dedicated to the Individuals with Disabilities Education Improvement Act (IDEA) rather than to "idea" in the general sense.

Additionally, AASA produces the *AASA Legislative Agenda* that goes through a proposal and adoption policy by the *AASA Executive Committee* and *AASA Governing Board.* This gives you a clear breakdown of what AASA supports with regards to federal and state education policy. You can review an example of this here:

2017 AASA Legislative Agenda: http://www.aasa.org/uploaded-Files/Banners/2017%20Legislative%20Agenda%20FINAL.pdf.

In line with the resources shared from the NASSP website with regards to the *What* and the *How,* AASA has a similar section on their website titled *Policy and Legislative Related Websites.* Here you will find much of the same information found on the *Capitol Hill Basics* portion of the NASSP website. You can access this portion of the AASA website here: http://aasa.org/Content.aspx?id=854. I particularly like the *Additional Information* portion of this webpage. More specifically, the *Best Evidence Encyclopedia* link, where one can access reliable reviews of research-proven educational programs.

If I were to report one advantage of the AASA website over the NASSP website, it would be the AASA webpage focused on *State Policy Trends*. Here, school/district leaders can easily access the gubernatorial elections, legislative trend reports, and state of the state addresses. Thus, one can easily find information pertaining to educational policy in their respective state by utilizing the resources on this webpage. You can access this section of the AASA website here: http://aasa.org/content. aspx?id=31794.

A great way to get involved quickly at AASA is to attend the annual Legislative Advocacy Conference in Washington, D.C., presented by AASA in conjunction with the Association of School Business Officials International (ASBO). This conference is an all-out full blitz of advocacy on Capitol Hill, and the lineup of individuals you will hear from and engage with during the conference is invaluable. For example, at the 2017 conference, such individuals include Liz King, the Director of Education Policy, Leadership Conference on Civil and Human Rights, Mary Kusler, Senior Director, Center for Advocacy, National Education Association, and David Cleary, Chief of Staff, to name a few. To see an example agenda and learn more about this conference, see: http://aasa. org/legconf.aspx.

Finally, if you are an aspiring or practicing school building/district leader in the rural setting, AASA has made an asserted commitment to rural education in the United States. The NREAC is made up of both state and national organizations concerned about educational opportunities for students who live in rural areas of the United States. Numerous resources exist on this section of the AASA website. You can access this information here: http://aasa.org/content.aspx?id=17140.

In addition to the NASSP and AASA website resources, I encourage you to join the advocacy groups of both organizations. Again, much as with the website resources, you can join the NASSP advocacy group regardless of whether you are a member or not, whereas you must be a member of AASA to join their advocacy group.

Advocacy Groups to Join

The following advocacy groups will allow you to stay abreast of advocacy opportunities as well as keep you informed of the federal (and state) legislation that affects your daily work as a school leader.

NASSP *Federal Grassroots Network*
https://nassp.org/advocacy

Via the NASSP website and *The Principal's Legislative Action Center*, you can voice concerns by utilizing their easily searchable and accessible legislative database found here: https://nassp.org/advocacy/principals-legislative-action-center-(plac).

Likewise, in addition to locating officials on the *The Principal's Legislative Action Center*, you can locate advocacy campaigns, legislation, and sign up to receive alerts (I would do this now to stay in the loop regarding federal policy). You can learn about NASSP's advocacy goals here: https://youtu.be/QPk8G1xjJZw.

In addition, I highly recommend joining NASSP's Federal Grassroots Network. You can do so here: https://echo4.bluehornet.com/form/100113/fgn/4.

Here is what NASSP writes about their Federal Grassroots Network (NASSP, 2017):

> Take your advocacy efforts to the next level. As a school leader, you advocate on behalf of your students and staff every day with the decisions you make. We need you to share your expertise and on-the-ground experiences with policymakers so they are better informed when making decisions on education policy. If advocacy is especially important to you, one way for you get more involved is to join the NASSP Federal Grassroots Network!

NASSP's Federal Grassroots Network brings together individuals who want to build close relationships with their members of Congress to inform them about how policies they create in Washington impact education in their districts and states. Members of the FGN can tap into the following resources:

- A community of advocates who commit to regularly meeting with their federal representatives to discuss state and federal policies that will benefit schools and students nationwide
- A monthly FGN email newsletter highlighting recent changes in federal education policy
- Weekly advocacy update blog posts on the School of Thought blog with the latest news and resources regarding federal education policy
- The opportunity to attend the annual NASSP Advocacy Conference, a unique event that brings like-minded education professionals together to share ideas and discuss the top education policy issues of the day
- Resources to become more effective advocates at all levels of government, including a basic guide on advocating on behalf of schools and principals

There has never been a more crucial time for you to voice your insight on effective school leadership and education policy. Join NASSP's Federal Grassroots Network today!

Additionally, I suggest visiting NASSP's *School of Thought* blog here: http://blog.nassp.org/microblog/principals-policy/.

NASSP also hosts an Advocacy Conference in Washington, D.C. This conference provides opportunities for school leaders to serve on panel discussions, attend a briefing, and meet and interact with congressmen and congresswomen, state senators, etc. You can learn more about this annual conference at: https://nassp.org/advocacy/federal-grassroots-network/nassp-advocacy-conference.

For those of you who just do not know where to start, visit the *basic guide on advocating on behalf of schools and principals* site at: https://nassp.org/advocacy/federal-grassroots-network/advocacy-materials.

Finally, here are some names you should know and become familiar with regarding advocacy at NASSP:

Amanda Karhuse – Director of Advocacy at NASSP.
Follow on Twitter at: @akarhuse

Zachary Scott – Manager of Advocacy at NASSP
Follow on Twitter at: @zachscott33

AASA *Legislative Corps* **and** *Advocacy Network*
http://www.aasa.org/content.aspx?id=104

In order to become more familiar with the *AASA Legislative Corps,* I recommend reading a brief overview here: http://www.aasa.org/uploadedFiles/Publications/Newsletters/Legislative_Corps_Weekly_Report/LegCorpsAugust17.pdf.

The *AASA Legislative Corps* allows you to access the *AASA Legislative Corps Weekly Report.* Within this report, you have access to a summary of all Washington news with an impact on public schools. Furthermore, you are encouraged to participate in advocacy and respond to occasional alerts, with an emphasis on voicing concerns to your own House and Senate members. Here, AASA creates universal emails that are easily accessed and personally tailored, and include key information as to how your House and Senate members vote will help or hurt schools. An example of the *AASA Legislative Corps Weekly Report* can be found here: http://www.aasa.org/uploadedFiles/Publications/Newsletters/Legislative_Corps_Weekly_Report/LegCorpsAugust17.pdf.

I personally have found the policy emails from AASA, namely the *AASA Legislative Corps,* to be very informative, timely, and to provide meaningful information as it applies to federal and state educational policy. Likewise, AASA Executive Director Dan Domenech regularly sends emails focused on advocacy. These emails usually contain advocacy and policy efforts aligned with the mission of AASA.

Finally, here are some names you should know and become familiar with regarding advocacy at AASA:

> Noelle Ellerson – Associate Executive Director of Policy and Advocacy at AASA
> Follow on Twitter at: @noellerson
>
> Sasha Pudelski – Assistant Director of Policy and Advocacy at AASA
> Follow on Twitter at: @spudelski
>
> Leslie Finnan – Senior Legislative Analyst at AASA
> Follow on Twitter at: @lesliefinnan

Hashtags to Follow

The following hashtags will connect you to the active advocacy efforts of school leaders throughout the nation. I have excluded specific hashtags such as ESSA (#ESSA), etc. Nevertheless, such hashtags exist and are what I consider to be "hot topic", i.e., more time sensitive. The hashtags shared here are usually attached to such "hot topic" hashtags and therefore should connect you to the same individuals.

#PrincipalsAdvocate
#PrincipalsinAction
#LovePublicEducation
#EduPolicy
#ThankAPrincipal

In summation, there is no doubt that the power of AASA (and NASSP) is being felt on Capitol Hill. Advocacy is an important aspect of effective school building/district leadership in the 21st Century. Due to developing and readily accessible technology, this type of educational policy information is increasingly is increasingly at the very fingertips of our nation's school building/district leaders. Furthermore, advocacy has never been easier, as several federal, state, and local organizations have utilized such technology and made advocacy efforts a streamlined process. This process includes strategies such as allowing individuals to provide electronic signatures with the click of a mouse, creating and sharing well-written and well thought out templated blanket emails (where school building/district leaders just plug in their personalized information), the utilization of hashtags alongside a slew of social media outlets (e.g., Twitter, Facebook, LinkedIn, Instagram, etc.), and annual conferences focused on getting school building/district leaders face-to-face with their representatives on Capitol Hill – just to name a few. If you are not currently involved or informed with regards to educational policy, it is not too late to get started. This chapter has aimed to provide you with an array of resources to assist all aspiring and practicing school building/district leaders in beginning to advocate for their stakeholders by numerous methods. Thus, I encourage you to join this coalition of school building/district leaders to ensure that decisions being made on Capitol Hill (and in your respective state) are made with one thought in mind, "what is best for students" – and in more recent years, might we add "what is best for public education?" as public education is seemingly under attack in the United States.

Finally, I cannot conclude this chapter without sharing information about a breakthrough documentary film my friend Chris Kay made titled *Of By For*. For anyone new to the American Political System in general, this documentary is an unbiased and in-depth analysis of the American Political System in the 21st Century, focused on political corruption. You might just be surprised by how much influence the *insiders* and *special interests* have in shaping the American Political System. You can access the *Of By For* website and trailer here: http://ofbyforfilm.com.

Enjoy!

Reflection

Questions for Practicing and Aspiring School Leaders

1. What steps will you take to ensure you stay up to date with the latest Bills (and educational policy in general) at the federal, state and local levels?
2. How will you aim to effectively advocate on behalf of your stakeholders: students, staff, parents, community members and business owners?
3. As a school district/building leader, what organizations might you join to stay abreast of current educational policy at the federal, state, and local levels?
4. As a school district/building leader, how might you use social media (and hashtags) to stay informed of hot topics (i.e., what is trending) with regards to educational policy?
5. What is the difference between advocacy and lobbying? Furthermore, how will you ensure you actively participate in both by all possible means (e.g., emails, letters, phone calls, Tweets, face-to-face meetings, etc.) as a school district/building leader?

Problem-based Scenario

The Uninformed Policy Maker

As a building (or district) school leader, you have recently been named the *State Administrator (or Superintendent) of the Year*. As part of this recognition, you have been invited to Washington, D.C. to advocate on Capitol Hill with all of the nation's school (or district) leaders who received this award in their respective states. After arriving in Washington, D.C., you are eager to meet with your Congressmen, Congresswomen, and State Senators, as well as their Educational Policy Advisors and Committees. However, after your first two meetings, it has become blatantly apparent that many of the individuals you have met with thus far are not well-versed in the Bills and/or policies you are advocating/lobbying for (or against). Furthermore, you realize your time with these individuals is short. That is, between the time you meet with them and the time you get your picture taken with them, there is a very short period in which to inform these individuals of how vital their vote is with respect to a particular Bill/policy, and perhaps most importantly, how the Bill/policy will affect your stakeholders. You have four more meetings scheduled. Please share how your approach might change with regard to the next four meetings based on the information shared within this scenario? What strategies might you use to build a relationship when meeting said individual while also sharing the necessary and key information as it applies to the Bill/policy, and how it will affect your stakeholders?

In addition, how might you follow up the first two meetings that have already happened, in order to share vital information you did not have time to share during the face-to-face meetings? Along these same lines, and thinking a little further ahead, how will you follow up the remaining (and future) meetings in order to ensure continued correspondence with such individuals? Finally, you are well aware that as a school building/district leader you will not be able to regularly fly to Washington, D.C. to meet face-to-face with these individuals. Nonetheless, you want to stay involved with advocacy efforts in any way, shape, or form that you can. Please share what steps you will plan to take in order to continue your advocacy efforts and stay abreast of educational policy at the federal, state, and local levels from your post at your school/district?

Choose Your School Setting

Choose your role and then choose your school building/district setting before you respond to the scenario above. As you draft your response, please be cognizant of how your setting might affect how you respond to the scenario. Essentially, based on the characteristics listed, think about what we generally know about these characteristics, and furthermore, how they generally impact schools/districts. How might they affect your decision-making with regards to the scenario, if at all? Be sure to clearly describe your school setting in your response.

Role: Superintendent, Principal, or Assistant Principal
Locale: Urban, Suburban, or Rural
Size: Small District, Medium District, or Large District
Diversity: No Diversity, Some Diversity, or Very Diverse
SES Status: 100% Free and Reduced Lunch (FRL), 50% FRL, or 0% FRL

Chapter 12

School Law

"Law is reason, free from passion." ~ *Aristotle*

Introduction

The aim of this chapter is to examine (albeit briefly) school law, which may affect you as a school building/district leader from several angles, and in some cases may determine whether or not you keep your job. Now, to cover school law in the amount of depth necessary for both aspiring and practicing school building/district leaders would require a book (or a series of books) dedicated only to school law. Nonetheless, that kind of depth is not intended in this chapter; rather the goal here is to introduce to you some of my general thoughts regarding school law, while highlighting what I believe is important to know about school law both historically and in the 21st Century, and to provide several resources for you to reference. In essence, my aim is to provide you with a "snapshot" of school law as it applies to school leadership, in general terms. As we know, understanding school law is extremely important to effective school leadership. Thus, I aim to offer key information I believe will be valuable to you as an aspiring or practicing school building/district leader. Finally, I have included a few books I highly recommend as it applies to school law. Enjoy!

School Law

Having taught school law in graduate programs for several years now, I am often conflicted by how to squeeze enough content into one semester to adequately prepare aspiring school leaders to be well-versed in all (or most) things school law. In fact, when I have been asked by colleagues what I teach in school law, I usually reply by saying, "enough for my students to keep their jobs and stay out of jail." Although I am only somewhat joking when I say this, in a lot of ways, it is true. Essentially, over the years, because of the vast amount of information that needs to be covered in a school law course, I have often felt that such courses should be split into two (i.e., *School Law I* and *School Law II*). Nonetheless, I have found it to be effective to approach the content of such a course with four main goals in mind: (1) to thoroughly review historical court cases and decisions (federal and state) that I deem to be significant to the PreK-12 educational setting; (2) to thoroughly review the current federal and state laws as they apply to the PreK-12 educational setting; (3) to review ethics as they apply to school leadership (refer to chapter five); and (4) to explain the role and structure of courts in the United States (e.g., judicial districts, regional circuits, U.S. court of appeals, district courts, etc.). This approach has been effective thus far in that at the conclusion of each course, I am confident my students will "keep their jobs and stay out of jail." Thus, I will approach this chapter with the same intent. However, and perhaps worth noting, I will not adequately cover all of the content I would present to my graduate students in their entire school law course. Nonetheless, I will touch briefly on several important items, all pertaining to school law.

Historical Court Cases and the Schoolhouse

Although one might rightfully argue and debate as to what court cases should be included in this section, I contend that the cases highlighted here had a significant impact in shaping the PreK-12 educational setting in some way, shape, or form. The cases presented in this chapter are what many consider to be landmark court cases and are often cited in case law[39]. Nonetheless, in keeping with the promised snapshot approach to the sections in this chapter, I will withhold the in-depth details and discussion surrounding each court case. Rather, I will outline each case, and elaborate on how each connects to the PreK-12 educational setting, focusing on the significance (what was at stake), outcome (decision), amendment

---

39 Case law refers to the process of using and citing a law established by the outcome of former cases to support a more recent case.

involved (if any), and reflection statement (to get you reflecting on how the court case/decision might apply to you as an aspiring or practicing school building/district leader). Please note that the court cases are in no particular order, however, I have tried to organize them with some kind of flow from one to the next. Although I have provided a snapshot for each court case, I encourage you to research each of them in greater detail.

Pierce v. Society of Sisters, 268 US. 510 (1925)

> Significance: Should parents (and guardians) have the right to choose how and where their children are educated (i.e., private schools, public schools, etc.)?
>
> Outcome: The state has the right to ensure children receive a proper education and regulate all schools; however, parents (and guardians) have the right and duty to choose the appropriate education preparation for their children.
>
> Amendment Involved: 14th Amendment
>
> Reflection Statement: Might this affect how you lead in the 21st Century with the charter school movement in full swing across the nation? Does it make you think of best practices and "customer service"? Parents have options, and many of those options mean money leaving your school building/district.

Brown v. Hot, Sexy, and Safer Productions, 68 F. 3d 525 (1st Cir. 1995)

> Significance: Do parents have rights once their children enter the schoolhouse doors? In this case, no option existed for parents to remove their child from a mandatory school-wide function (e.g., sex education presentation).
>
> Outcome: Parents (Brown) lost in federal district court and in the U.S. Court of Appeals for the 1st Circuit. The Supreme Court refused to review the 1st Circuit's ruling.
>
> Amendment Involved: 1st Amendment
>
> Reflection Statement: Regardless of the outcome of this case, should you not always give parents as many options as possible simply because it is best practice? As I tell my students, sure the parents lost the case, but do you really want to be involved in

such a court case? I recommend that you give parents choices, perhaps especially when it comes to items such as sexual education. If not, you just might end up being named in a court case we study in our school law courses someday.

Dixon v. Alabama, 294 F .2d 150 (5th Cir. 1961)

Significance: Can schools act *in loco parentis*[40] to discipline or expel their students in the education setting? Essentially, can students be disciplined without due process in the education setting?

Outcome: Students cannot be disciplined without due process, including notice of their alleged violations and an opportunity to be heard.

Amendment Involved: 14th Amendment

Reflection Statement: When it comes to suspending and/or expelling students, due process is required.

Tinker v. Des Moines ISD, 393 U.S. 503 (1969)

Significance: Do students lose their rights to free speech once they enter the schoolhouse doors? In this case, a planned, peaceful and silent protest (e.g., wearing armbands) against the Vietnam War.

Outcome: The Supreme Court ruled in favor of the students, agreeing that students' free speech rights should be protected and that students do not lose their constitutional rights when entering the schoolhouse.

Amendment Involved: 1st Amendment

Reflection Statement: So long as the free speech activities do not disrupt the learning environment, students have free speech rights (and all constitutional rights) in the schoolhouse.

Bethel v. Fraser, 478 U.S. 675, 682 (1986)

Significance: Can a public school punish a student for giving a lewd, indecent, and obscene speech at a school assembly?

---

40 The term *in loco parentis* is Latin for "in place of a parent."

Outcome: The constitutional rights of students at the public schoolhouse are not automatically coextensive with the rights of adults. In this case, The Supreme Court held that suspension of the student did not violate the 1st Amendment.

Amendment Involved: 1st Amendment

Reflection Statement: How will you aim to prevent students from giving lewd, indecent, or obscene speeches at the schoolhouse? That is, what checks and balances will you have in place to deter this type of speech/behavior?

Morse v. Frederick, 127 S. Ct. 2618 (2007)

Significance: Do school authorities violate the 1st Amendment (namely the free speech clause) when they prevent students from expressing views that may be interpreted as promoting illegal drug use?

Outcome: Morse (the principal) won in the U.S. District Court of Alaska. That is, it was determined that Frederick's (the student) action was not protected by the 1st Amendment. However, the U.S. Court of Appeals for the Ninth Circuit reversed the ruling and held that Frederick's banner (that read "Bong Hits 4 Jesus," held up by Frederick and other students as the Olympic torch passed through town) was constitutionally protected. The U.S. Supreme Court granted certiorari.[41]

Amendment Involved: 1st Amendment

Reflection Statement: Might you as a principal restrict the free speech of students at a school-supervised event when the speech is reasonably viewed as promoting illegal drug use? In this case, regardless of the outcome, the court supported schools taking steps and safeguards with regards to speech that can reasonably be regarded as encouraging illegal drug use.

---

41 Certiorari refers to a writ or order by which a higher court reviews a decision of a lower court. If "granted" (as mentioned in the *Morse v. Frederick* case), it essentially means the higher court has reviewed the decision of the lower court and agrees with that decision.

Hazelwood School District v. Kuhlmeier, 484 U.S. 260 (1988)

Significance: Are the 1ˢᵗ Amendment rights of students violated when school officials prevent the release and publication of particular items (in this case, articles in a school newspaper)?

Outcome: The 8th Circuit ruled that the students' 1ˢᵗ Amendment free speech rights were indeed violated when the principal prohibited the publishing of certain articles deemed to be inappropriate in the school newspaper. However, the Supreme Court reversed the decision of the 8ᵗʰ Circuit, and ruled in favor of the school principal.

Amendment Involved: 1ˢᵗ Amendment

Reflection Statement: This case and outcome is an excellent example of why school leaders can delegate tasks, but cannot delegate responsibility. Should you ensure that all school publications are approved by you before going to print? After all, everything should stop at your desk. Right? This does not mean micromanaging, but, as Ronald Reagan once said, "trust but verify."

Engel v. Vitale, 370 U.S. 421 (1962)

Significance: Can state officials compose an official school prayer and encourage its recitation in public schools?

Outcome: It is unconstitutional for state officials to compose an official school prayer and encourage its recitation in public schools.

Amendment Involved: 1ˢᵗ Amendment

Reflection Statement: How might this outcome apply to the Pledge of Allegiance? Or perhaps requirements for your Fellowship of Christian Athletes (FCA)?

Clear Creek ISD v. Jones, 977 F.2d 963 (1992)

Significance: Although state school officials (as mentioned in the previous case) cannot compose and/or encourage recitation of prayer in public schools, can students vote on their own account whether or not to have another student recite prayers during school (in this case at a graduation ceremony)?

Outcome: 5th Circuit of Appeals ruled that it is in fact constitutional for students to vote on having prayers during graduation ceremonies. However, the invocation should be nonsectarian and non-proselytizing (does not represent a specific religion and/or try to convert).

Amendment Involved: 1st Amendment

Reflection Statement: Will you allow prayers (invocation prayers and benediction prayers) at your graduation ceremony if they are led by students? Why? Why not?

Santa Fe ISD v. Doe, 530 U.S. 290 (2000)

Significance: Is student-led, student-initiated prayer at high school football games a violation of the 1st Amendment?

Outcome: A policy permitting student-led, student-initiated prayer at high school football games does in fact violate the 1st Amendment.

Amendment Involved: 1st Amendment

Reflection Statement: How might this outcome apply to prayers (e.g., the Lord's Prayer – Matthew 6:9-13) by your football team (led by your football coach) before each football game?

New Jersey v. T.L.O., 469 U.S. 325 (1985)

Significance: Does the 4th Amendment's prohibition (exclusionary rule) on unreasonable searches and seizures apply to searches conducted by public school officials?

Outcome: Yes, the 4th Amendment does apply to searches conducted by public school officials. However, school officials can conduct reasonable warrantless searches of students under their authority, notwithstanding the probable cause standards that would normally apply to searches under the 4th Amendment. Thus, the court did rule that in this case, the search by the assistant principal was reasonable given the circumstances.

Amendment Involved: 4th Amendment

Reflection Statement: How will you determine when (and if) a search of a student's possessions is reasonable?

Safford Unified School District v. Redding, 557 U.S. 364 (2009)

Significance: Does the 4th Amendment prohibit school officials from strip searching students suspected of possessing drugs? In addition, are school officials individually liable for damages in a lawsuit filed under 42 U.S.C. Section 1983?

Outcome: Searches must be reasonably related to the objectives of the search and not excessively intrusive, taking into consideration the age and gender of the student as well as the nature of the infraction. In this case, The Supreme Court held that school officials did not have sufficient suspicion to strip search the student. Furthermore, it was held that school officials were not individually liable for damages in a lawsuit filed under 42 U.S.C. Section 1983.

Amendment Involved: 4th Amendment

Reflection Statement: Might you think twice before strip searching a student?

Brown v. Board of Education, 347 U.S. 483 (1954)

Significance: Are state laws establishing separate public schools for black and white students unconstitutional?

Outcome: Court declared state laws establishing separate public schools for black and white students to be unconstitutional. This decision overturned the *Plessy v. Ferguson* decision from 1896, which had allowed state-sponsored segregation as it applied to public schools. The case is infamous, as it was a major victory for the Civil Rights Movement, stating that "separate educational facilities are inherently unequal." Worth noting, the outcome of this case did not spell out methods for ending racial segregation in schools. Furthermore, *Brown II*, 349 U.S. 294 (1955) only hinted at such methods, demanding that states desegregate schools "with all deliberate speed."

Amendment Involved: 14th Amendment

Reflection Statement: Are schools in the United States/21st Century still segregated? You might be surprised...read this article by McLaughlin (2017): http://www.cnn.com/2017/03/14/ us/cleveland-mississippi-school-desegregation-settlement/ index.html

Gebser v. Lago Vista ISD, 524 U.S. 274 (1998)

Significance: Are schools/school officials liable for what they do not know? That is, as it applies to this case, can a federally funded educational program or activity be required, under Title IX of the Education Amendments of 1972, to pay sexual harassment damages to a student who was involved in a secret relationship with a member of its staff?

Outcome: The Supreme Court ruled the answer is no. Essentially, The Supreme Court held that schools/school officials must be aware of forbidden conduct and there must be evidence that a school deliberately failed to respond in a proper manner.

Amendment Involved: Title IX of the Educational Amendments of 1972

Reflection Statement: What official procedures for reporting sexual harassment are in place at your school/district? What anti-harassment policies exist in your school/district? Please note that both are required by federal law.

Federal and State Law

Again, I will aim to point you in the right direction and highlight some federal laws you should be cognizant of as an aspiring/practicing school leader. With regards to state law, as they differ from state-to-state, I encourage you to become well-versed in your respective state laws. That is, it is vital for you to know the laws in the state in which you plan to practice as a school leader or are currently practicing as a school leader. In the 21st Century, most of this information (if not all) is easily accessible and readily available online. Likewise, most state departments of education and/ or state school board associations do an excellent job of maintaining such information (i.e., updates and the like). For example, you can easily access the Oklahoma State Department of Education's 2016 School Law Book (PDF format) via the Oklahoma State School Boards Association (2017) website at: https://www.ossba.org/wp-content/uploads/2015/11/2016-School-Law-book.pdf. In addition, one can purchase books focused on state school law. For example, if you aspire to practice or are practicing in the State of New York, you can purchase *School Law (New York School Law) 35th Edition* at: https://www.amazon.com/School-Law-New-York/dp/1632811642 or, if you are in the State of California you could purchase *California School Law 3rd Edition* at: https://www.amazon.com/California-School-Law-Frank-Kemerer/dp/0804785155. In addition to these types of resources, the United States Department of Education (2017) has created a webpage dedicated to a contact list of state departments of education (as well as other educational agencies) at: https://www2.ed.gov/about/contacts/state/index.html?src=ov. Again, I could go on and on here, but ultimately, it will be up to you to seek out the best resources and contacts for your respective state laws. Nonetheless, federal law affects us all. Thus, I will highlight several federal laws (with links) that directly affect your responsibilities as a school leader on a daily basis. Obviously, I do not plan to cover all of the federal laws affecting your work. Nevertheless, just as you should research and know the laws in your state, you should also research (use the links provided) and know the federal laws governing our nation's schools. Please note, when researching and learning about federal law, do so with the thought in mind that in the United States, the federal role in education is somewhat limited due to the 10th Amendment. Thus, a lot of the policy affecting the PreK-12 educational setting is decided at the state (and local) levels. Nevertheless, that is certainly not to say that federal policy does not affect the PreK-12 educational setting. In fact, I believe we all know better. The links provided here are derived from the *Law & Guidance* section of the United States Department of Education (2017) website:

Every Student Succeeds Act (ESSA). https://www.ed.gov/essa?src=policy

Individuals with Disabilities Act (IDEA). https://sites.ed.gov/idea/?src=policy-page and https://www.gpo.gov/fdsys/pkg/USCODE-2011-title20/pdf/USCODE-2011-title20-chap33.pdf

Civil Rights.

> *Disability discrimination.* https://www2.ed.gov/policy/rights/guid/ocr/disability.html

> *Protecting students with disabilities (Section 504 FAQ).* https://www2.ed.gov/about/offices/list/ocr/504faq.html

> *Sex discrimination (Title IX of the Education Amendments of 1972).*
> https://www2.ed.gov/policy/rights/guid/ocr/sex.html

> *Race and national origin discrimination (Title VI of Civil Rights Act of 1964).*
> https://www2.ed.gov/policy/rights/guid/ocr/racenational.html

Additionally, the following links are derived from the *Federal Laws, Regulations and Policy Guidance* section of the United Federation of Teachers (2017) website:

> *Family Educational Rights and Privacy Act (FERPA).* http://www.uft.org/teaching/federal-laws-regulations-and-policy-guidance#ferpa

> *Protection of Pupil Rights Amendment (PPRA).* http://www.uft.org/teaching/federal-laws-regulations-and-policy-guidance#ppra

Court structure in the United States.

In order to provide a general snapshot and introduction to the role and structure of the different courts in the United States, I have included a few links below derived from the *Court Role and Structure* section of the United States Courts (2017) website:

Court role and structure.
http://www.uscourts.gov/about-federal-courts/court-role-and-structure

Supreme court. https://www.supremecourt.gov

Courts of appeals. http://www.uscourts.gov/about-federal-courts/court-role-and-structure/about-us-courts-appeals

District courts.
http://www.uscourts.gov/about-federal-courts/court-role-and-structure

U.S. federal courts circuit map.
http://www.uscourts.gov/sites/default/files/u.s._federal_courts_circuit_map_1.pdf

It is my hope that after reading this section you now are familiar with some of the historical court cases (and decisions) shaping the work you do (or will do) on a daily basis in the PreK-12 educational setting. In addition, it is my hope that you have a better idea of where to locate information pertaining to key federal and state laws, and the court structure in the United States.

Recommended Books on School Law

The Law of Schools, Students, and Teachers by Kern Alexander and M. David Alexander

School Law and The Public Schools: A Practical Guide for Educational Leaders by Nathan L. Essex

Law and Ethics in Educational Leadership by David L. Stader

Reflection

Questions for Practicing and Aspiring School Leaders

1. As a school district/building leader, what steps will you take to ensure you stay up to date with school laws at the federal, state, and local levels?

2. As a school district/building leader, how will you aim to regularly inform your staff (this includes board members if you are a district leader) of current and recent changes to educational law?

3. As a school district/building leader, why might you believe it is vital for you to understand the historical court cases/decisions (such as shared in this chapter) affecting the PreK-12 educational setting?

4. As a school district/building leader, why might you believe knowing where to readily access school law information (i.e., federal, state and local) is key for your success as a school leader?

5. As a school district/building leader, why might you believe it is important for you to clearly understand the role and structure of the different courts in the United States?

Problem-based Scenario

"Do what is right, not what is easy." ~ Unknown

As an effective building (or district) school leader, you always attend Individualized Education Program (IEP) meetings in your school building. This particular IEP meeting includes the student, the parents of the student, several of the student's teachers, and the student's intervention specialist. Now, before we go on here, if you are choosing to be a district school leader for this scenario, let's assume for all intents and purposes that you have chosen to attend this particular IEP meeting of your own accord. However, note that most superintendents do not attend IEP meetings at the building level, and unfortunately, not all school building leaders (assistant principals and principals) attend IEP meetings – that is why "effective" was included at the beginning of the scenario, because effective school building leaders do in fact attend all IEP meetings in their respective school. That being said, at this particular IEP meeting, as the meeting progresses, it has become apparent to you that the student's IEP goals have not been reviewed, evaluated and/or updated from the previous academic school year. Furthermore, after a little investigating into the students IEP file/folder, it appears the intervention specialist just copied and pasted the IEP goals from the previous annual IEP meeting/past academic school year. You are aware that, by law, a student's IEP must be reviewed and evaluated each year as to whether or not the student is making progress towards their annual goals, and that new goals should be developed for the next academic school year based on this review and analysis of the student's present level of performance. Please share what you would do in this particular scenario. That is, carefully explain and lay out what steps you will take in order to ensure the IEP is compliant with the law. In doing so, please be cognizant that as the school/district administrative representative at this IEP meeting, you are required to, among other things, ensure the IEP is legally compliant. In addition, by signing your name to the IEP, you are indicating you were present at the meeting and approve the IEP/notes from the meeting.

Choose Your School Setting

Choose your role and then choose your school building/district setting before you respond to the scenario above. As you draft your response, please be cognizant of how your setting might affect how you respond to the scenario. Essentially, based on the characteristics listed below, think about what we know about these characteristics, and furthermore, how they generally impact schools/districts. How might they affect your decision-making with regards to the scenario, if at all? Be sure to clearly describe your school setting in your response.

Role: Superintendent, Principal, or Assistant Principal
Locale: Urban, Suburban, or Rural
Size: Small District, Medium District, or Large District
Diversity: No Diversity, Some Diversity, or Very Diverse
SES Status: 100% Free and Reduced Lunch (FRL), 50% FRL, or 0% FRL

Chapter 13

School Finance and Human Resources

Introduction

Just as with the previous chapter focused on school law (see chapter 12), a book (or series of books) could easily be dedicated to the two areas of school finance and human resources. Thus, the intent of this chapter is merely to provide you with a "snapshot" of these two areas, in general terms. In addition, I approached this chapter in a very reflective manner. That is, reflecting on my own experiences teaching each of these areas as a professor in educational leadership preparation programs in the higher education setting, as well as sharing my general thoughts and opinions based on my own practitioner experience in the PreK-12 educational setting. School finance and human resources practices can either positively or negatively affect your school building/district, and how you approach both is extremely important as it relates to effective school leadership and the success (or failure) of a given school building/district. In the area of human resources practices, school building/district leaders throughout the nation have become very inventive and downright innovative in how/where they have advertised jobs, their hiring processes, and what they implement effectively to retain staff. Likewise, school building/district leaders throughout our nation have become novel in how they utilize school funding formulas to their advantage, by becoming well-versed in exactly how their schools are funded at the local, state, and federal levels. In this chapter, I have aimed to highlight some of these innovative practices, as well as what I consider to be bad practices, in the areas of school finance and human resources.

Human Resources

Due to the fact that I am currently co-authoring a book titled *Human Resources: A Practical Guide for School Leaders,* due to be released by Rowman & Littlefield sometime in 2018-19, for this book and this section, I will aim to reflect briefly on some human resources practices (both good and bad) I have experienced as they apply to the building and district levels. Enjoy!

Please note: the following story has been somewhat altered to protect the identity of the individuals within the story. I once sat in the office of a veteran human resources director as part of a committee that was focused on how the district could better retain teachers and administrators in said district, as well as how we could improve the school climate and school culture. The district paid extremely well, well above most districts in the area, yet they experienced what many would consider a high rate of turnover at all levels, from teachers, to school building administrators, to district office personnel (however, worth noting here, never the human resources director), to the superintendent. During our conversation which focused on strategies to reduce the high turnover in the district, we discussed how we could better retain teachers, and possible ways to improve school climate and culture throughout the district. I discussed the idea of "celebrating everything and celebrating often." This particular aspect of the conversation led me to highlight that one of the director's administrators had recently been named *State Administrator of the Year,* and how that should have been celebrated. His/her quick response, much to my surprise and dismay, was, "we do not like to celebrate personal achievements in our school district." I will refrain from using the actual district name, but he/she followed that statement with, "It's the (insert city of the school district) way." As our conversation went on, it was apparent that the high turnover and negative school climate and culture that he/she called "the (insert city of the school district) way," started right in the human resources department. It was at this point in the conversation that I began to wonder who was responsible for evaluating the human resources director in this particular district? As I would find, no one was really performing such evaluations, and, to make matters worse, the current superintendent was on his/her way out. This deeply saddened me, as it became apparent that this was the root of the problem, and much of the district's difficulties in retaining teachers, and the school climate and culture emanated directly from his/her department (as well as other aspects/parts of the district office). As a result of being on this committee, I completed additional research and was shocked to learn just how seldomly/rarely they are evaluated. This led me to the decision to co-author a book on human resources, as it applies to school leaders at both the building level and district level. The story shared here aims to highlight just how much human resources directors and departments can affect areas such as retaining employees and the school climate and culture of a given school district. That is, when there is a large amount of turnover in a district (or a school building), there is usually a reason for it. Often, I found, "where there is smoke, there is fire." Furthermore, if the one constant is the human resources director and a small handful of district office employees (as with the district/story shared here), it may become apparent where the real issue is. I want to share some snapshot practices for school/district school leaders with regards to human resources, not only from a hiring standpoint, but also from the standpoint of how to best retain teachers and how such practices tie into school climate and culture.

Hiring. When it comes to hiring school employees, there are a few items I believe are worth noting in relation to human resources best practices. The practices shared are based upon my own experiences and I am sure we could add more to the list. Furthermore, I did not elaborate on each, as this type of information will be in the human resources book I am writing. Nevertheless, I believe you will find many of them are common sense. However, they would not be included in this chapter if they were the norm. In actuality, I have found many of these practices are not the norm at all. In no particular order:

- When hiring employees in a school/district, school leaders must work hand-in-hand with the human resources director/department in every step of the process.

- You should attempt to hire individuals that reflect the demographics (i.e., diversity) of your student body and community.
- You should "think outside the box" with regards to how the job posting/description is written and where the job is posted (e.g., social media, websites, etc.).
- The interview committee(s) should include as many stakeholders as possible: students, staff, parents, community members and local business owners.
- There should be several rounds of the interview process, each requiring different tasks of the individual interviewed (e.g., Q&A, teaching presentation, tests, essay/written responses to questions, etc.).
- You should <u>always</u> hire the best candidate regardless of anything else (e.g., how much they will be paid, how long you anticipate they will stay, etc.).
- You should always allow the candidate to tell you/the interview committee about themselves (i.e., background and experiences) at the beginning of the interview and end with the opportunity for the candidate to ask you/the interview committee any questions they may have.
- You should always include a tour of your district/building as part of the interview process (this may be more conducive as part of a later round of interview process).
- Elaborate on questions (attempt to do so naturally) and create an environment to make the interviewee as comfortable as possible.
- Ensure your interview questions are what you really want to know about a potential candidate.
- Offer the interviewee a drink of water before the interview starts (usually while the interviewee is waiting somewhere before they are interviewed).
- Include questions that allow the candidate to show they have completed some preliminary research on the school building/district.
- Know exactly what questions each interview committee member will ask, and in what order, before the interview starts.

- Require references and be sure to call them all. I would do this before the first round of interviews – right after you go through all applications and resumes with the interview committee.
- Email a thank you to all individuals who applied and were not chosen to be interviewed.
- Call (versus email or letter) and thank all individuals who interviewed and were not chosen to go to the next round and/or were not chosen for the position.
- Be open to innovative and irregular resume formats. Likewise, with presentations, if the interview calls for it.
- Ensure that the interview committee is reminded to execute what my grandma always reminded me of. That is, "firm handshakes and look them in the eye."
- Outline everything (with timelines) from the posting of the job to the final interview (and possibly include the board meeting you intend for the recommendation to be made to hire the candidate), and include with job posting.
- Don't hire individuals that you believe will "fit in"; rather, hire individuals you believe will change the world (not maintain the status quo, so to speak).
- Lastly, remember, nothing is official (i.e., contract) until the school board approves it. Proceed accordingly...

As you read through the aforementioned list, you may have found a common theme with regards to some of the content included within the bullet-points. That is, the mindset they are derived from comes from the quote "The most dangerous phrase in any organization is "we have always done it this way."" Please note this mentality applies to several of the bullet-points such as the interview protocol, the questions asked, how the job is posted (and where it is posted), the flexibility in resume and presentation design of the applicants, etc. Essentially, be open to innovation and change, especially if it is for the better. Oftentimes, we stick to what we have always done. For example, I remember being part of an interview committee as a school administrator. New to the district, we were conducting interviews in July hiring for the upcoming academic school year.

I remember sitting down and reading through the interview questions and thinking they were awful. As a school leader who has always challenged the status quo, I spoke up and expressed my concern. Much to my surprise, I had discovered the interview questions had been around for at least twenty years in that district. In fact, when we did decide to change them, we could not locate an electronic copy of the questions, as they had been copied over and over for years. This is just one example, as I could share many, but just because it is the way you/your building/district have always done things, does not mean it is the most efficient and most effective, and furthermore, what is best for students.

Retaining Staff. Much as with the snapshot of practices shared in the hiring section, here I have aimed to share some practices I believe help retain employees. This has become an area of focus due to the current national teacher shortage, teacher attrition and mobility issues as it applies to reciprocity from state-to-state (and in some cases, country-to-country, nation-to-nation, etc.). Again, some might be deemed as common sense, but, again, I would not be sharing them if they were the norm.

- It's all about relationships! Build them!
- Have the same mindset and approach to all of your employees as Virgin Records CEO, Richard Branson: "Train people well enough so they can leave, treat them well enough so they don't want to."
- Include effective teacher induction/orientation programs as part of your school/district policies and procedures. Ensure such programs are implemented!
- Always include a quality mentoring aspect as part of the teacher induction/orientation program.
- Create space in the master schedule for common planning time amongst staff, and sustained practice-based collegial learning opportunities.
- Conduct individualized professional development catered to the individual versus the whole group (when possible - there is certainly a time for whole-group professional development).
- Include goal setting (both short-term and long-term) as part of the teacher induction/orientation program.

- Lead a school/district you would want to teach/work in, and ensure your teachers lead a classroom they would want to learn in.
- Be cognizant of how best to foster a positive school climate and culture in your school/district.
- Protect your superstars, and don't give up on your slugs.
- Check on your new employees regularly as part of the teacher induction/orientation program.
- Ask yourself (and in some case, the employee) *why*, when your best employees become quiet.
- Ask your employees for feedback regarding your leadership (AKA the "humble pill").
- Create an environment that encourages and supports employees to try new things and fail at them.
- Complete evaluations in the constructive spirit, not the punitive spirit. On this note, make feedback meaningful and timely.
- Visit every classroom (or school building if you are a district leader) every day!
- Lastly, when you speak with employees, they will begin to associate what you speak about as important to you. So, if you talk about "Ohio State football" every time you speak with a teacher/administrator, then they will begin to think that is important to you. Whereas if you talk about "what is best for students" or "student achievement" every time you talk to a teacher, they might think that is important to you. Proceed accordingly ... That being said, it is okay to discuss Ohio State football every once in a while.

Systemic. Although I have trodden lightly throughout this book with regards to the "birds eye view" of the systemic changes necessary to improve the PreK-12 educational setting as a whole, here I wanted to provide several possible policy recommendations pertaining to human resources in schools, and how such policies and procedures can work to improve the teaching profession and attract (and retain) staff. In fact, many districts throughout our nation are already implementing many of the strategies shared here in order to attract the best talent to their districts (and keep them, I might add). However, this "poaching" from one district to another is certainly not best practice for students, as the research has shown that teacher (and administrator) turnover does, in fact, affect schools/districts negatively, especially when it comes to academic achievement. Nonetheless, as a school/district leader reading this book, these practices may help you both hire and retain the best talent. Many of these items shared are directly (or indirectly) affected by the educational system in the United States. That is, some of them are often out of the control of a given human resources director and/or school building/district leader. If you cannot control these items, then *advocate* for the necessary policy changes in your school/district (see chapter 11). Before I share suggestions pertaining to the systemic issues below, I want to share some statistics about our nation's teachers (Learning Policy Institute, 2017):

> U.S. teachers make about 20% less than other college graduates; 30% by mid-career.
>
> Salaries have lost ground since the 1990's.
>
> Average starting salaries in 2013 ranged from $27,000.00 (MT) to $44,000.00 (AK).
>
> In more than 30 states, a mid-career teacher heading a family of four is eligible for several forms of government assistance.

Let those statistics *sink in* for a minute. Now we see how important the workplace environment might be, given those statistics. Let's review the policies that are best for students. Worth mentioning here, the policy recommendations shared here are in large-part based on the findings of research conducted by the Learning Policy Institute (2017), as well as their policy recommendations based on those findings.

- Competitive/equitable salaries
- Financial incentives (e.g., stipends for commutes, degree obtainment, housing, child care)
- Forgivable loans and scholarships for years of service
- Enhanced opportunities for mobility (i.e., reciprocity from nation-to-nation, state-to-state as well as pension portability)

- Pipelines into teaching (such as high school career pathways)
- Collegial work environments
- Improved administrator training

Again, I am just scratching the surface. However, this will give you a start as it applies to the hiring process and retaining your employees. If we were to break human resources down, it really is about hiring and retaining employees. I know, easier said than done, right? Especially if you are in a district that does not have the same resources as a nearby district (resulting in the aforementioned poaching from one district to another). Nevertheless, I have also been in and visited school districts that are low paying and high achieving (even though staff often had limited resources). In all of those settings, if you were to ask individuals why they continue to stay, even though the pay is lower than nearby districts, and the same resources are not available, the answer will most always be that they love where they work, and, perhaps more importantly, they love who they work for (i.e., their principal or superintendent). As previously suggested, lead a school (or district) you would want to teach/work in and beware of the human resources directors out there that are culture/climate eradicators and enjoy turnover in their districts so they have something to do each year (as with the human resources director in my story shared earlier in this chapter). In essence, take care of people, treat them well, and do what you can to meet their needs. You might just be surprised how it will affect your school building/district. It is never too late to start, you can start right now!

Recommended Books on Human Resources

Human Resources: A Practical Guide for School Leaders by Dr. Denver J. Fowler and Dr. Douglas R. Davis

The Human Resource Function in Educational Administration by William B. Castetter and I. Phillip Young

Human Resources Administration: Personnel Issues and Needs in Education by L. Dean Webb and M. Scott Norton

Human Resources Administration: A School-Based Perspective by Richard E. Smith

Human Resources Administration in Education: A Management Approach by Ronald W. Rebore

Human Resources Management for Effective Schools by John T. Seyfarth

Human Relations for Career and Personal Success by Andrew J. DuBrin

Human Relations: Personal and Professional Development by David A. DeCenzo and Beth Silhanek

School Finance

Before we delve further into this section focused on school finance, I want to be clear about what should drive all of your decisions when you are working on your school building/district budget. That is, when it comes to school finance I have found it best to start with one single question: *How much money is actually making its way to the classrooms (in a given school building or throughout a district)?* Once you are able to accurately answer this question, you can begin to sort out the rest of your school building/district financial decisions and details based on what is best for students, and likewise, manage the money (and money processes) in such a way that the school building/district budget aligns with the overall strategic plan of a given district. That being said, in my experience school finance for a building principal can vary widely from district-to-district and school-to-school. Likewise, district leaders (such as superintendents) have varying degrees of involvement with school finance (and varying degrees of knowledge/understanding of school finance, and varying levels of desire to be involved in their school's finances). That is, depending on personnel as well as district policies and procedures, some of you may have significant involvement with school finances, whereas others will only have slight involvement. As a practitioner, I have experienced both. In some buildings/districts in which I worked, I personally maintained a budget. That is, I was in charge of every aspect of the account I managed, and only worked with district office in lesser respects. In contrast, in other districts I had only slight involvement with a budget. In both cases, as there should be, there were checks and balances in place with regard to what went in and came out of such accounts. That is, someone reviewed and approved such requests, for the most part. In addition, as one might imagine, when I personally maintained my own budget I was in a much smaller rural school district with fewer personnel. When I had little to no involvement, I was in a much larger urban school district with more personnel. This is not necessarily the rule, and therefore the reader should not assume this will be the case based on your school/district locale (i.e., rural, suburban, urban) or size (i.e., student enrollment). I report this perspective based solely on my own experiences and no assumptions should be made. Moreover, some districts employ a Chief Financial Officer (CFO) at the district level. This individual is responsible for all financial planning and record-keeping, and often provides financial reporting to the superintendent and school board. In both of my experiences, the district employed such an individual. However, whereas one had a more hands-off approach, the other was much more hands-on. That is, in one setting, the CFO was involved with the budgeting and allocations from the account I managed, whereas in the other setting, the CFO was only involved at the approval stage – approving what funds were allocated and for what purpose. Nevertheless, in both settings, everything went through the CFO (or someone in that office) at some step in the process of allocation. In short, when it comes to school finance there are really only a few things to be cognizant of. First, you need to be able to manage and budget an account (basic math skills). I would further argue that you need to be able to do so using technology (let it work for you). Secondly, decisions made on where money is allocated should be a collaborative process. That is, I never made spending decisions on my own; I always included others in the process. When making any decision in a school/district, collaborative decision-making is always going to be best practice. After all, much of your school/district budget is derived from tax payer dollars. It is not your money, it is your stakeholders'. Spend accordingly! The first two practices make sense, right? Simple enough – knowledge of simple math, learning to use technology (whatever your school/district uses) to manage your school/district accounts, and including as many stakeholders as possible in the decision-making process as to where taxpayer (and in some cases, fundraiser) money is spent. Thirdly, and perhaps most importantly, there needs to be a record of all funds going in and out of your account(s). It is in this connection that I have heard of individuals losing their jobs...not in connection with funds going out (that record is usually kept automatically), but rather, in connection with the record of funds going in (or in some cases, not going in at all). For example, one of the professors in my graduate program told us about a principal who he considered to be one of the best principals he had ever worked with. He went on to explain how this principal would hold open gyms every Sunday in his school building. As more and more individuals started coming to the open gyms, he decided to start asking individuals to pay/donate $3.00 each to participate. He did this for many years. He used this money to reward students and teachers for performance, etc. This included things like paying for classroom pizza parties, buying his students' lunches (if they did not have lunch money), additional school supplies, paying after school tutors, etc. Once word got out he had been doing this, the CFO at his district (at the request of another individual – remember, it only takes one upset parent) asked if he had record of the money he had been collecting and spending over the past couple of years. The fact was, he did not. He had kept the cash in his desk in his office and used it as he saw fit. Likewise, he had no receipts for the majority of the items he had spent the money on. In short, he was fired. You see, although one could assume he was honest about the amount of money he had collected and spent, the truth is, no official record existed. Therefore, no one really knew for sure. In the end, although his intentions might have been good, he lost his job.

This particular aspect of school finance is of great importance. As a school leader, all money collected and spent should be on record. This becomes particularly important when your school is conducting fund-raisers and the like, and has accounts linked to your Parent Teacher Association (PTA) or Parent Teacher Organization (PTO). Believe it or not, sometimes your PTO/PTA president is under the impression that they actually run the school/district (think the PTO/PTA president in the movie *Bad Moms*). If I were you, I would ensure you rein in such individuals. That is, I would discuss with them their role and where it begins and ends (there is a lot of research on *role theory* – clearly defining individuals' roles within a given organization). After all, remember, as a school leader, you can delegate tasks, but you cannot delegate responsibility, perhaps especially when it comes to money. Lastly, as a school leader, you should fully understand what ever formula is in place regarding how your school/district is funded at the federal, state and local levels. This varies from state-to-state, therefore you will need to become well-versed in your state's funding formula for public schools. I have provided several resources at the end of this section in order to help you find such information. As an example, let's look at the State of Ohio. Public school funding in the State of Ohio comes in large part from three main sources: the federal government, the state (from the Ohio Department of Education's general revenue funds and the Ohio Lottery profits), and local resources (based on locally levied property taxes and/ or income taxes approved by voters). Worth noting here, the Ohio Supreme Court declared the State of Ohio's system of funding public education based on property taxes was unconstitutional, and held that the legislature should create a more equitable system (Geneva, 2016). However, no new system exists to date. In addition, in recent years, the State of Ohio public schools have seen large portions of school funding diverted to charter and private schools. In some districts, this has been school funds in the millions of dollars. All that being said, the money used to operate a school district in the State of Ohio is voted on by community members in the form of a levy[42]. That is, school districts in Ohio can receive funding from property tax levies approved by voters. Here is a great resource on further understanding school levies (Ohio School Boards Association, 2017): https://www.ohioschoolboards.org/sites/default/files/OSBAUnderstandingLeviesFactSheet.pdf.

As you can see in this example, the way schools are funded in the State of Ohio may differ from that in your state, although most states do utilize local property taxes to fund public schools. Therefore, in the United States, a child's zip code often determines the type of education they receive, the type of school they attend, and more often than not, their future. This sad reality is further highlighted in chapter 10, titled *Leading for Inclusiveness*. This is why it is imperative that school/district leaders fully understand the funding formula in their state. Notably, in recent

---

42 A levy, as used here in this chapter, is a local property tax collected to help finance the education programs and operations of public schools. A levy can help supplement the general fund that pays for the operation of a given school district. This general operation can include items such as salaries, benefits, supplies, equipment, materials, utilities, fuel, and extracurricular activities.

years, several books have been authored focused solely on state-specific school finance. For example, if you are in Illinois, Virginia, Florida, Texas, or even Australia, the International Council of Professors of Educational Leadership (ICPEL) has you covered. See: http://www.ncpeapublications.org/index.php/ncpea-press-books. If you are in the State of Ohio, see: https://www.ohioschoolboards.org/catalog/publications/making-sense-school-finance. Ultimately, it will be up to you to seek out such resources for your state as well as learn the formula in your particular state, and perhaps most importantly, how best to navigate those waters to ensure you are doing what is best for your students. Worth noting, the school building/district leaders I know who best manage their school finances are the same school building/district leaders who are well-versed in how their schools are funded at the federal, state, and local levels. It may come as no surprise that these same individuals do an excellent job of keeping their stakeholders well-informed of the state funding formula in their respective state and how it affects the local school/district, as well as employing innovative approaches in how they manage their school's finances. In fact, many school districts highlight their finances in the yearly Quality Profile Report I shared with you in chapter 2. You see, if you manage your school building/district finances in a way that you can be proud of, and so can your community, you have nothing to hide. Thus, be transparent and ensure all stakeholders; students, staff, parents, community members and business owners, are familiar with the school building/district finances.

Recommended Books on School Finance

Visit the International Council of Professors of Educational Leadership (ICPEL) website at: http://www.ncpeapublications.org/index.php/ncpea-press-books.

For the State of Ohio, pick up a copy of *Ohio School Finance Blue Book* by Robert G. Stabile or *Making Sense Out of School Finance* by Dr. Howard Fleeter

For the State of California, pick up a copy of *School Finance: A California Perspective 10th Edition* by Arthur Townley and June Schmieder, or choose one of the books here: https://www.sscal.com/publications.cfm.

It is my hope that you found this chapter informative in the areas of school finance and human resources practices. The information shared does not nearly encompass all there is to know about the two areas highlighted, however, as previously mentioned, to do so adequately would take separate books (or series of books) focused on each area in their own right. Those books do exist, and I have shared several of them at the end of each section in this chapter. In this regard, I highly encourage you to seek out said books (and visit/access the many links shared within this chapter) in order to learn more about each area in greater detail, especially as it applies to your state.

Reflection

Questions for Practicing and Aspiring School Leaders

1. As a school district/building leader, what steps will you take to ensure you stay up to date with best practice as it applies to human resources?
2. As a school district/building leader, what steps will you take to ensure you stay up to date with best practice as it applies to school finance?
3. How will you aim to effectively manage your school/district finances?
4. As a school district/building leader, how will you work hand-in-hand with human resources and other staff to effectively hire individuals in your school/district?
5. As a school district/building leader, how will you work hand-in-hand with human resources and other staff to effectively retain individuals in your school/district?

Problem-based Scenario

Mo Money Mo Problems

As a building (or district) school leader, you have recently accepted a new administrative position. On your first day in the summer, the former administrator (who retired as the district's "sacred cow") has agreed to meet with you to "show you the ropes." That is, to help orient you to your new position. The meeting is going extremely well and thus far you are very grateful for his/her help in acclimating you to your new position. However, towards the end of your meeting, he/she mentions that there is a "slush fund" that he/she has been collecting for several years now. He/she does not mention how the slush fund has accumulated (i.e., where the money is from). As he/she opens the safe in your new office, he/she mentions that there is an estimated several thousand dollars in there. He/she goes on to list all the ways that he/she would spend the money…"flowers for my secretaries," "Christmas cards for my colleagues," "presents for my grandkids," and "coffee and donuts for building/district staff." Before he/she shuts that safe, you watch him/her take a few hundred dollars and stuff it in his/her pocket. After shutting the safe, he/she abruptly stands up with a smile and says, "I even take a little for myself from time-to-time," and winks at you. He/she goes on to welcome you again, and reminds you not to hesitate to reach out to him/her should you ever need anything or have any questions or concerns. After he/she leaves, you close your office door and sit down in your chair reflecting on what just happened. What would you do? What is your next step? How do you approach this issue without angering the "sacred cow" or any of his/her former colleagues that you now work with? Remember, as previously mentioned in this chapter, money unaccounted for leads to trouble, and possible termination. Please carefully, and in great detail, describe how you would handle such a situation given the information provided in this somewhat difficult scenario.

Choose Your School Setting

Choose your role and then choose your school building/district setting before you respond to the scenario. As you draft your response, please be cognizant of how your setting might affect how you respond to the scenario. Essentially, based on the characteristics listed below, think about what we know about these characteristics, and furthermore, how they generally impact schools/districts. How might they affect your decision-making with regards to the scenario, if at all? Be sure to clearly describe your school setting in your response.

Role: Superintendent, Principal, or Assistant Principal
Locale: Urban, Suburban, or Rural
Size: Small District, Medium District, or Large District
Diversity: No Diversity, Some Diversity, or Very Diverse
SES Status: 100% Free and Reduced Lunch (FRL), 50% FRL, or 0% FRL

Chapter 14

Tips for School Leaders

"A leader is one who knows the way, goes the way, and shows the way."   *~ John C. Maxwell*

Leading 101

Here I have decided to include some of my general thoughts with regards to school leadership, and life for that matter, in an effort to prepare you to be the best school leader possible. Enjoy!

> *Show me an excellent school leader... you've got my attention. Show me an excellent school leader who is also an excellent spouse, parent, has a strong faith, has strong morals, is ethical, and takes care of their health...now you you've got my undivided attention. You think that stuff doesn't matter, you're dead wrong. We're molding the future minds of our society.*

> *Do not maintain the status quo. "Status quo" is Latin for "the mess we're in." Be a change agent! After all, remember, the worst saying in any organization is "we have always done it this way."*

> *As a school leader, it is indeed true that you can delegate tasks (and you should). However, you can never delegate responsibility. At the end of the day, you are responsible for it all.*

> *If things aren't working out where you are, polish your resume and move on. But be careful not to burn any bridges before your departure. You can leave without things needing to get messy. My motto is, and will always be, "kill them with success, and bury them with a smile."*

Everyone is replaceable, to some degree. So be careful about who you hire, who you fire, and how you treat people. Perhaps most importantly, know how to treat your superstars. Don't be the Orlando Magic front office losing Shaquille O'Neal to the Lakers. Take care of your superstars!

In life, we say it is all about relationships. In schools, it is about the climate and culture. Sure, relationships are part of that, but I promise, no initiative will work without having the climate and culture of the school in order.

I have worked with some of the lousiest school administrators (and people) and I have worked with some of the best school administrators (and people). Both were great learning experiences!

People may schmooze more than you, but never let them outwork you. Let me tell you from experience, it feels a lot better to be rewarded for hard work than ass-kissing.

Be relentlessly, consistently, persistent in all that you do!

All my life I have been told I cannot do this or that. But what people were really saying is, "I cannot do this or that." Remember that, you can do anything you put your mind to!

People will always remember how you made them feel; much less will they remember anything you said. Proceed accordingly.

People couldn't care less how much you know, until they know how much you care. Proceed accordingly.

You can't fix everybody, so don't even try. It will be plenty of work trying to fix yourself. Focus accordingly.

Always give a firm handshake and look people in the eye. If you travel internationally, do the local equivalent.

Don't talk just to hear yourself speak. Say what you mean and mean what you say.

Don't have a chip on your shoulder towards folks that were born on third base (with a silver spoon in their mouth) when in contrast you were born in the on-deck circle or still up to bat at home plate. For the most part, someone somewhere along the way made major sacrifices for them (or their parent, or their parents, parents) to be born standing on third base. Out-work them and out-achieve them anyway! It feels great!

Every single day, do what is best for students. It's all that matters when nothing else does!

I was once asked how I became so successful, given my background. My answer: formidable 'to do' lists, a monthly planner, and elbow grease. Since I can remember, I have consistently made 'to do' lists and I always kept a monthly planner. Both help me stay focused and allow me to prioritize what I need to do next. As for the elbow grease, you can't replace hard work and enthusiasm with much of anything.

All that being said, I am still learning. I fall short of perfect each and every day. Chances are, you will too. Greatness lies in the striving for perfection, not the obtainment of it.

Life is short. Proceed accordingly.

Quotes and Insights

I have always been a fan of quotes. I often look to them for daily inspiration myself, as well as to inspire others. That is why I have always been a fan of Project Wisdom, a great resource for school district/building leaders. Essentially, Project Wisdom is a collection of thought-provoking messages designed to be read over the PA or in-house television system within your school building (Project Wisdom, 2016). Each day a thought-provoking message is shared, followed by a quote associated with the message, and then "Make it a great day, or not ... the choice is yours." If you are interested, you can find more information about this program at: www.projectwisdom.com. I highly suggest it for any school leader.

Below I have provided some of my favorite quotes and insights (in no particular order). Enjoy!

"Intent reveals desire. Action reveals commitment."
~ Unknown

"Kids don't fail schools, schools fail kids." ~ Sir Ken Robinson

"If you cannot find a leader who inspires you, be the leader you wish you had." ~ Simon Sinek

"People don't care how much you know, until they know how much you care." ~ Unknown

"People don't always remember what you said, but they always remember how you made them feel." ~ Unknown

"Insecure leaders never develop people. They replace them."
~ John C. Maxwell

"Children must have at least one person who believes in them. It could be you." ~ Marian Wright Edelman

"Knowing is not enough, we must apply. Willing is not enough, we must do." ~ Bruce Lee

"I can't understand why people are frightened of new ideas. I'm frightened by the old ones." ~ John Cage

"When we tell people to do their jobs, we get workers. When we trust people to get the job done, we get leaders." ~ Simon Sinek

"The leaders who will have real impact will be those who can move past compliance to creativity, beyond implementation to innovation." ~ Unknown

"If they say it's impossible, remember, that it's impossible for them, not you." ~ Unknown

"A leader is someone who demonstrates what's possible." ~ Mark Yarnell

"Every kid is one caring adult away from being a success story." ~ Josh Shipp

"You have enemies? Good! That means you've stood up for something sometime in your life." ~ Winston Churchill

"Your past does not have to define who you are or who you can become." ~ Dr. Thomas Tucker

"You are what you do. Not what you say you'll do." ~ Unknown

"If the purpose of learning is to score well on a test, we've lost sight of the real reason for learning." ~ Jeannie Fulbright

"I'm not interested in competing with anyone, I hope we all make it." ~ Unknown

"We need to be helping our students, create a future we will all want to live in." ~ Sir Ken Robinson

"It's all about relationships." ~ Unknown

"I speak to everyone in the same way, whether he/she is the garbage man or the president of the university." ~ Albert Einstein

"Children learn more from what you are than what you teach." ~ W.E.B. DuBois

---

"People may hear your words, but they feel your attitude."
~ John Maxwell

"Education is not preparation for life; education is life itself."
~ John Dewey

"Don't tell your problems to people. Eighty percent don't care, and the other twenty percent are glad you have them."
~ Lou Holtz

"No challenge can stop you if you have the courage to keep moving forward in the face of your greatest fears and biggest challenges. Be Courageous!" ~ Jon Gordon

"Success is to be measured not so much by the position that one has reached in life as by the obstacles which he/she has overcome." ~ Booker T. Washington

"Success is the result of perfection, hard work, learning from failure, loyalty, and persistence." ~ Colin Powell

"Culture is the sum of what you permit and what you promote." ~ Richard Fagerlin

"Faith and fear have one thing in common. They both believe in a future that hasn't happened yet. Choose to believe in a positive future." ~ Jon Gordon

"Don't chase a boy or a girl. Chase God, and if you see someone keeping up, introduce yourself." ~ Tom Allen

"Everything I did in my life that was worthwhile I caught hell for." ~ Unknown

"God, Family, Academics, Athletics, the Arts." ~ Dr. Denver J. Fowler

"Go into the world and do well. But more importantly, go into the world and do good." ~ Minor Myers, Jr.

"My goal is to build a life I don't need a vacation from." ~ Unknown

"I never lose. I either win or learn." ~ Nelson Mandela

"Take vacations, go as many places as you can. You can always make more money; you can't always make more memories." ~ Unknown

"Either write something worth reading or do something worth writing about." ~ Benjamin Franklin

"To thrive under pressure, focus on your love of competing and playing instead of your fear of failing. Worrying about the outcome and what people think steals your joy and sabotages your success, while loving and appreciating the moment energizes you and enhances your performance." ~ Jon Gordon

"Each day represents a fresh start; a new beginning to do what you believe is possible and accomplish what others say is impossible." ~ Jon Gordon

"A business [insert school] has to be evolving, it has to be fun, and it has to exercise your creative instincts." ~ Richard Branson

"Too often we underestimate the power of a touch, a smile, a kind word, a listening ear, an honest compliment, or the smallest act of caring, all of which have the potential to turn a life around." ~ Leo Buscaglia

"Whatever your role in your school is, commit to being a leader worth following." ~ Unknown

"In the end, we only regret the chances we didn't take." ~ *Unknown*

"Be diligent in believing what we do in the classroom could possibly echo for a lifetime in the heart of a student." ~ *Robert John Meehan*

"Integrity demands that I do what's right, even if it's unpleasant and unpopular." ~ *Dr. James Dobson*

"The secret to successful hiring is this: Look for people who want to change the world." ~ *Marc Benioff*

"You can't always be the most talented person in the room. But you can be the most competitive." ~ *Pat Summit*

"A low threshold for boredom and a hate for small talk." ~ *Sara Wheeler (describing Denys Finch Hatton)*

"The boundary between selfish and elusive is porous." ~ *Sara Wheeler (describing Denys Finch Hatton)*

"There's more to life than beer, barbeques, and ball games." ~ *Unknown*

"Say how you feel, leave the job you hate, find your passion, love with every ounce of your bones, stand up for things that matter, don't settle, don't apologize for who you are. Be brave." ~ *Unknown*

"Confidence is closely linked to mental toughness because it takes a strong mind to conquer fear, anxiety, and worry." ~ *Michael Kaplan*

"Every school in America has teachers working for free on a daily basis. Go by any school parking lot early in the morning, late in the afternoon, or even at night or on the weekends, and you will see them. No overtime, no bonuses or promotions on

the line – just doing it for their students! Teachers are using their free time, and often investing their own money, for children's literacy, prosperity, and future." ~ Unknown

"Your beliefs don't make you a better person. Your behavior does." ~ Unknown

"Leadership is one-part influence and two-parts responsibility: As people of influence, we must always take responsibility for our contribution to problems that arise around us." ~ Unknown

"If we don't focus on school culture, we might as well not waste our time on anything else." ~ Unknown

"Success is like reaching an important birthday and finding you're exactly the same." ~ Audrey Hepburn

"One day you'll be just a memory for some people. Do your best to be a good one." ~ Unknown

"Today is the oldest you've ever been and the youngest you'll ever be again." ~ Unknown

"Lead and inspire people. Don't try to manage and manipulate people. Inventories can be managed, but people must be led." ~ Ross Perot

"Contrary to popular belief, nobody owes you anything." ~ Unknown

"If you want your children to turn out well, spend twice as much time with them, and half as much money." ~ Abigail Van Buren

"If I can look at your zip code and I can tell whether you're going to get a good education, we've got a real problem." ~ Condoleezza Rice

"Have more than you show, speak less than you know."
~ Unknown

"Blaming, complaining, and defending, never solved a problem, achieved a goal, or improved a relationship."
~ Brian Kight

"If you don't sacrifice for what you want, what you want will be the sacrifice." ~ Unknown

"Sometimes the issue is simply that their ceiling is your floor."
~ Unknown

"Adversity requires you to make a choice: react on default or respond with discipline. The choice, not the adversity, is what matters most." ~ Tim Kight

"As leaders our ability to do "what is best for kids" often lies within our ability to inspire, influence, and support the adults in the system." ~ Shelley Burgess

From Steve Jobs:

1. *Learn* how to participate in the future
2. *Focus* on the positive
3. *Fail* forward
4. *Travel* the world
5. *Find* the right partner
6. Obstacles are *opportunities* in disguise
7. Take *risks*
8. Surround yourself with *great people*
9. Remember *you will be dead* soon
10. *Learn from others*

Book, Journal, Podcasts, and Other Recommendations

It is never too late to start a book club. In fact, I highly recommend you create one both with your administrative team and your staff. Book studies can have a positive and lasting impact on all things school. In addition, if you have a long commute to and from work, consider purchasing some audio books. Here is a great resource on *How to Improve Your Next Book Study in 6 Steps*. See: http://theeducationalleaders.com/improve-next-book-study-6-steps/.

In no particular order, I have provided a list of books and journals (both peer-reviewed and non-refereed), that I highly suggest for both aspiring and practicing school leaders. I have also provided a list of books I like or I have had the opportunity to be part of. In creating this list, I attempted to keep it concise enough that it would not be overwhelming for you, the reader (in fact, I actually cut the list in half before this book went to print). Thus, please know that much thought went into deciding what recommendations were made. Enjoy!

Books (that I have been/will be part of)

The 21st Century School Leader: Leading Schools in Today's World by Dr. Denver J. Fowler (Word & Deed Publishing) – You must have already bought this one! Good choice!

*Exploring the Impact of the Dissertation in Practice by Dr. Valerie A. Storey

The Contemporary Superintendent: (R)Evolutionary Leadership in an Era of Reform by Leigh Wallace and M. Mountford (Information Age Publishing)

The Principal Reader: Narratives of Experience by Darrin Griffiths and Scott Lowrey (Word & Deed Publishing)

School Type Diversification in England and the United States of America: Implications for School Leader Preparation Programs by Dr. Valerie A. Storey (Information Age Publishing)

Contemporary Perspectives on Social Capital in Educational Contexts by Dr. RoSusan Bartee and Dr. Phillis George (Information Age Publishing)

**Human Resources: A Practical Guide for School Leaders* by Dr. Denver J. Fowler and Dr. Douglas R. Davis (Rowan & Littlefield)

**I'm Your Huckleberry: A Completely True Story of Perseverance, Resilience, Persistence, and Triumph* by Dr. Denver J. Fowler (TBD)

**A Guide for teaching Ethics* by Dr. Denver J. Fowler (TBD)

**Educational Technology for Teacher and School Leaders* by Dr. Denver J. Fowler, John Riley, and Marlena Bravender (NCPEA Publications)

**Transformative Leadership for Educational Leaders* by Dr. Denver J. Fowler and Dr. Sarah M. Graham (Word & Deed Publishing)

*I have written or will write a chapter within this book

**In progress, not yet in print

Book List

The 360° Leader by John C. Maxwell

Notes to Myself by Hugh Prather

Strengthsfinder 2.0 by Tom Rath

Everything School Leaders Need to Know About Assessment by W. James Popham

Answers to Essential Questions About Standards, Assessments, Grading, & Reporting by Thomas R. Guskey and Lee Ann Jung

Schools and Data: The Educator's Guide for Using Data to Improve Decision Making by Theodore B. Creighton

Educational Research: Planning, Conducting, and Evaluating Quantitative and Qualitative Data by John W. Creswell

Quantitative Data Analysis Using Microsoft Excel by Gerard Babo and Leonard H. Elovitz (Please note: The authors have created two editions, a PC edition and a Mac edition. The blue cover is for PC users, whereas red cover is for Mac users)

An Administrators Guide to Student Achievement & Higher Test Scores by Marcia Kalb Knoll

Quantitative Research in Education by Wayne K. Hoy

Qualitative Research in Practice by Sharan B. Merriam

What Great Principals Do Differently: 18 Things That Most Matter by Todd Whitaker

Principals of Inclusion by Darrin Griffiths

Leading with Integrity by Clarence G. Oliver, Jr.

10 Traits of Highly Effective Principals by Elaine K. McEwan

Leadership: Key Competencies for Whole-System Change by Lyle Kirtman and Michael Fullan

The Energy Bus by Jon Gordon

How Full Is Your Bucket by Tom Rath and Donald D. Clifton

American Education by Joel Spring

Reign of Error by Diane Ravitch

Building Engaged Schools by Gary Gordon and Steve Crabtree

Educational Administration by Wayne K. Hoy and Cecil G. Miskel

The Education of a Lifetime by Robert Khayat

The Measure of Our Days by Andrew P. Mullins, Jr.

50 Myths & Lies that Threaten America's Public Schools: A Real Crisis in Education by David C. Berliner, Gene V. Glass, and Associates.

Leadership for Low-Performing Schools by Daniel L. Duke

Beyond Theory: Practical Strategies for Making a Difference in Schools by Tyrone Olverson, Dr. Catherine L. Barnes, and Scott Taylor

FISH! by Stephen C. Lundin, Harry Paul, and John Christensen

Using Quality Feedback to Guide Professional Learning: A Framework for Instructional Leaders by Shawn Clark and Abbey Duggins

The School Leader's Guide to Formative Assessment by Todd Stanley and Jana Alig

A Framework for Understanding Poverty by Ruby K. Payne

Collaborative School Improvement by Trent E. Kaufman, Emily Dolci Grimm, and Allison E. Miller

Integrating Educational Technology into Teaching by M.D. Roblyer

What's in Your Space? 5 Steps for Better School and Classroom Design by Dwight Carter, Gary Sebach, and Mark White

Impact: How Assistant Principals can be High Performing Leaders by Christopher Colwell

Publication Manual of the American Psychological Association (APA)

Emotional Intelligence 2.0 by Travis Bradberry and Jean Greaves

International Perspectives on Designing Professional Practice Doctorates by Dr. Valerie A. Storey

Mere Christianity by C.S. Lewis

The Slow Professor: Challenging the Culture of Speed in the Academy by Maggie Berg and Barbara K. Seeber

Research in Education: A Conceptual Introduction by James H. McMillan and Sally Schumacher

School Crisis Prevention and Intervention by Mary Margaret Kerr

Beginning the Principalship by John C. Daresh

Wild at Heart by John Eldredge

Accountability for Learning: How Teachers and School Leaders Take Charge by Douglas B. Reeves

Achieving Success for New and Aspiring Superintendents: A Practical Guide by Mary Frances Callan and William Levinson

Meeting the Ethical Challenges of Leadership by Craig E. Johnson

Proactive School Security and Emergency Preparedness Planning by Kenneth S. Trump

Modern School Business Administration: A Planning Approach by James W. Guthrie, Christina C. Hart, John R. Ray, I. Carl Candoli, and Walter G. Hack

On Common Ground: The Power of Professional Learning Communities by Richard DuFour, Robert Eaker, Rebecca DuFour

Understanding and Evaluating Educational Research by James H. McMillan and John F. Wergin

A Casebook for Exploring Diversity by George L. Redman

The Gate-Keepers: Inside the Admissions Process of a Premier College by Jacques Steinberg

Leadership Secrets from the Executive Office: Revised and Updated by George Hathaway

The MOO Factor: Margin of Opportunity by Dr. Dennis Schone

Outliers by Malcolm Gladwell

Character Compass: How Powerful School Culture Can Point Students Toward Success by Scott Seider

Using Technology with Classroom Instruction that Works by Howard Pitler, Elizabeth R. Hubbell, Matt Kuhn, and Kim Malenoski

School and Society: Historical and Contemporary Perspectives by Steven E. Tozer, Guy Senese, and Paul C. Violas

David and Goliath by Malcolm Gladwell

HBR's 10 Must Reads: On Leadership by Peter F. Drucker

Conflict of Interests: The Politics of American Education by Joel Spring

Lessons from the Classroom: 20 Things Good teachers Do by Hal Urban

Making Summer Count: How Summer Programs Can Boost Children's Learning by Jennifer S. McCombs, Catherine H. Augustine, Heather L. Swartz, Susan J. Bodilly, Brian McInnis, Dahlia S. Lichter, and Amanda Brown Cross

Content-Area Writing: Every Teacher's Guide by Harvey Daniels, Steven Zemelman, and Nancy Steineke

The Ethics of School Administration by Kenneth A. Strike, Emil J. Haller, and Jonas F. Soltis

Learning from Lincoln: Leadership Practices for School Success by Harvey Alvy and Pam Robbins

The Ethics of Educational Leadership by Ronald W. Rebore

Ethics for Educational Leaders by Weldon Beckner

Ethical Leadership in Schools by Kenneth A. Strike

Ethics in a New Millennium by Dalai Lama

Cage-Busting Leadership by Frederick M. Hess

Fulfilling the Promise of the Differentiated Classroom: Strategies and Tools for Responsive Teaching by Carol Ann Tomlinson

Understanding by Design: Professional Development Workbook by Jay McTighe and Grant Wiggins

Pushing the Envelope: Critical Issues in Education by Allan C. Ornstein

I used to think ... And now I think ... by Richard F. Elmore

Placed-Based Education: Connecting Classrooms & Communities by David Sobel

Why Community Matters: Connecting Education with Civic Life by Nicholas V. Longo

Instructional Rounds in Action by John E. Roberts

The Blind Advantage by Bill Henderson

A Repair Kit for Grading: 15 Fixes for Broken Grades by Ken O'Connor

Fair Isn't Always Equal: Assessing & Grading in the Differentiated Classroom by Rick Wormeli

Total Literacy Techniques: Tools to Help Students Analyze Literature and Informational Texts by Pérsida Himmele, William Himmele, and Keely Potter

Leadership for Increasingly Diverse Schools by George Theoharis and Martin Scanlan

Learning from the Best: Lessons from Award-Winning Superintendents by Sandra Harris

Leading the Way to Success by Dr. Warren Bennis, Jack Canfield, Kevin Hub, and James Kouzes

Classroom Management that Works: Research-Based Strategies for Every Teacher by Robert J. Marzano

Classroom Management for Secondary Teachers by Edmund T. Emmer, Carolyn M. Evertson, and Murray E. Worsham

Personalizing 21st Century Education: A Framework for Student Success by Dan Domenech, Morton Sherman, and John L. Brown

Journal List
Review of Education Research

Educational Researcher

UCEA Review

Any of the Journals produced by the International Council of Professors of Educational Leadership

International Journal of Education and Teaching

Athens Journal of Education

AASA Journal of Scholarship & Practice

Journal of Educational Administration

Journal of Cases in Educational Leadership
    The Journal of Research on Leadership Education

Magazine List

School Administrator by AASA

Principal Leadership by NASSP

Educational Leadership by ASCD

AMLE Magazine by AMLE

Other Great Resources

BAM! Radio Network
See: http://www.bamradionetwork.com/

The Principal Center Radio Show
See: https://www.principalcenter.com/radio/

We Love Schools Podcast by Joel Gagne and Carole Dorn-Bell
See: http://www.weloveschoolspodcast.com

Here are two *We Love Schools* podcasts that I have been part of:

Episode 27
Developing Leaders in Our Schools
http://www.weloveschoolspodcast.com/2016/06/
developing-leaders-in-our-schools/

Episode 24
A Close Look at Trends in Education: Looking at Mississippi and Beyond
http://www.weloveschoolspodcast.com/2016/05/a-close-look-at-
trends-in-education-looking-at-mississippi-and-beyond/

Book Notes from Jim Mahoney
See: http://hosted.vresp.com/1820435/dc1346f35a/572894461/26c
22c4445/

Mr. Carter's Office by Dwight Carter
See: https://dwightcarter.edublogs.org/

Chapter 15

The Epilogue

As I sat down to write this epilogue, it has now been several months since I first wrote *The 21st Century Leader: Leading Schools in Today's World*. I am certainly very proud of it, but more importantly, it is my hope the content of this book was both meaningful and useful for you, the reader. Please know that much thought and effort went into "what to include" within each chapter as well as "what not to include" – as it applies to leading schools in the 21st Century. Nonetheless, it may go without saying that new educational technology is rapidly advancing as well as being created each and every day. In fact, it was reported that $8.15 billion was invested in edtech companies in the first 10 months of 2017 alone (TechCrunch, 2018). Thus, I do have dreams of going back and adding to a few of the sections/chapters of this book. However, at some point an author must let go and accept the book as complete...an extremely hard task when you are writing about the 21st Century and beyond – as again, new innovations and revelations are shared instantaneously, on a continual basis, each and every day. Now, to encompass all educational technology would be nearly impossible, as somewhere, somebody, is working on something we never even dreamed of. Thus, I will certainly plan for future editions of this book to include any and all of the new, and perhaps most importantly, effective, educational technology that comes along in future years, and furthermore, how it can be utilized with school building/district leadership – as a 21st Century School Leader (and beyond). That said, I could not resist sharing a few more tidbits. Enjoy!

- Augmented reality ... I am surprised this is not utilized more in the educational setting. In fact, my buddy who teaches within the History Department at West Point recently shared with me that they use it all the time. For an example of how augmented reality works, download the Living Wine App on your smart phone and scan a bottle of 19 Crimes wine. Very cool!

- Associate Degree and High School Diploma...more and more "Early College High Schools" are handing their graduates both a High School Diploma and Associate Degree when they graduate from High School. I strongly believe we will see this trend across all high schools in the near future...and if not, why not?
- Other Apps worth checking out ...that were not mentioned in the book ...
  - o GeoGuessr
  - o Listenwise
  - o Edpuzzle
  - o TodaysMeet
  - o Pear Deck Flash Card Factory
  - o Google Tour Builder
  - o 360 Cities
  - o Viewpure
  - o SMMRY
  - o Rewordify
  - o VideoScribe
  - o VIPKID
  - o FlipGrid (ensure student voice in your classrooms)
  - o Scanner for Me
  - o YouTube (for screencast video and transcription – use with the Google Docs dictation feature)
  - o Canva (for graphic design, creating fliers, infographics, etc.)
  - o MakeMagazinDE
  - o MakerSpace
  - o Sketchnotes
  - o Classroom Clips
- New podcast launched by The Wallace Foundation – *The Principal Pipeline*

- o See: http://www.wallacefoundation.org/knowl-edge-center/pages/podcast-principal-pipelines-epi-sode-1-building-the-pipeline.aspx
- o I could not help but to include the visual shared by The Wallace Foundation via their podcast site. Please see below.

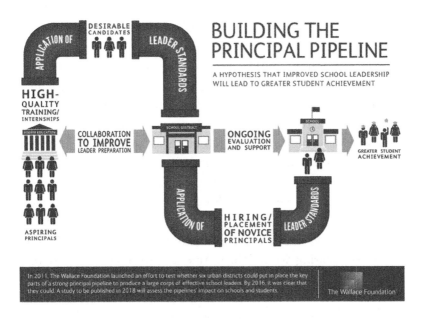

Finally, as someone who still spends quite a bit of my time in school buildings and school districts across the nation and around the globe, I am continually reminded of why I decided to write this book. As I reported earlier in the introduction, I still find that a majority of prac-ticing school leaders out there are leading their schools much like we have in the distant past. Furthermore, I still find that a majority of school leaders are great managers, but often less much instructional leaders. I could go on and on here, but it is also important to note that there are many innovative school leaders out there who are what I would deem to be 21st Century School Leaders. Leaders who are constantly looking for strategies and techniques to improve teaching and learning in their respective school buildings and districts, who truly lead for equity, who are life-long learners, and make every decision based on what is best for students. In more recent weeks, I have attempted to come up with one word to describe such 21st Century School Leaders. After much thought and deliberation, the one word I settled on was "avant-garde." This word describes those school leaders who regularly think outside the box, are experimental, and often radical, or unorthodox, in their approach to school leadership. Leaders who are forward-thinking, pioneering, revolutionary, trailblazing, inventive, and ahead of the times. Leaders who relentlessly, consistently, and persistently look to identify how to best serve all stakeholders: students, staff, parents, community members, and business owners, in the 21st Century and well beyond. Leaders who see the extraordinary in the ordinary world. These are the school leaders who often find innovative answers to the most difficult questions facing educators in the PreK-12 educational setting – in the 21st Century. These school leaders are a lot like Dr. Paul Bartsch. Do you know that name? If not, you should. Let me end this book with a short version story of someone I believe was "avant-garde" during their lifetime. Dr. Bartsch was someone who certainly had the ability to see the extraordinary in the ordinary world. During World War I, American troops were devastated by mustard gas. In essence, by the time our soldiers noticed the mustard gas in the trenches, it was too late. Thus, the United States had to come up with a way to detect the mustard gas far in advance of when humans could naturally detect it – as again, that was far too late. The answer to this problem came from the world of limax maximus. That is, Dr. Bartsch found the answer to the problem in ordinary garden slugs. He discovered that slugs could detect and visibly indicate their discomfort to mustard gas far in advance of humans. Essentially, he discovered that slugs closed their breathing aperture when exposed to mustard gas. In the end, the slug was sent to the World War I trenches and proved to save many American lives (by some estimates, hundreds of thousands). Dr. Bartsch was certainly someone I would call "avant-garde." It should probably also be noted that Dr. Bartsch was a genius in his own right, inventing the underwater camera among other things. Nonetheless, I share this story to make a point. Sometimes, in life, the answer to the most difficult questions are found in the most unlikely of places. To be a 21st Century School Leader, someone I call "avant-garde," we must look in the most unlikely of places for the answers to the most difficult questions in the educational setting. We owe it to our nation's school aged children to re-think our approach to school leadership, and in general, the PreK-12 educational setting as a whole. We must be "avant-garde" in our approach to attempting to solve the most arduous questions. After all, if not now, then when? If not you, then who? If we do not start being more experimental, more radical, more unorthodox, more forward-thinking, more pioneering, more revolutionary, more trailblazing, more inventive, and more ahead of the times, and regularly thinking outside the box, we will most certainly have a nation generation at risk.

Afterword by Dr. Thomas Tucker

"It is my hope that any individual aspiring to the superintendency will take the time to read this text."

As a practicing superintendent and lifelong educator, I have certainly witnessed the changing landscape of the PreK-12 educational setting firsthand. It was not too long ago that iPads and the like did not exist. In fact, when I think back to my early years as a school teacher, much of the technology that currently exists in our world (and classrooms) did not exist then. The question we must ask ourselves is "What does this mean for school leaders?" In proposing this very question, I believe Denver  has answered it from an array of angles within his book. Not only does he answer this question, he expands well beyond it within the content of each chapter. Thus, it is my hope that any individual aspiring to the superintendency will take the time to read this text.

For practicing (and aspiring) school building leaders and superintendents, I strongly believe the content specifically focused on 21st Century school leadership skills (chapters 1, 2, 4 & others) will be especially beneficial to the reader. In addition, information on leading for inclusiveness (chapter 10) is particularly insightful. As it applies to what most would describe as good leadership in any arena, Denver goes into great detail focusing on ethics in leadership (chapter 5), the importance of being a lifelong learner (chapter 3), an advocate for education (chapter 11), and networking (chapter 9), while also making suggestions for work-life balance (chapter 8) and provides numerous tips for school leaders (chapter 14). Perhaps some of the richest content is found within chapter 4 (Closing the Achievement Gap) and chapter 7 (School Climate & School Culture) where proven best practices are shared from a practitioners' perspective, supported by the extant research. As it applies to being an effective school leader, Denver has left no stone unturned. What sets this book apart is the vast amount of resources included in addition to the content of the book. In each chapter, Denver shares his recommendations on where to find key information as it applies to the content of each chapter, which allows the reader to easily locate this information. In addition, he includes journal and book recommendations as it relates to the content of each chapter. This practice and approach to the writing of the book is extremely helpful, and as such, I believe the reader will especially enjoy this particular aspect.

Finally, I believe it would be a disservice of me not share that I have rarely met any other individual that has the same passion, commitment, and desire to move the needle of education forward in both the United States and globally, than that of Denver. As his former superintendent (when he was still a teacher), his mentor during his superintendent internship, and now someone I consider a close friend, colleague, and leading expert on educational leadership, I continue to be amazed by all of his accomplishments and contributions to our field as a whole. He exemplifies what it means to be a great person and 21st Century school leader.

References

American Association of School Administration (2017). *Policy and advocacy.* American Association of School Administrators. Retrieved from: http://aasa.org/content.aspx?id=104

American Association of School Administrators (2017). *Code of ethics: AASA's statement of ethics for educational leaders.* American Association of School Administrators. Retrieved from: http://www.aasa.org/content.aspx?id=1390

American Association of School Administrators (2017). *Professional Standards for the Superintendency.* American Association of School Administrators. Retrieved from: http://www.aasa.org/content.aspx?id=1844

Barker, B. (2006). Rethinking leadership and change: A case study in leadership succession and its impact on school transformation. *Cambridge Journal of Education, 36*(2), 277-293.

Beecher, M., & Sweeny, S. (2008). Closing the achievement gap with curriculum enrichment and differentiation. One school's story. *Journal of Advanced Academics, 19*(3), 502-530.

Black, W. (2008). The contradictions of high-stakes accountability 'success': A case study of focused leadership and performance agency. *International Journal of Leadership in Education, 11*(1), 1-22

Blink, R. (2007). *Data-driven instructional leadership.* New York, NY: Routledge.

Body for Life. (2017). *Body for life.* Abbott. Retrieved from: http://bodyforlife.com/

Brookover, W. & Lezotte, L. W. (1979). *Changes in school characteristics coincide with changes in student achievement.* Occasional paper No. 17. East Lansing, MI: The Institute for Research in Teaching, Michigan State University.

Broszat, M. (2017). *Say goodbye to boring PD: Rethinking technology's role in professional development.* EdSurge. Retrieved from: https://www.edsurge.com/news/2017-02-07- say-goodbye-to-boring-pd-rethinking-technology-s-role-in-professional-development

The 21ˢᵗ Century School Leader

Brown, M., Trevino, L., & Harrison, D. (2005). Ethical leadership: A social learning perspective for construct development and testing. *Organizational Behavior and Human Decision Processes, 97,* 117-134.

Brown, K., & Fowler, D. (2018). Data driven decisions: Using equity theory to highlight implications for underserved students. *AASA Journal of Scholarship & Practice.*

California Performance Assessments for Teachers and Leaders (2017). *About CalAPA.* California Performance Assessments for Teachers and Leaders. Retrieved from: http://ctcpa.nesinc.com/about_calapa.asp

Carter, D. (2016). *My beliefs about students.* Mr. Carter's Office. Retrieved from: https://dwightcarter.edublogs.org/my-beliefs-as-an-education-administrator/

Cashmore, P. (2006). *MySpace, America's Number One.* Mashable. Retrieved from: http://mashable.com/2006/07/11/myspace-americas-number-one/#1K46EcZh8kqV

Center for Civic Education (2015, June 1). We The People: The Citizen and the Constitution [Website]. Retrieved from: http://www.civiced.org/national-finals-2015-about

Center for Creative Leadership (2017). *Four facets of self –awareness.* Retrieved from: http://ccllead.me/Bsk1WK

Chang, H.C., & Iyer, H. (2012). Trends in Twitter hashtag applications: Design features for value-added dimensions to future library catalogues. *Library Trends, 61*(1), 248-258.

Ciulla, J. (2004). *Ethics, the heart of leadership.* Westport, CT: Quorum Books.

Coleman, J. S. (1966). Equality of Educational Opportunity (COLEMAN) Study (EEOS). ICPSR06389-v3. Ann Arbor, MI: Inter-university Consortium for Political and Social Research [distributor], 2007-04-27. http://doi.org/10.3886/ICPSR06389.v3

Commission on Teacher Credentialing (2017). *Standards: Educator preparation.* Retrieved from: https://www.ctc.ca.gov/educator-prep/stds-prep-program

Commission on Teacher Credentialing (2014). *California Professional Standards for Education Leaders.* Retrieved from: https://www.ctc.ca.gov/docs/default-source/educator- prep/standards/cpsel-booklet-2014.pdf?sfvrsn=71b5d555_0

Cuddy, A. (2012). *Your body language may shape who you are.* TEDxTalk. Retrieved from: https://www.ted.com/talks/amy_cuddy_your_body_language_shapes_who_you_are/up- next

David, J. L., & Talbert, J. E. (2012). *Turning around a high-poverty school district: Learning from Sanger Unified's success.* Pal Alto: Bay Area Research Group and Stanford, CA: Center for Research on the Context of Teaching.

Department of Education and Science (2000). *Learning for life: Paper on adult education.* Retrieved from: http://files.eric.ed.gov/fulltext/ED471201.pdf

DeGraff, J. (2014). *Digital natives vs. digital immigrants.* The Huffington Post. Retrieved from: http://www.huffingtonpost.com/jeff-degraff/digital-natives-vs-digita_b_5499606.html

DeMichele, T. (2016). *Understanding Explicit Bias and Implicit Bias.* Retrieved from: http://factmyth.com/understanding-explicit-bias-and-implicit-bias/

DeShazo, K. (2016). *Laremy Tunsil, the NFL draft, and social media lesson for student athletes.* Fieldhouse Media. Retrieved from: http://www.fieldhousemedia.net/laremy-tunsil-the-nfl-draft-and-social-media-lessons-for-student-athletes/

Dreisbach, C. (2009). *Ethics in criminal justice.* New York, NY: McGraw-Hill Education.

EdGlossary (2017). *One-to-one.* Retrieved from: edglossary.org

England, J.T. (1992). Pluralism and education: Its meaning and method. Retrieved from ERIC: https://eric.ed.gov/?id=ED347494

Ferlazzo, L. (2017). *Using "Google Story Builder" to encourage students to study English over the summer.* EduBlogs. Retrieved from: http://larryferlazzo.edublogs.org/2017/06/03/using-google-story-builder-to-encourage-students-to-study-english-over-the-summer/

Fountas, I. & Pinnell, G.S. (2015, May 28). Benchmark Assessment System, 2nd Edition: Overview [Website]. Retrieved from http://www.heinemann.com/fountasandpinnell/BAS2_Overview.aspx

Forbes (2017). *13 Leadership skills you didn't need a decade ago that are now essential.* Forbes. Retrieved from: http://www.forbes.com/sites/forbescoachescouncil/2016/12/13/13- leadership-skills-you-didnt-need-a-decade-ago-that-are-now-essential/#730b4a2669ad

Fowler, D., Edwards, R. & Hsu, H. (2018). An investigation of state superintendents in the United States: Ethical leadership perspectives, state leader demographics, and state education characteristics. *Athens Journal of Education.*

Fowler, D. (2017). Leading for school improvement: Collecting, analyzing, and disseminating achievement data to guide instructional practices in schools. In D. Griffiths & S. Lowery (Eds.). *The Principal Reader: Narratives of Experience.* Ontario, Canada. Word & Deed Publishing.

Fowler, D. (2016). Using data to close the achievement gap: The secret to success in data deployment is the data team. *Principal Leadership 16*(7), 52-57.

Fowler, D. (2015). Using data in urban schools to close the achievement gap. *The GAP E- Magazine: America's Elite Diverse Education Forum 1*(1), 28-36.

Fowler, D. & Riley, J. (2015). *How to Build Your PLN on Twitter.* THE Journal: Transforming education through technology. Retrieved from: https://thejournal.com/articles/2015/09/11/how-to-build-your-pln-on-twitter.aspx

Fowler, D., & Johnson, J. (2014). An investigation of ethical leadership perspectives among Ohio school district superintendents. *Education Leadership Review of Doctoral Research. 1*(2), 96-112.

Fowler, D. (2016). Cats in the cradle: My work-life balance. *School Administrator 73*(3), 11-12.

Geneva, J. (2016). *History of Ohio Public School Funding.* Cleveland Heights University City School District. Retrieved from: http://www.chuh.org/HistoryofOhioSchoolFunding.aspx

Gibson, D., Ostashewski, N., Flintoff, K., Grant, S., and Knight, E. (2013). Digital badges in education. *Education and Information Technologies 20*(2), 403-410.

Gilsbach, T. (2017). *Understand FERPA requirements to train employees and protect your institute from social media liabilities.* AudioSolutionZ: Business Solutions for Every Industry. Retrieved from: https://www.audiosolutionz.com/education/social-media- education-ferpa-compliance.html

Godin, S. (2017). *A tribe is.* Pinterest. Retrieved from: https://www.pinterest.com/pin/185492078382655505/?lp=true

Goleman, D. (2010). *What makes a leader?* in Harvard Business Review: On Leadership. pp. 1- 22.

Gordon, J. (2017). *Servant leadership and a sandwich.* The Jon Gordon Companies. Retrieved from: http://www.jongordon.com/positive-tip-servant-leadership.html

Gordon, J. (2015). *You Win in the Locker Room First: The 7 C's to Build a Winning Team in Business, Sports, and Life.* Hoboken, NJ: John Wiley & Sons.

GovTrack (2017). *What are the different types of bills?* GovTrack. Retrieved from: https://govtracknews.wordpress.com/2009/11/11/what-are-the-different-types-of-bills/

Grady, M. (2011). *Leading the Technology-Powered School.* Thousand Oaks, CA: Corwin.

Gupta, R. (2016). *NOKIA CEO ended his speech saying this "we didn't do anything wrong, but somehow, we lost.* LinkedIn. Retrieved from: https://www.linkedin.com/pulse/nokia-ceo- ended-his-speech-saying-we-didnt-do-anything-rahul-gupta

Hallinger, P. (1992). The evolving role of American principals: From managerial to instructional to transformational leaders. *Journal of Educational Administration, 30*(3). Retrieved from: http://dx.doi.org/10.1108/09578239210014306

Harris, D. N., & Herrington, C. D. (2006). Accountability, Standards, and the Growing Achievement Gap: Lessons from the Past Half-Century. *American Journal of Education, 112,* 209-238.

Holtz, L. (2017). *Trust, commitment, love.* Goalcast. Retrived from: https://www.youtube.com/watch?v=TSae0t8xtiY

Howard, J., Nitta, K., & Wrobel, S. (2010). Implementing Change in an Urban School District: A Case Study of the Reorganization of the Little Rock School District. *Public Administration Review, 934-941.*

Kannapel, P. J., Clements, S. K., Taylor, D., & Hibpshman, T. (2005). Inside the Black Box of High-Performing High-Poverty Schools. *Report, Prichard Committee for Academic Excellence.*

Kirwan Institute for the Study of Race & Ethnicity, The Ohio State University (2017). *Understanding implicit bias.* Retrieved from: http://kirwaninstitute.osu.edu/research/understanding-implicit-bias/

Kosoff, M. (2014). *Selfie sticks are the new tool everyone is using to help take pictures of themselves.* Business Insider: Tech Insider. Retrieved from: http://www.businessinsider.com/selfie-stick-2014-7

Kuttner, P. (2015). *The problem with that equity vs. equality graphic you're using.* Cultural Organizing. Retrieved from: http://culturalorganizing.org/the-problem-with-that-equity- vs-equality-graphic/

Learning Policy Institute, (2017). *Addressing Teacher Shortages by Building a Profession of Teaching.* Lecture presented by Dr. L. Darling-Hammond at CelebrateEd in Sacramento, California.

Leishman, S. (2012). *4 benefits of joining Twitter chats.* MIT Connect. Retrieved from: http://connect.mit.edu/blog/4-benefits-joining-twitter-chats

Lewis, C.S. (1952). *Mere Christianity.* New York, New York: Harper Collins.

Library of Congress (2016). *Thomas Jefferson: Jefferson's library.* Library of Congress. Retrieved from: https://www.loc.gov/exhibits/jefferson/jefflib.html

Loukas, A. (2016). *What is School Climate?* Paper presented at the 2nd Panhellenic Conference, Larissa, Greece. Abstract received from: https://www.researchgate.net/publication/265306026_What_Is_School_Climate

Loukas, A. (2007). What is School Climate? *NAESP Leadership Compass, 5*(1), 1-3

Martin, M., Fergus, E., & Noguera, P. (2010). Responding to the Needs of the Whole Child: A Case Study of a High-Performing Elementary School for Immigrant Children. *Reading and Writing Quarterly, 26,* 195-222.

Martinez-Carter, K. (2014). *In defense of the selfie stick.* The Huffington Post. Retrieved from: http://www.huffingtonpost.com/map-happy/selfie-stick_b_6074954.html

Mayer, J. (2015). *10 best guided mediations on YouTube.* Live the Life You Love. Retrieved from: http://www.ilivethelifeilove.com/10-best-guided-meditations/

McLaughlin, E. (2017). *Mississippi school district ends segregation fight.* CNN. Retrieved from: http://www.cnn.com/2017/03/14/us/cleveland-mississippi-school-desegregation- settlement/index.html

Midgley, S., Stringfield, S., & Wayman, J. (2006). *Leadership for data-based decision-making: Collaborative educator teams.* Paper presented at American Educational Research Association, San Francisco, CA.

Molay, K. (2007). *Webinar or webcast: What's the difference.* The Webinar Blog. Retrieved from: http://wsuccess.typepad.com/webinarblog/2007/03/webinar_or_webc.html

Muilenburg, L. & Berge, Z. (2016). *Digital Badges in Education: Trends, Issues, and Cases.* New York, NY: Routledge.

National Association of Secondary School Principals (2017). *Take your advocacy to the next level.* NASSP. Retrieved from: https://nassp.org/advocacy/federal-grassroots-network

National Association of Secondary School Principals (2017). *Learning the basics of advocating on behalf of schools and principals.* NASSP. Retrieved from: https://nassp.org/advocacy/federal-grassroots-network/advocacy-materials?SSO=true

National Policy Board for Education Administration (2016). *NPBEA formally acquires new professional standards for educational leaders (PSEL).* Retrieved from: http://www.npbea.org/

National Policy Board for Education Administration (2015). *Professional Standards for Educational Leaders.* Retrieved from: http://www.npbea.org/wp/wp-content/uploads/2014/11/ProfessionalStandardsforEducationalLeaders2015forNPBEAFINAL-2.pdf

NELP Standards Overview (2016). *National educational leadership preparation standards: what they are, how they were developed and what purpose they serve.* Retrieved from: www.npbea.org/wp/wp-content/uploads/2016/.../NELP-Standards-Introduction.docx

Northouse, P. (2016). *Leadership: Theory and Practice.* Thousand Oaks, CA: SAGE Publications.

Ohio Department of Education (2017): *Ohio Superintendent Evaluation System.* Ohio Department of Education. Retrived from: http://education.ohio.gov/getattachment/Topics/Teaching/Educator-Evaluation- System/Ohio-s-Superintendent-Evaluation-System/reducODE2009-SES- FULLv3.pdf.aspx

Ohio Department of Education (2017). *Ohio Standards for Superintendents.* Ohio Department of Education. Retrieved from: https://education.ohio.gov/getattachment/Topics/Teaching/Educator-Equity/Ohio-s-Educator-Standards/Standards-for-Superintendentsfinal_nov2008.pdf.aspx

Ohio Department of Education (2017). *Ohio Principal Evaluation System.* Ohio Department of Education. Retrieved from: https://education.ohio.gov/getattachment/Topics/Teaching/Educator-Evaluation-System/Ohio-Principal-Evaluation-System-OPES/Principal-Performance-Ratings/OPES- Model-111715.pdf.aspx

Ohio Department of Education (2017). *Standards for Ohio Educators.* Ohio Department of Education. Retrieved from: https://education.ohio.gov/getattachment/Topics/Teaching/Educator-Equity/Ohio-s-Educator-Standards/StandardsforEducators_revaug10.pdf.aspx

Ohio Department of Education (2016). *Columbus City School District: Financial Data.* Retrieved from: http://reportcard.education.ohio.gov/Pages/District- Report.aspx?DistrictIRN=043802

Ohio Department of Education (2015, May 29). *Ohio's New Local Report Cards* [PDF]. Retrieved from: http://old.akronschools.com/dotAsset/7cc68f94-da81-4ccc-a8af- dafecb2abe18.pdf

Ohio School Boards Association (2017). *Understanding School Levies.* OSBA. Retrieved from: https://www.ohioschoolboards.org/sites/default/files/OSBAUnderstandingLeviesFactShe et.pdf

Oklahoma State School Boards Association (2017). *School Law Book.* OSSBA. Retrieved from: https://www.ossba.org/wp-content/uploads/2015/11/2016-School-Law-book.pdf

Oliver, C.G. (2015). *An administrator's guide-Leading with Integrity: Reflections on Legal, Moral and Ethical Issues in School Administration.* Bloomington, IN: AuthorHouse.

Olsen, S. (2006). *Google's antisocial downside.* CNET. Retrieved from: https://www.cnet.com/news/googles-antisocial-downside/

Online Course Report (2017). *The 50 Most Popular MOOCs of All Time.* Rankings. Retrieved from: http://www.onlinecoursereport.com/the-50-most-popular-moocs-of-all-time/

Pastiloff, J. (2017). *Find your tribe.* Pinterest. Retrieved from: https://www.pinterest.com/explore/tribe-quotes/?lp=true

Perception Institute: Research Representation, Reality (2017). *Explicit bias.* Retrieved from: https://perception.org/research/explicit-bias/

PerformancePLUS (2015, May 29). PerformancePLUS a PLUS 360 application [Website]. Retrieved from: https://guilderlandschools-ny.perfplusk12.com/default.as p

Pierson, R. (2013). *Every kid needs a champion.* TEDxTalk. Retrieved from: https://www.ted.com/talks/rita_pierson_every_kid_needs_a_champion#t-391466

Ramalho, E., Garza, E. & Merchant, B. (2010). Successful school leadership in socioeconomically challenging contexts: School principals creating and sustaining successful school improvement. *International Studies in Educational Administration, 38*(3), 35-56.

Reeves, D. B. (2003). High performing in high poverty schools: 90/90/90 and beyond. *Center for performance assessment,* 1-20.

Renaissance Learning, Inc. (2009). *Key Questions STAR enterprise can help you answer.* [Brochure]. Gahanna, OH: Author.

Rennie Center for Education Research & Policy. (2011). A focus on achievement at excel high school: A best practices case study. *Journal of Education, 190*(2), 1-11.

R&L Education (2017). *Professional standards for the superintendency.* Rowman & Littlefield. Retrieved from: https://rowman.com/ISBN/0876522029#

SAS EVAAS for K-12. (2015, May 28). Retrieved from http://www.sas.com/en_us/industry/k- 12-education/evaas.html

Schwartz, B. (2010). *Using our practical wisdom.* TEDxTalk. Retrieved from: http://www.ted.com/talks/barry_schwartz_using_our_practical_wisdom

Seymour, B. (2017). *Teaching and learning with technology.* SeymourEducate. Retrieved from: https://seymoureducate.com/about/

Siemer, K. (2013). *Facing the consequences: Poor social media choices lead to lost jobs and scholarships.* Browse. Retrieved from: https://storify.com/Katie_M_Ritter/facing-the- consequences-poor-social-media-choices

Sivers, D. (2010). *Leadership lessons from dancing guy.* YouTube Channel. Retrieved from: https://www.youtube.com/watch?v=fW8amMCVAJQ

Snow, C. (2014). Rigor and realism: Doing educational science in the real world. *Educational Researcher, 44*(9), 460-466.

Strahan, R. & Gerbasi, K.C. (1972). Short, homogenous versions of the mar-lowe-crowne social desirability scale. Journal of Clinical Psychology, 28, 191-193.

Stringfield, S., Reynolds, D. & Schaffer, E. (2001, January). Fifth-year results from the High Reliability Schools project. Symposium conducted at the meeting of the International Congress for School Effectiveness and Improvement, Toronto, Canada.

Swanson, K. (2016). *Why EdCamp?* Edutopia. Retrieved from: https://www.edutopia.org/blog/why-edcamp-kristen-swanson

Tarte, J. [justintarte]. (2017, Jul 05). We promote what we permit. A culture can never rise above the worst behavior that is allowed. It all starts with #leadership & example. #hr [Tweet]. Retrieved from: https://twitter.com/justintarte/status/882576477119795203

Theoharis, G., & Scanlan, M. (2015). Leadership for increasingly diverse schools. New York, NY: Routledge.

Ungarino, R. (2015). *For more poor Americans, smartphones are lifelines.* CNBC. Retrieved from: http://www.cnbc.com/2015/04/01/for-more-poor-americans-smartphones-are- lifelines.html

UNICEF (2007). *Promoting the rights of children with disabilities.* Retrieved from: http://www.un.org/esa/socdev/unyin/documents/children_disability_rights.pdf

United Federation of Teachers (2017). *Federal laws, regulations and policy guidance.* United Federation of Teachers. Retrieved from: http://www.uft.org/teaching/federal-laws- regulations-and-policy-guidance#ppra

United States Courts (2017). *Court role and structure.* United States Courts. Retrieved from: http://www.uscourts.gov/about-federal-courts/court-role-and-structure

United States Department of Education (2017). *Laws & guidance.* U.S. Department of Education. Retrieved from: https://www2.ed.gov/policy/landing.jhtml

United States Department of Education (2009). *Selected statistics on enrollment, teachers, dropouts, and graduates in public school districts enrolling more than 15,000 students, by state: 1990, 2000, 2006.* National Center for Education Statistics: Institute of Education Sciences. Retrieved from: https://nces.ed.gov/pubs2009/2009020.pdf

Welch, J. (2017). *Developing others: The gauge of true leadership.* WordPress. Retrieved from: https://sagegenx.wordpress.com/2016/10/26/developing-others-the-gauge-of-true- leadership/

Whitaker, T. (2016). *ASCD shorts: Climate and culture with Todd Whitaker.* ASCD YouTube. Retrieved from: https://www.youtube.com/watch?v=4IwZubnyr_c

Wilkins, K. (2012). *Ain't nobody got time for that.* YouTube. Retrieved from: https://www.youtube.com/watch?v=zGxwbhkDjZM

Wiseman, R. (2002). *Queen Bees and Wannabes.* New York: NY. Three Rivers Press.

About the Author

Dr. Denver J. Fowler is currently an Assistant Professor of Educational Leadership and Policy Studies at California State University, Sacramento (CSUS), in the Department of Graduate and Professional Studies in Education, within the College of Education. In addition to this role, he currently serves as an elected Senator on the Faculty Senate at CSUS, as well as the Department Representative for the California Faculty Association. His research is focused on educa-tional leadership in the PreK-12 educational setting. More specifically, he is interested in how the ethical leadership perspectives of school leaders vary according to leader demographics and district characteristics. Dr. Fowler has presented his research both nationally and internationally, including presentations in China, Greece, Italy, Cuba, Puerto Rico, and Africa. He is the author of numerous publications in the areas of education and school leadership. A former practitioner, he has over a decade of successful experience in the PreK-12 educational setting, having served as a coach, teacher, athletic director, technology coordinator, and school administrator. He was named the National Association of Secondary School Principals (NASSP) and Ohio Association of Secondary School Administrators *Assistant Principal of the Year* in the State of Ohio and was nominated for the NASSP *National Assistant Principal of the Year* in the United States. Dr. Fowler received Congressional Recognition from the United States House of Representatives and the State of Ohio House of Representatives for his efforts in the PreK-12 educational setting. A strong supporter of education and policy reform, he has advocated for school leaders, teachers, and education (in general) on Capitol Hill in

Washington, D.C. In addition to his PreK-12 experience, he has over seven years of successful teaching and research experience in the Higher Education setting. Prior to his arrival at CSUS he held appointments at The Ohio State University, The University of Mississippi, Bowling Green State University, and University of West Florida, where he was responsible for teaching courses (both online, hybrid, and face-to-face) in educational leadership, teacher education, and educational technology, at the undergraduate, graduate, and doctoral levels. Dr. Fowler received his Bachelor of Science in Education (B.S.) from The Ohio State University, Master of Arts in Education (M.A.) from Mount Vernon Nazarene University, and Doctor of Education (Ed.D.) from Ohio University. In addition to his degrees, he also completed a School Leadership Institute program at Harvard University and he is a licensed Superintendent, Principal, Teacher, and holds a Private School Administration/Teaching license (all administration, all grade levels, and all subject areas). Dr. Fowler is a member of and/or actively involved in several professional organizations including *Educational Leaders Without Borders*, AERA, UCEA, AASA, ICPEL (formerly NCPEA), CAPEA, AMLE, ASCD, NASSP, OASSA, MAPEL, ODK, BASA, and NEA, to name a few. He is also actively involved in his local community, church, and Rotary. Dr. Fowler resides in Cameron Park, California with his wife Anna, and three children, Haley, Beckett, and Teagan. Additional family members at the Fowler household include a dog named Cannoli, and two fish.

Help Us Build A School in Peru

My wife Anna and I are raising money to help build a school in Peru. Please consider donating to our campaign by visiting our GoFundMe page to learn more about our proposed project at:

https://www.gofundme.com/helpusbuildaschoolinperu

"In every child who is born, under no matter what circumstances, and no matter what parents, the potentiality of the human race is born again; and in him/her, too, once more, and of each of us, our terrific responsibility towards human life; towards the utmost idea of goodness, of the horror of error, and of God."

~ James Agee